DATE DUE

~~MR 1 6 '99~~		
~~AG 5 '99~~ ~~8 18~~		

DEMCO 38-296

CHILDREN
AS RESEARCH SUBJECTS

CHILDREN AS RESEARCH SUBJECTS

Science, Ethics, and Law

Edited by
Michael A. Grodin
Leonard H. Glantz

New York Oxford
OXFORD UNIVERSITY PRESS
1994

Kuala Lumpur   Singapore   Hong Kong   Tokyo
Nairobi   Dar es Salaam   Cape Town
Melbourne   Auckland   Madrid

and associated companies in
Berlin   Ibadan

Published by Oxford University Press, Inc.,
200 Madison Avenue, New York, New York 10016

Oxford is a registered trademark of Oxford University Press

Library of Congress Cataloging-in-Publication Data
Children as research subjects :
science, ethics, and law /
edited by Michael A. Grodin, Leonard H. Glantz.
p.   cm.   Includes bibliographical references and index
ISBN 0–19–507103–4
1. Pediatrics—Research—Moral and ethical aspects.
2. Children—Research—Moral and ethical aspects.
3. Human experimentation in Medicine.
4. Children—Legal status, laws, etc.
I. Grodin, Michael A.
II. Glantz, Leonard H.
[DNLM: 1. Human Experimentation—in infancy & childhood.
2. Ethics, Medical.   3. Child Advocacy.
W 20.5 C536 1994]   174′.28—dc20   DNLM/DLC for Library of Congress   93–3589

9 8 7 6 5 4 3 2 1

Printed in the United States of America
on acid-free paper

*This book is dedicated
to the advocates for the care
and welfare of children
—past, present, and future*

Preface

Research with children presents some vexing and challenging questions to those who conduct, review, regulate, and participate in this activity. Such research presents a powerful tension between two sometimes conflicting social goals: protecting individual children from harm and exploitation, while at the same time increasing our body of knowledge about children in order to develop beneficial medical, psychological, and social interventions. While research with adults raises some similar questions, adults can make choices for themselves, regarding whether or not to volunteer to become research subjects. Children, on the other hand, are presumed to be incapable of making this and other important decisions for themselves. Parents are considered the primary protectors and decision makers for their children. However, parents have this authority because they are presumed to act as protectors of their children's interests. But do parents violate this trust when they ''volunteer'' their children to become research subjects?

The state is also supposed to act as a protector of children. Indeed, when parents abuse their power or are insufficiently protective, the state is expected to intervene in the parent–child relationship to ensure the child's welfare. How then can the state permit children to be research subjects?

Finally, the term *child* includes individuals with greatly varying capacities and needs. Infants depend entirely on their parents or other caregivers for nurturance and protection, and obviously are unable to participate in any decisions. Adolescents approaching adulthood have a great deal of independence from their parents and can usually participate meaningfully in important decisions that affect them. What, then, should the child's role be in the decision to become a research subject?

Some dramatic medical interventions have involved children. A transplant of a heart from a baboon into a human was performed on an infant, and kidneys have been removed from healthy children to be transplanted into their ill siblings. Trials with polio vaccine, a staple of childhood immunization programs today, had been widely conducted on children. And it is likely that many, if not most, of the genetic engineering techniques that are a major focus of current basic science research will be conducted on children who suffer from genetically caused diseases. But interventions do not need to be this dramatic to constitute research. Interviewing minors about their sexual or drug-using behavior is increasingly common. Even testing the efficacy of a new math or reading curriculum in the school makes children research subjects.

Several years ago, the editors of this book realized that despite recognition of the unique problems associated with the participation of children in biomedical and behavioral research, and despite a small but growing literature, there was no integrated, comprehensive text dedicated to these issues.* We decided to produce a text that would be a useful resource to physicians, psychologists, educators, lawyers, ethicists, institutional review board members, child advocates, and others who are involved in performing or reviewing research with children.

A full examination of the issues regarding research with children must extend across disciplinary borders. Science provides the rationale for conducting research with children, while ethics and law can provide a framework for balancing individual and societal interests. As a result of this interdisciplinary focus, we sought collaborators for our project. We drafted detailed outlines for each chapter and sent them to potential authors. The purpose of this exercise was to enable us to develop a coherent book, with as few redundancies as possible, rather than a series of essays. Much to our delight, all of the authors we hoped would agree to write chapters accepted the invitations. We also were pleased that they carefully addressed the issues we presented to them in the outlines. If we have succeeded in producing a useful text, it is because of the superb effort they made.

We would encourage readers to read the book from beginning to end. Because the chapters appear to be independent works, there will be a temptation to read only the chapters that seem to be of particular relevance to the reader's discipline. The chapters *do* stand on their own, but we feel one chapter builds on another, and the reader who selects chapters will lose some of the richness the text provides as a result of the cross-fertilization between chapters.

There are also several appendixes that provide primary source materials, particularly the relevant federal regulations, as well as some practical guidelines to help both researchers and reviewers evaluate the many considerations of research with children.

We hope that the readers of this book will find it not only a useful resource, but also a stimulus for further exploration of the complex issues and conflicting values found throughout the text. One of the pervasive values in American society today is that scientific progress will lead to improvements in human

---

*There is an excellent British text: R. H. Nicholson, ed., 1986, *Medical Research with Children: Ethics, Law and Practice,* Oxford University Press, Oxford.

health and well-being, which in turn will lead to the good life. While no one can doubt the importance science has played in improving our lives, one should also keep in mind philosopher Hans Jonas' caution: "Let us also remember that a slower progress in the conquest of disease would not threaten society, grievous as it is to those who have to deplore that their particular disease be not yet conquered, but that society would indeed be threatened by the erosion of those moral values whose loss, possibly caused by too ruthless a pursuit of scientific progress, would make its most dazzling triumphs not worth having."*

Boston   M.A.G.
May 1993   L.H.G.

---

*Philosophical reflections on experimenting with human subjects. In Paul A. Freund, ed., *Experimentation with Human Subjects* (New York: George Braziller, 1969), pp. 1–31.

Acknowledgments

It is not possible to pay adequate tribute to George Annas and Wendy Mariner, our colleagues in the Law, Medicine and Ethics Program at Boston University. They are the very best of scholars, critics, teachers, and friends, and our work and lives have been enriched by our long association. We would also like to thank Norman Scotch, Robert Meenan, Joel Alpert, and Aram Chobanian of Boston University Schools of Medicine and Public Health for their ongoing support. We thank the many researchers and members of institutional review boards we have had the privilege of working with over the past years. We would also like to acknowledge Jay Katz at Yale University Law School, whose extraordinary book, *Experimentation with Human Beings,* not only served as our introduction to this field many years ago, but also set the standard for all books on this topic. Betty Ollen provided editorial assistance on several chapters, and Lisa Goitein provided able research assistance. We were fortunate to have the skillful word processing and proofreading support of Aida Valentin, Donna-Marie Rios, and Chris Chaisson. We would like to thank our editor, Jeff House of Oxford University Press, who has provided insight and guidance throughout. Finally, we will never be able to adequately express our love and appreciation to Nancy Nozick Grodin and Barbara F. Katz whose patience, support and unfailing nurturance make it all possible.

Contents

II Practical Problems

Contributors

DAN W. BROCK, PH.D.
Professor of Philosophy and Biomedical
  Ethics
Director, Center for Biomedical Ethics
Brown University

ROBERT E. COOKE, M.D.
Emeritus, Professor of Pediatrics
State University of New York at Buffalo
Chairman, Scientific Advisory Board
Joseph P. Kennedy, Jr. Foundation

LEONARD H. GLANTZ, J.D.
Professor of Health Law
Boston University Schools of Medicine
  and Public Health

MICHAEL A. GRODIN, M.D., FAAP
Professor of Health Law, Pediatrics,
  Socio-medical Sciences and
  Community Medicine
Adjunct Professor of Philosophy
Director, Program in Medical Ethics
Boston University Schools of Medicine
  and Public Health

RALPH E. KAUFFMAN, M.D., FAAP
Professor of Pediatrics and Pharmacology
Wayne State University
Childrens Hospital of Michigan

PATRICIA KEITH-SPIEGEL, PH.D.
Reed Voran Honors Distinguished
  Professor of Social and Behavioral
  Sciences
Ball State University

GERALD P. KOOCHER, PH.D.
Associate Professor
Harvard Medical School
Chief of Psychology
Childrens Hospital, Boston

SUSAN E. LEDERER, PH.D.
Associate Professor
Department of Humanities
The Pennsylvania State University College
  of Medicine

DAVID G. SCHERER, PH.D.
Assistant Professor of Psychology
University of South Carolina

LOIS A. WEITHORN, PH.D., J.D.
San Mateo, California

ESTHER H. WENDER, M.D., FAAP
Chief, Division of Developmental and
  Behavioral Pediatrics
Schneider Children's Hospital
Long Island Jewish Medical Center
Professor of Pediatrics
Albert Einstein College of Medicine

CHILDREN
AS RESEARCH SUBJECTS

Historical Overview:
Pediatric Experimentation

SUSAN E. LEDERER
MICHAEL A. GRODIN

In order to understand the nature, scope, and limits of the use of children as research subjects, it is necessary to consider the history of childhood and the family, of medicine, of pediatrics, of human experimentation, and of the protection of children as research subjects. Together, these histories frame the context for a contemporary analysis of the science, ethics, and law related to the use of children as research subjects.

Antiquity

The history of childhood resists easy generalizations. In the past, children's lives, like those of adults, were often harsh. In most cases social concern for child welfare was subordinated to the needs of the state or the interests of parents. In the precarious ecologies of the premodern era, famine and disease contributed to infant and child mortality and low life expectancies. Children often were not seen to be worthy of attachment or social concern. In many cultures, from antiquity through the Renaissance, the practice of abandoning infants and children carried little social stigma. Some abandoned children were fostered by other adults, others sold into slavery or prostitution, and many died as a result of their "exposure" or subsequent neglect (Boswell, 1988). One of the most famous "abandoned" children of antiquity was the infant Moses, whose mother placed him in a basket in the Nile in an effort to avoid death because of the Egyptian policy of slaughtering all male Hebrew infants.

In some societies, concern about declining birth rates and high child mortality led to some protections for children. During the reign of the Emperor Augustus (27 B.C.E.–14 C.E.), policies to increase the number of children included state subsidies to households with foster children and a special tax on bachelors. Three centuries later the Emperor Constantine ordered state subsidies for impoverished families with children. These policies reflected the interests of the state, rather than a concern for child welfare (Rudolph, 1987). Through increasing the population, the state would have more subjects to work, pay taxes, and serve in the military.

The history of pediatric care reflects the relative social invisibility of children. Although the Hippocratic texts (third century B.C.E.) included discussion of childhood diseases and suggested that children were different from adults, there was no systematic discussion of medical care for children. In the second century, the great physician Galen (130–200 C.E.) described some specific afflictions of children in his medical writings. The *Canon* of Avicenna (980–1063 C.E.), the leading medical textbook of the Western and Eastern worlds for several centuries, included descriptions of specific childhood diseases. Thomas Phaire's *Book of Children* (1545) probably was the first medical text in the English language devoted to pediatrics. The text included descriptions of more than forty diseases of children, as well as an extensive discussion of therapies.

The Eighteenth Century

In the eighteenth century, medical interest in infants and children intensified. The pathologist Giovanni Morgagni performed large numbers of autopsies on children. A number of early "medical experiments" in immunization involved children, since lack of prior experience with a disease and proximity to the experimenter made children good subjects for early experiments. The children and servants or slaves of physicians often served as initial subjects. Children were the population at greatest risk in England. Smallpox was endemic among children there and epidemic in the North American colonies. In 1721, when the Puritan religious leader Cotton Mather suggested the practice of variolation against smallpox, Zabdiel Boylston first attempted the procedure on his two sons and his two slaves (Blake, 1985). At the end of the eighteenth century, the development of a vaccination for smallpox again involved the children of physicians and institutionalized children. After observing that the experience of cowpox or swinepox offered immunity from smallpox, Jenner vaccinated his one-year-old son. Jenner's next subject was an eight-year-old boy, whose vaccination was challenged by an inoculation of smallpox material. When the physician Benjamin Waterhouse, who played a leading role in the introduction of vaccination in the United States, received his initial shipment of vaccine from London, he first administered the vaccine to his son. Waterhouse subsequently vaccinated seven of his children; in order to test their protection from the disease, he exposed three of them to smallpox patients (Blake, 1957). In Philadelphia, in 1802 when smallpox again visited the city, Thomas C. James, accoucheur to the almshouse, tested the Jennerian vaccine on forty-eight of the children under his care. He later challenged their immunity to the disease by inoculating the children with smallpox (Radbill, 1979).[1]

Similar attempts were made to protect children against another dreaded childhood disease, measles. In 1759, after promising a payment to their parents, the Scottish physician Francis Home inoculated twelve children with blood taken from a patient with measles. "The prejudices of mankind," Home explained, made it difficult to collect the blood, and "much more difficult to find subjects for inoculation" (Still, 1965, pp. 430–431). Several American physicians attempted to replicate Home's efforts. In 1799 a Rhode Island physician inoculated "three young persons in his circle" with blood taken from measles patients (Hektoen, 1905).[2] In 1801, in an attempt to determine if measles was infectious, Nathaniel Chapman performed a series of inoculations involving children from the Philadelphia Almshouse. Chapman's failure to infect the children with the blood, tears, mucus, bronchial secretions, and the material from skin eruptions from children already infected with measles led him to conclude that measles was noncontagious.[3] In the 1850s a Chicago physician attempted to immunize the children under his care at a local orphan asylum. Using blood drawn from children already ill with measles, John E. M'Geer inoculated three children in the asylum. After these children developed mild cases of measles, M'Geer proceeded with additional injections (M'Geer, 1851;[4] Cassedy, 1984, p. 138).

Nineteenth Century

In the first half of the nineteenth century, the attitudes and practices of American adults involving children changed dramatically. The Industrial Revolution helped transform child labor into a valuable commodity. Children as young as six joined their families in the workplace. As a result of this exploitation, the public gradually began to recognize the need for childhood protection. The Romantic movement helped generate interest in the purity, naturalness, and individuality of children. Children were increasingly regarded as distinct from adults, and childhood became a period of life worthy of being recognized and extended. The special responsibilities of child rearing provided a new justification for family existence. The great increase in child-rearing books and manuals, as well as the development of a distinct literature for children, reflected the new interest in children and child welfare. The celebration of a child's birthday dates from the nineteenth century (Degler, 1981).

Childhood became a focus of social reform in the nineteenth century. Reformers organized a wide range of institutions for children, establishing schools, orphanages, reformatories, foundling homes, and hospitals (Halpern, 1988). In the 1850s the first hospitals for children opened in New York City and Philadelphia. In 1873 the American Medical Association established a specific section on diseases of women and children. In 1888 the growing number of specialists in medical care for children formed the American Pediatric Society to foster the study of children's diseases and establish pediatrics as a branch of the medical sciences. In 1930 the American Academy of Pediatrics was founded to benefit the health and welfare of children. The 1931 American Academy of Pediatrics' constitution reads, "The object of the Academy shall be to foster and stimulate interest in pediatrics and correlate all aspects of the work for the welfare of children. . . . "

The social conditions of child life in late nineteenth-century America prompted pediatricians to investigate the health problems of children. Mortality remained high in children's institutions as a result of inadequate nutrition and recurrent epidemics. Foundling homes and children's hospitals became important training sites for pediatricians (English, 1984). The health needs of institutionalized children encouraged pediatric experimentation. In the first decade of the twentieth century, when Alfred F. Hess, a prominent New York pediatrician, became medical director of the Hebrew Infant Asylum in New York City, he instituted a series of experiments involving the children under his care. Hess acknowledged that research on institutionalized children offered scientific advantages because the standardized conditions in the asylum approximated those "conditions which are insisted on in considering the course of experimental infection among laboratory animals, but which can rarely be controlled in a study of infection in man" (Hess, 1914). In addition to trials of pertussis vaccine, Hess undertook extensive studies of the anatomy and physiology of digestion in infants. In 1911 he reported the development of a duodenal tube for infants that could be used to sample gastric secretions. Although conceding the difficulty of predicting the value of any new device, he subsequently used the instrument in a number of studies of both normal and diseased infants and children (Hess, 1911). Other investigators reported similar studies on institutionalized children, including Walter Reed and George Miller Sternberg, who studied immunity from smallpox in children in Brooklyn orphanages (Sternberg and Reed, 1895). In the second decade of the twentieth century, Joseph Goldberger conducted several studies for the United States Public Health Service on the value of diet in the prevention of pellagra at orphanages in Mississippi. Supplementing the poor diet in these institutions with fresh milk, vegetables, and eggs, Goldberger reported a dramatic decrease in the cases of pellagra among the children (Goldberger, 1916). He repeated this experiment at orphanages in other parts of the South (Etheridge, 1972).

The study of the diseases of childhood received enormous impetus from changes in medical science. The germ theory of disease spawned multiple experiments involving children and adults. The lack of appropriate animal models led investigators to involve children and adults as the "animals of necessity" in the search for the bacterial causes of disease. In the efforts to establish the causative agents of cancer, leprosy, syphilis, gonorrhea, tuberculosis, and yellow fever, deliberate attempts were made to infect human beings, including children. In the 1880s a California physician, serving as a health officer in a Hawaiian leprosarium, injected six leprous girls under the age of twelve with "the virus of syphilis" (Fitch, 1892). In 1895 New York physician Henry Heiman reported his successful production of gonorrhea in a four-year-old "idiot with chronic epilepsy"; a sixteen-year-old boy, who was also an "idiot"; and a twenty-six-year-old man in "the final stages of tuberculosis" (Heiman, 1895). More than forty reports of experimental infections with gonorrheal cultures, including the application of gonorrheal organisms into the eyes of sick children, appeared in the medical literature in the late nineteenth and early twentieth century (Hill, 1943). When an outbreak of molluscum contagiosum occurred in a Philadelphia orphanage, the pediatrician F. C. Knowles infected two children in order to study the process (Knowles, 1909). In 1931 three Japanese experimenters reported the experimental production of scarlet fever in eight children from three to seven years of age. Following the lead of American investigators who produced scarlet fever in adult volunteers, the Japanese physicians obtained their subjects through "the good will of friends who had an understanding of the circumstances" (Toyoda, Futagi, and Okamota, 1931, p. 351).

Establishing the infective agent was only the first step. Physicians also used child and adult subjects in the development of diagnostic tests and vaccines. Some efforts were spectacularly successful. In 1885 the French scientist Louis Pasteur administered the first rabies vaccination to Joseph Meister, a nine-year-old boy who had been bitten fourteen times by a rabid dog. Undertaken in desperation and apparently before sufficient tests on animals were completed, the first human trial of rabies vaccine caused considerable anguish for Pasteur (Geison, 1978). Search for a similar treatment for diphtheria, the leading cause of mortality in nineteenth-century children, led to the successful development of anti-toxin treatment for the disease.[5] In 1893–1894 the first large-scale testing of diphtheria antitoxin was conducted on foundlings in Paris institutions (English, 1985). The success of diphtheria serum therapy played an important role in altering public attitudes toward medical science and perhaps toward experimentation with human beings (Weindling, 1992).

Not all efforts to develop new vaccines were as successful. Some of the early vaccine trials may have actually increased susceptibility to disease, and the attempts to challenge the protection offered by immunization through intentional exposure to the infection may have also placed child subjects at greater risk. In this period, physicians pursued such investigations informally and with few explicit guidelines. In 1887 a New Jersey physician, Joseph W. Stickler, approached several pediatricians with his newly developed vaccine for scarlet fever, which consisted of the contagious material of equine foot and mouth disease. Although the distinguished pediatrician Abraham Jacobi and several other doctors tried to dissuade Stickler from experimentation with this material, the doctor injected himself and several young children with the "vaccine." He next challenged the protection of the inoculation by exposing his young subjects to scarlet fever patients and infected bed linens (Stickler, 1887). Fortunately, the children did not develop the disease, and Stickler later died apparently convinced of his great "discovery" (Pearce, 1914).

Physicians differed in their concerns about potential risks in these early vaccine trials. In 1912 the physician Gerald Webb expressed considerable apprehension about "inoculating the uninfected" with his live vaccine for tuberculosis. But circumstances enabled him to proceed when "a distinguished scientist dying of tuberculosis" asked Webb to vaccinate his two children, aged nine months and three years (Webb, 1912). Another physician attempting to develop a vaccine for tuberculosis harbored no similar concerns. That same year, Karl von Ruck tested his tuberculosis vaccine on 262 children at a Baptist orphanage in North Carolina.[6] At the request of the United States Senate, the Public Health Service conducted an investigation in 1914 and reported that guinea pigs who received the von Ruck vaccine yielded more quickly to tubercular infection than those not vaccinated (U.S. Senate, 1914). Some critics of the von Ruck vaccine charged that "If the 'animals so treated exhibited increased susceptibility,' what of the hundreds of little children used by Dr. von Ruck; do they show a like 'increased susceptibility'?" (Vivisection Investigation League, n.d.).

In the first two decades of the twentieth century, attempts to develop immunizations for measles, chickenpox, mumps, and whooping cough all involved testing on children in hospitals or orphanages. In 1915 Charles Hermann of New York obtained the consent of a mother to apply measles "virus" to the nasal mucosa of her four-month-old infant in an effort to immunize the child, and then proceeded "cautiously" to inoculate thirty-nine other infants (Hermann, 1915). Other efforts at measles immunization involved injections of serum from patients recovering from measles (Richardson and Connor, 1919). At the Hebrew Infant Asylum in New York City, Alfred Hess and Sophie Rabinoff attempted to immunize children against mumps and chickenpox. Children who never had mumps received prophylactic injections of blood from convalescent donors and were then placed in mumps wards (Hess, 1915). Sophie Rabinoff's enthusiastic report of successful efforts to stem the spread of varicella through vaccinations encouraged May Michael to repeat the attempt when chickenpox developed in Chicago's Home for Jewish Friendless in 1917. She administered vaccines to thirty-two children, but drew few conclusions (Rabinoff, 1915; Michael, 1917).

Twentieth Century

In the first part of the twentieth century, the availability of new drugs and new technologies also fostered increased experimentation with child subjects (Mitchell, 1964, p. 722). The invention of the X-ray prompted considerable experimentation on both normal children and adults. Physicians applied the X-rays to the study of the normal development of children, including the fetus in utero. Physicians Eli Long and E. W. Caldwell studied carpal ossification in 200 children, including "idiots" (Long and Caldwell, 1911). In order to determine the normal size and shape of the infant stomach, physicians Godfrey Pisek and Leon T. LeWald performed serial X-rays on sick and healthy children, ranging in age from two days to twenty months.[7]

The study of human digestion was a major focus of American medical research. Before 1880 the study of digestion in infancy was confined to animal experiments or autopsies on dead infants (Clarke, 1909a, pp.874–75). First introduced as a therapeutic measure for the gastrointestinal diseases of infancy, the stomach tube became an important research tool. Physiologists studied the motility of the stomach, gastric secretion, and the mechanisms of hunger in human newborns in Europe and America (Carlson, 1916). Metabolic studies in both normal and sick infants and children were also reported (Carpenter and Murlin, 1911). In 1908 concerns about the safety of the food additives saccharin and sodium benzoate led to government-sponsored investigations, which included testing the chemicals in adult volunteers (who received payment for their services) and in newborn infants and children (Grulee and Buhlig, 1911; see also Young, 1975). Interest in the duration of digestion of a meal led some physicians to use chemicals to identify the passage of a test meal. As early as the 1870s, physicians used dyes and other chemicals for gastrointestinal studies in adults. Beginning about 1909 pediatricians conducted similar studies in infants and children. In 1915 A. Hymanson, a New York physician, reported results from a carmin test in two sets of infants: a group of healthy newborn infants and twenty-five sick children ranging in age from six weeks to six years (Hymanson, 1915).

The technical requirements associated with research on pediatric patients prompted considerably more discussion in medical journals than the ethics of research with these populations. Research tools for studies in adults required modifications for use in children. Some investigators noted the surprising ease with which even young infants swallowed the stomach tube for gastric studies. "Most of the children, after having overcome the initial fright, and having become slightly used to the procedure, made very little effort to cry and some seemed quite content to suck on the tube" (Clarke, 1909b). Other projects required the active cooperation of the child or her parents. In their 1911 study of the metabolic processes of mothers and their infants before and after birth, Thorne Carpenter and John Murlin noted that while their respiration calorimeter studies did not entail "any particular hardship," the willingness of patients "to observe directions to the strictest letter was essential to the satisfactory outcome of the determinations" (Carpenter and Murlin, 1911). In his observations on a fourteen-year-old "child" with a gastric fistula, R. S. Lavenson reported that the girl could not be persuaded to repeat an experiment with stomach bitters because the bitter taste was so objectionable (Lavenson, 1909, 273).

The collection of blood and the products of metabolism from infants and young children was sometimes impeded by their smaller size and "unruly" behavior. Some investigators declined to study children because of difficulties associated with their smaller size.[8] Efforts to achieve compliance with research protocols in some instances may have placed children at greater risk than the experimental procedure itself. For example, when a child's activity interfered with attempts to obtain results of normal electrical response to galvanic current, investigators observed that "constant resistance necessitated mild chloroform narcosis in a few cases" (Wilcox, 1911, p. 399).[9] Some physicians reported that X-ray studies on active infants required the use of anesthesia for information about the normal anatomy and physiology of the infant stomach (Pisek and LeWald, 1913). Despite the fact that dangers associated with X-ray exposure were known to practitioners, ambiguity about what levels of exposure constituted harmful levels of radiation persisted (Serwer, 1977). Children were used as subjects in a number of experiments involving X-rays in which risk was deemed unremarkable.

Some nutrition studies required restraining infants and young children on an apparatus for the collection of metabolic products. In one study of a baby with a "rather happy disposition," investigators placed the infant on the apparatus for a second period of "prolonged confinement" of seven days. After the baby lost weight, the investigators removed the child from the frame despite his lack of obvious discomfort, noting they "carried the observation as far as was advisable with a human subject" (Bosworth, Bowditch, and Ragle, 1915). Some pediatric investigators reported that these devices used to restrain a child for the collection of excreta, while comfortable for the child, "roused unfavorable comment from nurses, parents, and visitors." The concerns of "anxious parents" led to the development of less conspicuous equipment to restrain children for metabolic studies (Dubois, 1911, p. 416).

The Vivisection of Children

In the late nineteenth century, the use of children in biomedical research provoked criticism from the American opponents of unrestricted animal experimentation. Animal protectionists who had established the first societies for the prevention of cruelty to animals also promoted societies for the prevention of cruelty to children. In many states, child and animal protection were the joint responsibility of humane societies (Shultz, 1968).

One of the targets of this early criticism was a Boston pediatrician. In August 1896 Arthur Howard Wentworth, a recent graduate of the Harvard Medical School and outpatient physician to the Children's Hospital in Boston, reported the results of forty-five lumbar punctures of infants and children. Wentworth explained that he first performed the operation of tapping the spinal canal in a child with a questionable case of tubercular meningitis. Although the child proved free of meningitis, she responded unfavorably to the puncture, leading Wentworth to suspect that the spinal tap was not as harmless as many believed. He then resolved to attempt "control experiments on normal cases," explaining:

> The diagnostic value of puncture of the subarachnoid space is so evident that I considered myself justified in incurring some risk in order to settle the question of its danger. If it proved to be harmless, then one need not wait until a patient becomes moribund before resorting to it. (Wentworth, 1896)

Wentworth subsequently withdrew spinal fluid from twenty-nine hospitalized children ranging in age from a few months to a few years, concluding that although "the momentary pain of the puncture" caused children occasionally to shrink back and cry out, the procedure itself was harmless and would prove to be a useful diagnostic tool.[10]

Wentworth presented his results to both the Suffolk County Medical Society and the American Pediatric Society in 1896, where he received encouraging responses. Publication of the article, however, provoked angry comment from another physician. A Philadelphia physician, John B. Roberts, labeled Wentworth's procedures "human vivisection," reminding his readers:

> It must be remembered that there were no therapeutic indications for the operation such as often lead us to justly and properly adopt operative treatment, the positive value of which is still undetermined. These operations were purely and avowedly experimental. . . . (Roberts, 1896)

Using the children in the hospital without explaining his plan to their mothers or gaining their permission, Roberts explained, intensified public fear of hospitals, especially among the poor. Amid the tumult over his lumbar punctures, Wentworth resigned his position at the Harvard Medical School. Furor over the Wentworth case, however, did not disappear.

Wentworth's descriptions of "control experiments on normal infants" intensified the debate over "human vivisection" (Lederer, 1992a). Arguing that human experimentation would result from the failure to restrict experimentation on animals, American antivivisectionists assailed the use of children and other helpless populations in medical research. Reports that a Swedish physician experimented on institutionalized children because they were "cheaper than calves" led to attacks on medical science and scientists (Humane Society, n.d.). Several proposals to outlaw experimentation on children and pregnant women were introduced into the United States Senate in 1900 and 1902. Antivivisectionists also pursued legislation at the state level to protect vulnerable patients—children, the insane, and pregnant women—from experimenters. In 1905 and 1907 proposals "to prohibit such terrible experiments on children, insane persons and certain women as have been performed of late years" and to ensure "that no experiment should be performed on any other human being without his intelligent written consent" were introduced in the Illinois legislature (Taber, 1907). In 1914 New York State Senator Herrick called for a commission to investigate the extent of experimentation on children in New York hospitals. In 1923 the New York legislature considered a bill prohibiting experimentation on children. None of these proposals were enacted (Shultz, 1968).

Several American pediatricians became the targets of antivivisectionist criticism for their use of orphans in trials of new diagnostic methods. Clinical trials of tuberculin for diagnosis of tuberculosis generated considerable controversy. In 1909 the eminent pediatrician Luther Emmett Holt, a professor of diseases of children at the Columbia University's College of Physicians and Surgeons, was attacked in the Hearst newspaper chain and in the antivivisectionist press for his "astonishing callousness" in performing 1000 tuberculin tests on "sick and dying babies" in his practice at New York Babies' Hospital (Holt, 1909). Unlike Wentworth, Holt weathered the attacks on his medical practice (Duffus and Holt, 1940). Antivivisectionists also branded three Philadelphia pediatricians "human vivisectors" for clinical trials of tuberculin involving infants at a Catholic orphanage in Philadelphia (Hamill, Carpenter, and Cope, 1908). The controversy over using infants as "guinea pigs" brought an abrupt end to further research at the St. Vincent's Home, "an institution ideally suited for investigations under controlled conditions" (Stokes, 1957). In 1914 a Rockefeller Institute researcher's trials of a newly developed test for syphilis using orphans and hospitalized children led the New York Society for the Prevention of Cruelty to Children to institute a formal complaint with the Manhattan district attorney. Although the physicians who enabled Hideyo Noguchi to conduct the trials acknowledged that they lacked the authority to give consent for the children's participation, the district attorney dropped the charges against the researcher (Lederer, 1985).

Criticism of clinical research involving infants and children was generally confined to Hearst publications and the antivivisectionist press. One notable exception was the condemnation of Alfred Hess's research at the Hebrew Orphan Asylum. In 1921 Konrad Bercovici, a social worker and journalist, criticized Hess and his associate Mildred Fish for using "orphans as guinea pigs" in studies of the dietary factors in rickets and scurvy (Bercovici, 1921). Bercovici described Hess's studies on scurvy, which involved withholding orange juice from institutionalized infants until they developed the characteristic small hemorrhages associated with the disease (Hess and Fish, 1914). He also quoted the employment of similar methods by Hess and his associates to discover a diet that would induce rickets (Hess and Unger, 1919–20). Although Bercovici acknowledged the importance of studying the effects of different diets on children, he explicitly rejected the idea of producing the disease in nonvolunteers, especially when some of the children did not fully recover from the effects of the disease:

> No devotion to science, no thought of the greater good to the greater number, can for an instant justify the experimenting on helpless infants, children pathetically abandoned by fate and intrusted to the community for their safeguarding. Voluntary consent by adults should, of course, be the *sine qua non* of scientific experimentation. (Bercovici, 1921)

Bercovici's assessment of the scurvy and rickets research prompted at least one medical journal to consider the ethics of using institutionalized children in nontherapeutic experiments. The editors of *American Medicine* conceded that experimentation on human beings should be limited to adult volunteers or "to children as may be utilized with parental consent" (Orphans and dietetics, 1921, p. 394). The physicians' efforts to minimize risks to the orphans and the scientific utility of the controlled feeding studies (which promised "a large return to the community for the care devoted to them") allowed the editors to justify the studies and exonerate the medical community (Orphans and dietetics, 1921, p. 396).

The criticism of the research exploitation of children and other helpless populations in the first half of the twentieth century did not generate formal guidelines about the ethics of human experimentation. Concern about antivivisectionist accusations led some researchers to monitor the use of children and other human subjects in biomedical experiments (Lederer, 1992b). In 1941 Francis Peyton Rous, editor of the *Journal of Experimental Medicine,* rejected the manuscript of a San Diego physician, noting:

> I cannot let this occasion pass without saying that in my personal view the inoculation of a twelve month old infant with herpes virus obtained from an adult was an abuse of power, an infringement on the rights of the individual, and not excusable because the illness which followed had implications for science. The statement that the child was "offered as a volunteer"—whatever that may mean—does not palliate the action. (Rous, 1941)

Despite the strong criticism, the physician, William Black, published the article in the *Journal of Pediatrics,* which included the report of application of herpes simplex virus to "S. D., a white girl twelve months old offered as a volunteer" (Black, 1942, p. 153).

In the first half of the twentieth century the conduct of human experimentation was left to individual investigators. Physicians clearly recognized some limits to experimentation. When his experimental gelatin injections provoked "alarming symptoms of prostration and collapse" in three normal children (including a "feeble-minded" four-year-old girl), the Chicago physician Isaac Abt discontinued his pediatric experiments, and began studies on rabbits (Abt, 1903, p. 290). In some cases, the pressures of scientific competition and the urgency of the need to protect children from dreaded disease prompted "premature human trials" (Paul, 1971). Criticism over the failure of trials involving child subjects could exert a deleterious effect on medical research. In the 1930s the search for a vaccine to control the scourge of polio involved thousands of American children in trials of untested vaccines. The high costs of raising and maintaining monkeys as research animals led investigators to involve child subjects after preliminary work on only sixty-two animals (Paul, 1971). The physicians involved were not unconcerned about their child subjects. The pathologist

John Kolmer, who advocated a live virus polio vaccine, first tested the safety of his vaccine on himself, his two children, and twenty-three other children "all immunized at the request or with the written consent of the parents" (Kolmer, Klugh, and Rule, 1935, p. 456). After initial success with the vaccine, Kolmer conducted trials of the vaccine on more than 300 children. During the same decade Maurice Brodie, a Canadian physician, developed an alternative vaccine for polio consisting of weakly immunogenic virus. Together with William H. Park, director of the New York Board of Health's Bureau of Laboratories, Brodie tested his vaccine on adult volunteers (himself and six employees of the bureau). He then administered the vaccine to twelve children "volunteered by their parents" (Berk, 1989). Similarly encouraged by his results, he initiated a large-scale polio vaccination program involving 1600 children in Kern County, California. Several thousand children ultimately participated in trials of both vaccines (Paul, 1971).

The large-scale vaccination programs of Brodie and Kolmer came to an abrupt end in 1935, following two special conferences sponsored by the American Public Health Association. Investigators denounced both vaccines as unsafe; one researcher from the United States Public Health Service branded Kolmer a virtual "murderer" for the *deaths* associated with his live virus vaccine (Paul, 1971, p. 259; Berk, 1989, p. 334). The criticism cost Brodie his position, but Kolmer survived the controversy and went on to pursue research in other aspects of medicine.

The 1935 controversy over human trials of polio vaccine retarded research with polio vaccines for nearly two decades (Berk, 1989). The deaths associated with the 1935 vaccine trials made investigators hesitant to involve human subjects. But vaccine research also was interrupted by a transforming event in the history of modern medical research—the outbreak of World War II.

Medical Research in the Second World War and After

World War II offered enormous impetus to medical science. Established by President Franklin D. Roosevelt in 1941, the Office of Scientific Research and Development formed a Committee for Medical Research (CMR), which coordinated medical research on an unprecedented scale (Rothman, 1987). The CMR sponsored some 600 studies, many involving human subjects, in search of solutions for the medical problems of soldiers. Investigators used civilian institutions, including orphanages, for many of these studies. Indeed, access to such populations enhanced an investigator's research application to the CMR. In 1943 a number of boys and girls from the Ohio Soldiers and Sailors Orphanage participated in studies of dysentery, a major research focus during the war.

Injections of various suspensions of killed bacteria caused serious side effects in many of the children (Rothman, 1991, pp. 31, 33–35, 53).

After World War II, medical research continued to expand at an extraordinary rate. The growth of the National Institutes of Health (NIH) and the availability of government funding facilitated the massive increase in medical experimentation. Government appropriations for NIH grew from approximately $700,000 in 1946 to over $36 million in 1955. By 1970 the NIH received nearly $1.5 billion yearly and administered more than 11,000 grants (Rothman, 1991).

The spectacular growth in medical research initially did not spark much interest in the ethics of human experimentation. After the war, the world was outraged at the murders carried out in the name of science by Nazi physicians during World War II. Perhaps the most hideous experiments were conducted on the children of Auschwitz by Dr. Josef Mengele (Lagnado and Dekel, 1991). Despite the revelation of and recoil from Nazi medical experimentation, few American researchers applied the precepts of the newly formulated Nuremberg Code (see Appendix B) to their own research practices (Annas and Grodin, 1992). The cornerstone of the Nuremberg Code—the informed, uncoerced, and voluntary consent of the subject—would have excluded the participation of children as research subjects (Grodin and Alpert, 1988). Yet experimentation on children did not cease. In 1964 the World Medical Association's Declaration of Helsinki (see Appendix C) recognized a place in medical research for experimentation in special populations and called for some protections for these groups, including a process of surrogate decision-making.

In 1966 the Harvard anesthesiologist Henry K. Beecher challenged the medical profession with an ethical critique of clinical experimentation. Published in the *New England Journal of Medicine,* Beecher's report detailed twenty-two cases in which investigators endangered "the health or the life of their subjects" (Beecher, 1966).[11] Beecher's exposé and the public outcry over the Tuskegee Syphilis Study, a forty-year study of untreated syphilis in black males, and the Jewish Chronic Disease Hospital study, wherein elderly patients received injections of live cancer cells without their knowledge, hastened the establishment of protections for the human subjects of biomedical research (Jones, 1981).

Beecher's twenty-two cases included two studies conducted with institutionalized mentally retarded children and two studies using newborn infants. In one case, in order to determine whether ureteral reflux could occur in the normal bladder, investigators performed vesicourethrography in twenty-six normal infants less than forty-eight hours old, involving multiple X-ray exposures of the infants (Beecher, 1966). But the most notorious case involving children was undoubtedly the hepatitis study conducted at a New York institution for the mentally retarded. As Saul Krugman, lead researcher in the hepatitis studies, observed in 1986, "The name 'Willowbrook' has become synonymous with medical research gone astray" (Krugman, 1986).

Willowbrook

From the 1950s to the 1970s a research team led by Saul Krugman of New York University conducted studies of hepatitis virus at Willowbrook State School, an institution for the severely mentally retarded. These studies included the systematic infection of newly arrived children with strains of the virus.

Severe overcrowding and chronic underfunding at the Willowbrook School contributed to high rates of endemic and epidemic diseases among the children. Krugman, who joined the staff as a consultant in infectious disease, hoped to control the spread of hepatitis through the development of a vaccine. Believing that most newly admitted children would develop hepatitis, the investigators decided to study the effects and the natural history of hepatitis in children infected for experimental purposes. The team provided a "specially equipped, specially staffed unit" where the children would be protected from the other infectious diseases at the school. Krugman's team obtained the consent of parents for the child's participation in the studies in a process that evolved during the course of the hepatitis studies. Parents who consented to enroll their children in the studies were assured a more rapid admission to this special unit. Krugman noted that children who were wards of the state (and lacked parents to consent on their behalf) were never included in the study (Krugman, 1986, p. 160).

Parental consent for pediatric experimentation was the exception rather than the rule in the 1950s and 1960s. It may have been more common in the area of infectious disease because of the publicity surrounding polio, both the unsuccessful vaccine trials in the 1930s and the successful development of a vaccine in the 1950s. Polio researcher Jonas Salk conducted tests in institutionalized mentally retarded children and adults after he obtained the permission of their parents or guardians. The polio vaccine, although untested, offered some benefit to the initial recipients at two Pennsylvania institutions, the Polk State School and the D. T. Watson Home for Crippled Children. After the initial trials of the polio vaccine, field trials of the Salk vaccine proceeded with the written permission of parents (Smith, 1990).

In the development of a vaccine for measles, investigators also sought parental permission in the early trials. In 1958 researcher John Enders acknowledged the consent of parents or guardians for the initial trial of a live attenuated measles vaccine in eleven "mentally defective institutionalized children" (Enders, 1961–1962, p. 250). Similar written permission from mothers of infants born at a correctional institution for women was obtained by pediatricians who conducted further trials of the vaccine in 1960 (Stokes et al., 1960). After a 1960 measles epidemic at the Willowbrook School left sixty children dead, Krugman's team initiated similar trials of Enders' live attenuated measles vaccine, trials for which parents "signed consents for their [children's] inclusion in the vaccination study" (Krugman, Giles, and Jacobs 1960).

Unlike these vaccine trials, the Willowbrook studies involved the deliberate infection of the children with the hepatitis virus. The issue of parental consent for the experiment became the subject of controversy. In 1970 Henry Beecher once again questioned whether parents were informed of the risks for their children in the study and challenged the legal status of parental consent when no therapeutic benefit for the child was anticipated. He also questioned the failure to protect the children at the Willowbrook School against hepatitis with injections of gamma globulin, citing new evidence of the therapeutic efficacy of such injections. Beecher moreover criticized the admissions policy at the Willowbrook School that expedited entry into the overcrowded institution for children whose parents consented to participation in the hepatitis experiments (Beecher, 1970, pp. 122–127). The respected theologian Paul Ramsey joined Beecher in condemnation of the study, as did the editors of the British journal *Lancet,* who published a critical letter in 1971 and apologized to their readers for failing to move earlier against the study (Faden and Beauchamp, 1986). Other critics took issue with Krugman's claim that children at the institution, given the poor conditions, would have "inevitably" developed hepatitis. Linking the hepatitis project to a "study in nature," Krugman argued, would serve to mitigate the harm or ethical violation that ensued from the deliberate infection of the children (Rothman, 1982).

The ethics of the Willowbrook study continue to be controversial, but no one should doubt the impetus that the public controversy over the deliberate infection of mentally retarded children with a serious disease gave to the demand for the protection of the rights of human subjects.

The Call to Regulation

As criticism mounted in the press, the medical science community became increasingly aware of the conduct of unethical research. Public outcry arose over the U.S. Public Health Service Tuskegee syphilis study on poor black adult men and the initiation of fetal and abortus research (Levine, 1986, pp. 297–320). In 1973, the U.S. Department of Health, Education and Welfare (HEW), now the Department of Health and Human Services (HHS), published the first set of proposed regulations concerning the protection of human subjects in biomedical and behavioral research. On May 30, 1974, specific legal guidelines for clinical investigators were published (45 *CFR* 46). These regulations did not, however, specifically address research with children.

In July 1974, Congress passed the National Research Act as Public Law 93–348, establishing a National Commission for the Protection of Human Subjects in Biomedical and Behavioral Research. The commission deliberated from 1975 to 1978. Two of its published reports had a direct impact on the use of children as research subjects. On September 6, 1977, the commission issued an extensive appendix entitled ''Report and Recommendations: Research Involving Children'' (National Commission, 1977). This 156-page report was the first formal attempt to identify the unique problems associated with the use of children as research subjects (see Chapter 9). A year later, the commission issued the ''Belmont Report: Ethical Principles and Guidelines for the Protection of Human Subjects of Research'' (National Commission, 1978). The Belmont Report identified the ethical framework and relevant principles on which to base regulations. The three basic ethical principles identified as particularly relevant to the ethics of research on human subjects were respect for persons, beneficence/nonmaleficence, and distributive justice (see Chapters 4 and 5).

In 1977 the American Academy of Pediatrics published its first set of professional guidelines on ''Ethics of Drug Research.'' These physician-generated standards were an attempt to formally establish the ethical boundaries for conducting biomedical research with children.

Specific federal regulations governing ''Additional Protections Pertaining to Research Development and Related Activities Involving Fetuses, Pregnant Women, and Human In Vitro Fertilization'' were published in 1981 (45 *CFR* 46, Subpart 9). On March 8, 1983, a new set of regulations specifically governing ''Additional Protections for Children Involved as Subjects in Research'' was published (45 *CFR* 46, Subpart D, 1983). On June 18, 1991, a final ''Federal Policy for the Protection of Human Subjects'' in the form of a common rule was promulgated to integrate and consolidate existing non-HHS governmental regulations on human subjects (Federal Policy, 1991). The 1983 protections for children involved as subjects of research remained intact in the 1991 final policy. This regulation was accepted by the U.S. Office of Science and Technology Policy and has been adopted by HHS and fourteen other federal departments and agencies (see Appendix D).

Conclusions

The history of pediatric experimentation is largely one of child abuse. The vulnerable and disadvantaged were repeatedly exploited to further the ''medical advances'' of physicians and scientists. A preponderance of the children subjects were poor, institutionalized, mentally ill, physically disabled, or chronically ill. However, just as physicians often experimented on themselves, the children of the medical scientists themselves also served as convenient research subjects.

Eventually, the need to protect the rights and welfare of children as a uniquely vulnerable population was recognized. As children gain higher value in society, so has the goal of appropriate balancing of research risks and benefits. This goal has been supported by groups of pediatricians, social workers, and child-welfare advocates. Well-designed, carefully conducted, and ethically justified experimentation with childhood subjects can be safe, effective, and beneficial.

Notes

1. In New York, Boston, and Baltimore, almshouse children were also among the first to receive the vaccine. See also S. X. Radbill, "Centuries of Child Welfare in Philadelphia," *Philadelphia Medicine 71:*279–291, 319–327, 359–377, 1975.

2. Hektoen also cites the efforts of Hungarian, Italian, German, and English investigators to produce measles immunity in children. Dr. Green of Greenwich, Rhode Island, is discussed in J. Stewart, *A Practical Treatise on the Disease of Children,* 2d ed., New York: Langley, 1844, p. 416.

3. W. P. Dewees briefly cites Chapman's lectures on the noncontagiousness of measles in *A Treatise on the Physical and Medical Treatment of Children,* H. C. Carey and I. Lea, 1825, Philadelphia, p. 417. See also S. X. Radbill, "Centuries of Child Welfare in Philadelphia," *Philadelphia Medicine 71:*369, 1975.

4. In "Experimental Measles" (*Journal of Infectious Diseases 2:*238–255, 1905), Hektoen cites him as McGirr. See also J. H. Cassedy, 1948, *American Medicine and Statistical Thinking, 1800–1860,* Cambridge, Mass.: Harvard University, p. 138.

5. For whooping cough, see "Anti-vivisection Notes," *Journal of Zoophily* 22:11, 1913.

6. See the article on the government's testing of von Ruck's vaccine in the *New York Tribune,* March 30, 1913, p. 20; and "A Practical Method of Prophylactic Immunization against Tuberculosis," *Journal of the American Medical Association 58:*1504–1507, 1912.

7. Pisek and LeWald X-rayed both normal and sick infants from two days old to 20 months. See their article, "The Further Study of Anatomy and Physiology of the Infant Stomach based on Serial Roentgenograms," *Transactions of the American Pediatric Society 25:*150–165, 1913. See also *American Journal of Diseases of Children 6:*232–244, 1913.

8. For reports of "numerous but unsuccessful attempts to obtain blood" from infants and children, see p. 194 of F. S. Churchill and C. P. Clark, "The Bacteriology of the Blood in Early Life," *American Journal of Diseases of Children 1:*193–202, 1911.

9. In one case, a urine collection tube on the penis of an infant caused swelling and was removed before the end of the observation period. See also O. Schloss and J. L.

Crawford, "The Metabolism of Nitrogen, Phosphorous and the Purin Substances in the Newborn," *American Journal of the Diseases of Children 1:*203–230, 1911.

10. S. Benison, A. C. Barger, and E. L. Wolfe list twenty-seven children as subjects and, more significant, they downplay the experimental nature of the spinal taps, an aspect that Wentworth explicitly emphasized, in *Walter B. Cannon: The Life and Times of a Young Scientist,* Cambridge, Mass.: The Belknap Press of Harvard University, 1987, pp. 176–177.

11. For Beecher's two other "ethical lapses" involving children, see R. M. Zollinger, M. C. Lindem, R. M. Filler, J. M. Corson, and R. E. Wilson, "Effect of Thymectomy on Skin-Homograft Survival in Children," *New England Journal of Medicine 270:*707–709, 1964; and H. D. Ticktin and H. Y. Zimmerman, "Hepatic Dysfunction and Jaundice in Patients Receiving Triacetyloleandomycin," *New England Journal of Medicine 267:*964–968, 1962.

References

Abt, I. A. (1903). Hemorrhages in the newborn. *Journal of the American Medical Association 40:*284–291.

American Academy of Pediatrics (1977). Committee on Drugs. *Pediatrics 60:*91–101.

Annas, G. J., and Grodin, M. A. (1992). *The Nazi Doctors and the Nuremberg Code: Human Rights in Human Experimentation.* New York: Oxford University Press.

Beecher, H. K. (1966). Ethics and clinical research. *New England Journal of Medicine 274:*1354–1360, 1359. (See also R. Lich, Howerston, L. W., Goode, L. S., and Davis, L. A., 1964, The ureterovesical junction of the newborn, *Journal of Urology 92:*436–438.)

Beecher, H. K. (1970). *Research and the Individual: Human Studies.* Boston: Little, Brown and Company.

Bercovici, K. (1921). Orphans as guinea pigs. *The Nation 112:*911–913.

Berk, L. B. (1989). Polio vaccine trials of 1935. *Transactions and Studies of the College of Physicians of Philadelphia 11:*321–336.

Black, W. C. (1942). The etiology of acute infectious gingivostomatitis (Vincent's stomatitis). *Journal of Pediatrics 20:*145–160.

Blake, J. B. (1957). *Benjamin Waterhouse and the Introduction of Vaccination: A Reappraisal.* Philadelphia: University of Pennsylvania, pp. 14–15.

Blake, J. B. (1985). The inoculation controversy in Boston, 1721–1722. In *Sickness and Health in America,* ed. J. W. Leavitt and R. L. Numbers. Madison: University of Wisconsin, p. 348.

Boswell, J. (1988). *The Kindness of Strangers.* New York: Pantheon Books.

Bosworth, A. W., Bowditch, H. I., and Ragle, B. H. (1915). Whey in infant feeding. *American Journal of Diseases of Children 9:*124.

Carlson, A. J. (1916). *The Control of Hunger in Health and Disease.* Chicago: University of Chicago. (Cited in K. S. Nicholson, 1917, Anti-vivisection notes, *Journal of Zoophily 26:*187–188.)

Carpenter, T. M., and Murlin, J. R. (1911). The energy metabolism of mother and child just before and just after birth. *Archives of Internal Medicine 7:*184–222. (Also see Benedict, G., and Talbot, F., 1912, Some fundamental principles in studying infant metabolism, *American Journal of Diseases of Children* *4*:129–136.)

Cassedy, J. H. (1984). *American Medicine and Statistical Thinking, 1800–1860*. Cambridge: Harvard University Press.

Clarke, T. W. (1909a). Gastric digestion in infants: A review of the literature. *American Journal of Medical Sciences 137*:674–685.

Clarke, T. W. (1909b). The effect of certain so-called milk modifiers on the gastric digestion of infants. *American Journal of Medical Sciences 137*:872–888. (Also see Cowie, D. M., and Lyon, W., 1911, Further observations of the acid control of the pylorus in infants, *American Journal of Diseases of Children 2*:252–261, esp. p. 253.)

Curran, W. J. (1973). The Tuskegee syphilis study. *New England Journal of Medicine 289*:730.

Degler, C. N. (1981). *At Odds*. New York: Oxford University Press, p. 71.

Dubois, E. (1911). An apparatus for the collection of the excreta of infants. *American Journal of Diseases of Children 2*:415–418.

Duffus, R. L., and Holt, L. E., Jr. (1940) *L. Emmett Holt: Pioneer of a Children's Century*. New York: D. Appleton-Century Company.

Enders, J. F. (1961–1962). Vaccination against measles: Francis Home redivivus. *Yale Journal of Biology and Medicine 34*:239–260.

English, P. C. (1984). Pediatrics and the unwanted child in history: Foundling homes, disease, and the origins of foster care in New York City, 1860 to 1920. *Pediatrics 73*:699–711.

English, P. C. (1985). Diphtheria and theories of infectious disease: Centennial appreciation of the critical role of diphtheria in the history of medicine. *Pediatrics 76*:1–9.

Etheridge, E. W. (1972). *The Butterfly Caste: A Social History of Pellagra in the South*. Westport, Conn.: Greenwood.

Faden, R., and Beauchamp, T. (1986). *A History and Theory of Informed Consent*. New York: Oxford University Press., p. 163.

Federal Policy for the Protection of Human Subjects: Notices and Rules (1991). *Federal Register*, vol. 56, no. 117, Tuesday, June 18.

Fitch, G. L. (1892). The etiology of leprosy. *Medical Record 42*:293–298.

Geison, G. L. (1978). Pasteur's work on rabies: Reexamining the ethical issues. *Hastings Center Report 8*:26–33.

Goldberger, J. (1916). Pellagra: Causation and a method of prevention. *Journal of the American Medical Association 66*:471–476.

Grodin, M. A., and Alpert, J. J. (1988). Children as participants in medical research. *Pediatric Clinics of North America 35*:1389–1401.

Grulee, C. G., and Buhlig, W. H. (1911). Investigation of the action of sodium benzoate in artificially-fed infants. *Archives of Pediatrics 28*:849–869.

Halpern, S. A. (1988). *American Pediatrics: The Social Dynamics of Professionalism, 1880–1980*. Berkeley: University of California Press.

Hamill, S. M., Carpenter, H. C., and Cope, T. A. (1908). A comparison of the Von Pirquet, Calmette and Moro tuberculin tests and their diagnostic value. *Archives of Internal Medicine 2*:405–447.

Heiman, H. (1895). A clinical and bacteriological study of the gonococcus (Neisser) as found in the male urethra and in the vulvo-vaginal tract of children. *Medical Record 47*:769–778.

Hektoen, L. (1905). Experimental measles. *Journal of Infectious Diseases 2:*238–255.

Hermann, C. (1915). Immunization against measles. *Archives of Pediatrics 32:*503–507.

Hess, A. F. (1911). A duodenal tube for infants. *American Journal of Diseases of Children 1:*365. (See also Hess, A. F. 1913. The gastric secretion of infants at birth. *American Journal of Diseases of Children 6:*264–276.

Hess, A. F. (1915). Antimumps inoculation. *American Journal of Obstetrics 72:*183–185.

Hess, A. F. (1914). The use of a series of vaccines in the prophylaxis and treatment of an epidemic of pertussis. *Journal of the American Medical Association 63:*1007.

Hess, A. F. (1934). See Gerstenberger, H. J. Obituaries: Alfred Fabian Hess, M.D. *American Journal of Diseases of Children 47:*635–639.

Hess, A. F., and Fish, M. (1914). Infantile scurvy: The blood, the blood vessels, and the diet. *American Journal of Diseases of Children 8:*386–405.

Hess, A. F., and Unger, L. J. (1919–1920). Dietaries of infants in relation to the development of rickets. *Proceedings of the Society for Experimental Biology and Medicine 17:*220–221.

Hill, J. (1943). Experimental infection with neisseria gonorrhoeae, I. Human inoculations. *American Journal of Syphilis 27:*733–771.

Holt, L. E. (1909). A report upon one thousand tuberculin tests in young children. *Archives of Pediatrics 26:*1–9. (Also see *Vivisection—a menace to hospital patients,* New York: Vivisection Investigation League, n.d. p. 3.)

Humane Society (n.d.). *Human Vivisection: Foundlings Cheaper than Animals.* Washington, D.C.: Humane Society.

Hymanson, A. (1916). Carmin test for the duration of the complete food passage in infants and children. *American Journal of Diseases of Children 11:*112–116.

Jones, J. H. (1981). *Bad Blood: The Tuskegee Syphilis Experiment.* New York: Free Press.

Knowles, F. C. (1909). Molluscum contagiosum: Report of an institutional epidemic of fifty-nine cases. *Journal of the American Medical Association 53:*671–673.

Kolmer, J. A., Klugh, G. F., and Rule, A. M. (1935). A successful method for vaccination against acute anterior poliomyelitis. *Journal of the American Medical Association 104:*456–460.

Krugman, S. (1986). The Willowbrook hepatitis studies revisited: Ethical aspects. *Reviews of Infectious Diseases 8:*157–162, on pp. 157, 160.

Krugman, S., Giles, J. P., and Jacobs, A. M. (1960). Studies on an attenuated measles-virus vaccine. *New England Journal of Medicine 263:*174–177, on p. 175.

Lagnado, L. M., and Dekel, S. C. (1991). *Children of the Flames: Dr. Joseph Mengele and the Untold Story of the Twins of Auschwitz.* New York: William Morrow and Co.

Lavenson, R. S. (1909). Observations on a child with a gastric fistula in relation to recent advances in the physiology of gastric digestion. *Archives of Internal Medicine 4:*271–290.

Lederer, S. E. (1985). Hideyo Noguchi's luetin experiment and the antivivisectionists. *Isis 76:*31–48.

Lederer, S. E. (1992a). Orphans as guinea pigs: American children and medical experimenters, 1890–1930. In *In the Name of the Child: Health and Welfare, 1880–1940,* ed. Roger Cooter. London: Routledge, pp. 96–123.

Lederer, S. E. (1992b). Political animals: The shaping of the biomedical research literature in twentieth-century America. *Isis 83:*61–79.

Levine, R. J. (1986). *Ethics and Regulation of Clinical Research.* 2d ed. Baltimore, Munich: Urban and Schwarzenberg.

Long, E., and Caldwell, E. W. (1911). Some investigations concerning the relation between carpal ossification and physical and mental development. *American Journal of Diseases of Children 1:*113–138.

M'Geer, J. E. (1851). Inoculation in rubeola. *Eclectic Medical Journal 10:*322–324.

Michael, M. (1917) Prophylactic vaccination against chicken-pox. *Archives of Pediatrics 34:*702–706.

Mitchell, R. G. (1964). The child and experimental medicine. *British Medical Journal 1:*721–727.

National Commission for the Protection of Human Subjects of Biomedical and Behavioral Research (1977). Report and Recommendations: Research Involving Children. HEW Publication (OS) 77–004. Washington D.C.

National Commission for the Protection of Human Subjects of Biomedical and Behavioral Research (1978). *The Belmont Report: Ethical Principles and Guidelines for the Protection of Human Subjects of Research.* HEW Publication (OS) 78–0012, Appendix 1; HEW Publication (OS) 78–0013, Appendix II; HEW Publication (OS) 78–0014. Washington, D.C.

Orphans and dietetics (1921). *American Medicine 27:*394–396.

Paul, J. R. (1971). *A History of Poliomyelitis.* New Haven: Yale University Press, pp. 252–262.

Pearce, R. M. (1914). *The Charge of "Human Vivisection" as Presented in Anti-Vivisection Literature.* Chicago: The American Medical Association.

Pisek, G. R. and LeWald, L. T. (1913). The further study of the anatomy and physiology of the infant stomach based on serial roentgenograms. *American Journal of Diseases of Children 6:*232–244.

Rabinoff, S. (1915). Prophylactic vaccination for varicella. *Archives of Pediatrics 32:*651.

Radbill, S. X. (1979). The use of children in pediatric research. Paper delivered at American Association for the History of Medicine, Pittsburgh, Pa. 4 May 1979.

Richardson, D. L., and Connor, H. (1919). Immunization against measles. *Journal of the American Medical Association 72:*1046–1048.

Roberts, J. B. (1896). Human vivisection. *Philadelphia Polyclinic 5:*357.

Rothman, D. J. (1987). Ethics and human experimentation: Henry Beecher revisited. *New England Journal of Medicine 317:*1195–1199.

Rothman, D. J. (1982). Were Tuskegee and Willowbrook "studies in nature"? *Hastings Center Report 12:*5–7.

Rothman, D. J. (1991). *Strangers at the Bedside.* New York: Basic Books.

Rous, F. P. (1941). Rous to William C. Black, 21 July 1941, F. Peyton Rous Papers, Folder: JEM-Black, American Philosophical Society Library.

Rudolph, R. S. (1987). Aspects of child health. In *Pediatrics,* ed. A. M. Rudolph, et al. Norwalk, Conn.: Appleton & Lange, p. 1.

Serwer, D. P. (1977). The rise of radiation protection: Science, medicine and technology in society, 1896–1935, unpublished Ph.D. thesis, Princeton University.

Shultz, W. J. (1968). *The Humane Movement in the United States, 1910–1922.* New York: AMS Press.

Smith, J. S. (1990). *Patenting the Sun: Polio and the Salk Vaccine.* New York: Anchor Books.

Sternberg, G. M., and Reed, W. (1895). Report on immunity against vaccination conferred upon the monkey by the use of the serum of the vaccinated calf and monkey. *Transactions of the Association of American Physicians 10:*57–69.

Stickler, J. W. (1887). Foot-and-mouth disease as it affects man and animals. *New York Medical Journal 32:*725–732. (See also in *Medical Record 32* [1887]: 745–746; and *Boston Medical and Surgical Journal 117* [1887]: 607–609.)

Still, G. F. (1965). *The History of Paediatrics.* London: Dawsons of Pall Mall.

Stokes, J., Jr. (1957). Samuel McClintock Hamill (1864–1948), in *Pediatric Profiles,* ed. B. S. Veeder. St. Louis: Mosby, pp. 93–94, especially pp. 96–97.

Stokes, J., Reilly C. M., Hillman, A. R., and Buynak, E. B. (1960). Use of living attenuated measles-virus vaccine in early infancy. *New England Journal of Medicine 263:*230–233.

Taber, S. R. (1907). Shall vivisection be restricted? Letter to editor of *Chicago Record-Herald,* 12 May 1905. See also *Reasonable restriction vs. absolute license in vivisection.* Chicago: Vivisection Reform Society.

Toyoda, T., Futagi, Y., and Okamoto, M. (1931). Experimental production of scarlet fever by means of a scarlatinal hemolytic streptococcus. *Journal of Infections Diseases 48:*350–357.

U. S. Senate (1914). *Treatment of Tuberculosis.* Senate document 641, 63d Congress, 3d session. Washington, D.C.: Government Printing Office.

Vivisection Investigation League (n.d.). *The Rise and Fall of a Vaccine.* New York.

Webb, G. B. (1912). Studies in tuberculosis. *Bulletin of the Johns Hopkins Hospital 23:*233.

Weindling, P. (1992) From isolation to therapy: Children's hospitals and diphtheria in *fin de siecle* Paris, London, and Berlin. In *In the Name of the Child: Health and Welfare, 1880–1940,* ed. Roger Cooter. London: Routledge, pp. 124–145.

Wentworth, A. H. (1896). Some experimental work on lumbar puncture of the subarachnoid space. *Boston Medical and Surgical Journal 135:*133.

Wilcox, H. (1911). The diagnosis of infantile tetany. *American Journal of Diseases of Childhood 1:*393–416.

Young, J. H. (1975). Saccharin: A bitter regulatory controversy. In *Research in the Administration of Public Policy,* ed. F. B. Evans and H. T. Pinkett. Washington, D.C.: Howard University Press.

Science, Ethics, and the Law

Scientific Issues in Biomedical Research with Children

RALPH E. KAUFFMAN

The dynamic process of growth, differentiation, and maturation is what sets children apart from adults. In addition to overall growth, dramatic changes in body proportions, composition, and physiology take place during childhood. Growth and development are particularly rapid during the first two years of life. Major organ systems differentiate, grow, and mature. Body weight typically doubles by five to six months of age, and triples by the first birthday. Body length increases by 50 percent during the first year. Body surface area doubles by one year of age. During the first eighteen months of life, the child becomes ambulatory, develops socialization, and learns verbal language.

The respective proportions of body weight contributed by fat, protein, and water change substantially during infancy and childhood. At birth total body water constitutes approximately 80 percent of body weight, whereas water accounts for only 60 percent of body weight by five months of age and remains relatively constant thereafter. Although the proportion of body weight comprised by total body water does not change after late infancy, there is a progressive decrease in extracellular water throughout childhood and into young adulthood. As the proportion of body water decreases, the percentage of body weight contributed by fat doubles by four to five months of age. Protein mass increases during the second year of life as the child becomes ambulatory. This metamorphosis becomes apparent as the child changes from a pudgy infant into a wiry and active toddler.

Major organ systems also change in relative size as well as function during childhood. For example, the weights of the liver and kidneys relative to body size are approximately ten times in the preschool child what they are in the young adult (Maxwell, 1984). Likewise, the surface area covered by the skin, relative to body size, in the preschool child is approximately two-and-a-half times that in the adult (Maxwell, 1984, p. 96; Spino, 1985). Functional changes accompany changes in relative size. Hepatic clearance of many substrates is physiologically decreased during the newborn period, rapidly increases during the first three months of life, significantly exceeds adult clearance in the preschool child, and declines to adult levels during puberty (Kauffman, 1991; Wichmann, Rind, and Gladtke, 1968). Renal clearance of endogenous as well as exogenous substances follows a similar pattern. It is physiologically decreased in the newborn, increases to normal adult range during the first year of life, exceeds the adult level in the preschool child, and declines to the normal adult range during puberty (Kauffman, 1991). The absorptive surface of the small intestine is proportionately greater and gastrointestinal transit time may be shorter in infants and younger children compared with adults. Gastric acid production is temporarily decreased during the neonatal period, but approaches adult values by three months of age (Kearns and Reed, 1989). Exocrine pancreatic function also matures during the first year of life (Kearns and Reed, 1989).

Methodological Considerations When Conducting Research in Children

Because of the anatomical and physiological dynamics of growth and development, special considerations apply when conducting biomedical research with children. In addition, children have unique fears, anxieties, and perceptions of body threat at various ages to which the investigator must be sensitive. These factors require modification of methods or development of new methods for conducting research in children that may not be necessary or relevant when engaging in research with adult subjects.

Biomedical research frequently involves interventions that may be invasive and/or may introduce some degree of increased risk to the subject. Because of this, normal, healthy children rarely are included in this type of research. Research with children usually is conducted in the context of medical care of the subjects and therefore involves the participation of children who have a chronic health problem or are acutely ill. Conducting clinical research in the health-care delivery setting introduces a number of logistical and technical issues that the investigator must address.

First, it is essential that the research interventions cause minimal interference with the patient's medical care. The patient's welfare must always take priority. At the same time it is important that the investigator maintain the integrity of the study protocol. For this reason, it rarely is possible to rely on the health-care personnel who are primarily responsible for the subject's care to carry out the maneuvers required to successfully conduct the study. Their overriding responsibilities are to the patient as well as other patients for whom they are responsible and they should not be distracted from their primary responsibilities by research-related tasks. It is highly desirable therefore to have an appropriate professional available whose only responsibility is to assure that the study procedures are followed and who coordinates the study procedures with the child's care. Certain kinds of studies ideally are carried out in pediatric clinical research centers, if such facilities are available, where the caregivers are trained to provide the required medical care while conducting the research.

The success of any clinical study depends on successful enrollment of subjects who meet the protocol criteria. Many study proposals have met with failure, not because they were poorly conceived or poorly designed, but because the investigators were unable to enroll a sufficient number of participants to successfully complete the study. When involving children in research, the investigator needs to remember that the parents also are deeply involved and their interests, concerns, and fears—as well as those of the child—must be considered. A variety of factors influence an investigator's success in recruiting subjects for a study (Kauffman and Kearns, 1992). These include the degree of underlying concern and anxiety the parents and child have regarding the child's illness, the amount of discomfort or inconvenience associated with the study, the perception of patient and parents of the benefits versus the risks entailed in the study, and the way in which the patient and parents are approached with an invitation to participate in the study. The receptiveness of patient and parents to participating in a study is in direct proportion to the degree of rapport the investigator is able to establish. It is important that the investigator have a genuine concern for the welfare of the patient and clearly communicate this to patient and parents. This process includes a thorough knowledge of the patient's condition and treatment along with concurrence by the child's attending physician (if different from the investigator) that the child is an appropriate candidate for the study. The purpose and rationale for the study, all potential benefits and risks, and all procedures required should be described to the patient and parents. All questions should be answered. This allows the parents and, when appropriate, the patient to truly become informed about the study, and therefore give truly informed consent. When done with empathy and compassion, this process establishes a rapport that will lead to successful participation in the majority of cases. Since much of biomedical research in children depends on the availability of an appropriate population of children under medical treatment, it is most efficiently and successfully carried out in institutions or by collaborative groups of pediatric centers that provide care for sizeable populations of children.

Biomedical research frequently requires obtaining samples of body fluids or tissues, most commonly blood and urine. Many protocols require periodic or repeated sampling over some specified time interval. Blood samples may be necessary to follow the effects of a disease or treatment or to measure the time course of the concentration of an investigational drug after a dose has been administered. Venipuncture and capillary stick are the most frequently used methods to obtain blood samples. While these procedures may be done safely and are part of usual medical care, they are painful and frightening to most children. In many instances the anticipatory fear is more painful to the child than the actual physical pain of the procedure. It is important to take whatever steps are feasible to minimize the fear and discomfort associated with blood drawing. Various methods should be used to accomplish this. When feasible, samples for research use may be obtained at the same time blood required for the patient's care is drawn, thereby obviating the need for additional needle sticks. Certain types of patients have indwelling catheters placed to facilitate their care. Sometimes blood samples may be obtained through these catheters, avoiding the need for venipuncture. When repeated blood samples are required by a study, a commonly used technique is to place a small gauge heparinized silastic cannula or metal ''butterfly'' needle in a vein and secure it in place (Kauffman and Kearns, 1992). Once in place a small cannula is not painful and can be used for obtaining repeated samples without subjecting the child to repeated venipunctures or capillary sticks. Cannulae placed in the hand or forearm allow painless repeated sampling and do not restrict movement of the extremity. This is an efficient as well as humane approach to repeated blood sampling and is much less painful and frightening than repeated capillary sticks or venipunctures.

Urine sampling is less threatening and painful than blood sampling but is not without its negative aspects. School-aged children and adolescents may experience embarrassment with the perceived loss of privacy associated with urine collection. The infant or toddler who is not toilet trained presents unique problems. It is very difficult to obtain a complete and accurate quantitative urine collection in younger children without taping an external collection device on the perineum or placing a catheter in the urinary bladder. Neither is without some risk or discomfort. The adhesive from external collection devices may irritate and macerate the skin; a catheter is painful to place and increases the risk of urinary tract infection. Additional pain and discomfort introduced by a study protocol can be avoided in those instances when urine for investigational purposes can be collected simultaneously with samples required for the patient's care. For example, patients in intensive-care settings frequently have urinary catheters placed to monitor their urine output. No additional discomfort is imposed on the patient by collecting urine from the catheter for investigational use.

Other painful or invasive procedures that are required by an experimental protocol also should be conducted in concert with procedures required for medical care to minimize added suffering or risk caused by the research. Several examples help illustrate this point: Bone marrow obtained as part of research into the causes or treatment of childhood cancer may be obtained at the same time bone marrow for diagnosis or follow-up care is obtained; spinal fluid to assess diffusion of a new antibiotic into the central nervous system may be obtained at the time a diagnostic spinal tap is performed; biopsy of the small intestinal mucosa for study of mucosal enzymes may be obtained at the time of diagnostic endoscopy; a small sample of tissue from an organ of interest might be obtained during a therapeutic surgical procedure. Approaches such as these can allow essential research in children to occur without subjecting the child to any significant increased risk or discomfort over and above that entailed in the child's medical care.

Investigators conducting research with children must always be sensitive to the size of samples obtained for study. This is particularly important with regard to blood samples. It is essential that the volume of blood obtained in the course of a research project not significantly reduce the blood volume or red blood cell mass of the child. A common rule of thumb is to limit total blood loss to less than 10 percent of the child's blood volume. This introduces a substantial constraint when carrying out research with infants whose total blood volume may not exceed 250 ml. Likewise, the volume of urine available for analysis from an infant is quite limited compared to an older child or adult. Limitations in sample size require development of analytical methods that use much smaller sample volumes than typically are employed in adult studies. For example, assays that may require 3 to 5 ml of blood for adult studies may need to be modified to use one tenth that volume for similar studies in children.

Recent advances in analytical methodology offer the promise of less-invasive methods for obtaining certain types of new information in children, or the ability to acquire information that until now was not accessible. Nuclear magnetic resonance (NMR) technology has been applied in a very limited way to obtaining pharmacokinetic and drug metabolic data noninvasively in vivo (Malet-Martino and Martino, 1991). To date, drug metabolic studies have relied on noncontinuous invasive methods such as repetitive blood and tissue sampling.

In vivo NMR technology offers the prospect of being able to continuously and directly monitor the distribution and time course of metabolism of some drugs without invasive sampling. Several technical problems remain to be resolved before this becomes a reality, but the promise does exist. Another exciting advance in technology is positron emission tomography (PET) (Wagner, 1991; Baron et al., 1983). PET scanning allows observation of complex functions such as organ and cellular biochemistry, cell energy metabolism, incorporation of nucleotides into DNA, regional blood flow, and the time course of drug concentration in specific organs in the intact organism with minimally invasive techniques. However, PET scanning is not completely noninvasive because it requires administration of a short-lived, positron-emitting isotope and may, in some instances, require sedation and blood sampling during the procedure. The application of this technology to human research, especially in children, is quite limited at present but undoubtedly will expand dramatically during the coming decade.

The use of breath analysis following administration of substances labeled with a stable isotope offers another noninvasive approach to research with children. Several investigators have described the use of caffeine labeled with a stable isotope of carbon, ^{13}C, to noninvasively study oxidative drug metabolism in children (Lambert, et al., 1986; Levitsky, et al. 1989). This is an elegant example of a noninvasive research technique. The children simply were asked to ingest a soft drink containing ^{13}C-labeled caffeine and then to breathe into a sealed container. The quantity of exhaled ^{13}C-labeled CO_2 was measured, and from that the rate of oxidative 3-N-demethylation of caffeine could be determined. This technique—which requires no painful, unpleasant, or frightening procedures—has been used to study the effect of growth hormone on drug metabolism in children during puberty.

Differences Between Children and Adults in Types and Expression of Diseases

Children not only differ from adults anatomically and physiologically, they also differ in the types of diseases from which they suffer and the manifestations of diseases they have in common with adults. Although numerous examples can be cited, only a few will be mentioned to illustrate this concept.

Newborn respiratory distress syndrome (RDS), also known as hyaline membrane disease (HMD), is unique to the premature newborn. It is caused by a deficiency of phosphatidylcholine in the immature lung. Phosphatidylcholine is produced by the alveolar cells of the developed lung and serves as a surfactant agent to prevent collapse of the terminal alveoli during expiration. Since this is a disease that only occurs in the premature newborn infant, it can only be studied in this population. One of the major recent advances in therapy of this condition is the administration of exogenous surfactant by inhalation to the premature infant (American Academy of Pediatrics, Committee on Fetus and Newborn, 1991; Long et al., 1991). The clinical trials of exogenous surfactant had to be conducted exclusively in newborn infants since the condition does not occur in adults.

A serious sequela that affects many infants who are born with immature lungs and develop RDS during the newborn period is bronchopulmonary dysplasia (BPD) (Bancalari and Gerhardt, 1986). Bronchopulmonary dysplasia is thought to be secondary to lung immaturity as well as the administration of high concentrations of oxygen under high pressures by assisted ventilation required to treat RDS. BPD is a chronic lung disease characterized by pulmonary fibrosis, decreased ventilatory capacity, reactive airway disease, and increased susceptibility to lung infections. The disease is unique to infants who survive RDS and there is not an analogous adult disorder. As with RDS, increased understanding of the pathophysiology and treatment of BPD must come from clinical studies involving infants suffering from this condition.

Retinopathy of prematurity is a condition that primarily afflicts premature infants of birth weights less than 1500 g. It is characterized by initial vasoconstriction of the immature retinal vessels followed by permanent vascular occlusion, vasoproliferation within the retina, fibrosis, hemorrhage, and retinal detachment leading to some degree of visual loss, depending on severity (Hoyt, Good, and Petersen, 1991). New approaches to preventing and treating this condition have been explored through large multicenter studies involving large numbers of affected infants, since there is no analogous condition in adults from which comparable information can be obtained (Cryotherapy for Retinopathy of Prematurity Cooperative Group, 1988).

Certain malignancies occur only in children. Neuroblastoma and Wilms tumor are, with rare exception, solid tumors of childhood. The median age of diagnosis is approximately two years for neuroblastoma and three years for Wilms tumor. As a result of advances in treatment of these two childhood malignancies during the past two decades, today there is a greater than 90 percent survival rate at four years after diagnosis in children with stage I-III Wilms tumor and also at two years in children with stages I and II neuroblastoma (Leventhal, 1992). These advances in treatment would have been impossible without research involving infants and children afflicted with these malignancies since these cancers rarely, if ever, occur in adults.

Congenital heart defects occur in approximately ten per one thousand live born infants (Hoffman, 1990). Although mild forms of congenital heart malformations may occasionally persist undetected into adulthood, most congenital heart lesions are diagnosed and treated during infancy and childhood. There is no opportunity to study these conditions in adults and extrapolate the information to pediatric patients. Therefore, research on the pathophysiology and treatment of congenital heart disease must be carried out in infants and young children.

Certain infectious illnesses such as rubella, rubeola, mumps, pertussis, and *Hemophilus influenza* type B occur primarily during childhood. Therefore, studies to document the ability of vaccines to prevent these illnesses must be carried out in children. Furthermore, young children respond to vaccines differently than adult patients so data derived from studies in adult subjects cannot be extrapolated to young children. For example, in contrast to older children and adults, children less than twenty-four months of age did not develop protective immunity to *Hemophilus influenza* type B from the first commercially available vaccine (Peltola et al., 1977). Subsequently, a conjugated vaccine was developed that confers immunity in children under twelve months of age (Shapiro, 1990). The difference in antibody response to the two vaccines had to be documented in young children since the dissimilar response was unique to that age group.

Exposure to excessive lead in the environment can lead to lead poisoning at any age. However, preschool aged children are particularly susceptible to the toxic effects of lead. Several factors contribute to this. Young children are more likely to be exposed to lead in their environment because of their high level of hand-to-mouth activity and their propensity for ingesting nonfood substances. In addition, they absorb a greater fraction of ingested lead from their intestinal tract than adults. Because of their rapid growth and development, young children are uniquely susceptible to the toxic effects of lead on their hematopoietic, skeletal, and nervous systems. Therefore, they are vulnerable to toxicity from lower-body lead burdens than are adults. Some of the most critical indicators of toxicity in children, such as subtle neurological dysfunction and abnormal epiphyseal growth, do not occur in adults and would not be predicted from studies in adults. Current Centers for Disease Control guidelines (Centers for Disease Control, 1991) reflect these differences between children and adults; the guidelines place children at increased risk for neurological toxicity when they have blood lead concentrations greater than 10 μg/ml, whereas risk of toxicity in adults is associated with concentrations exceeding 40 μg/ml. The developmental difference in susceptibility to lead toxicity requires that studies of the pathophysiology and treatment of lead poisoning in children be conducted in children.

A diverse group of diseases are caused by inborn errors of metabolism of amino acids, carbohydrates, lipids, purines, pyrimidines, mucopolysaccharides, and abnormalities of other assorted enzymes and proteins that are critical to normal function. Most inborn errors of metabolism that are severe enough to cause clinical disease express themselves early in life, frequently during infancy. Many of these inherited abnormalities are associated with mental retardation, motor deficits, seizures, failure to grow and develop, organomegally, and chronic illness. Those that become apparent during the newborn period typically are severe and frequently are lethal if not treated promptly. These diseases can only be studied in the children affected by them since they rarely present during adulthood, and their treatment, when available, must be initiated during early childhood to be effective.

HIV infection and Acquired Immune Deficiency Syndrome (AIDS) may occur at any age. Whereas the infection is transmitted in adults predominantly by sharing contaminated needles or through sexual contact, the majority of pediatric cases are due to vertical transmission from an infected mother to her infant during gestation (Caldwell and Rogers, 1991). The clinical course of the infection in infants differs in several important aspects from adult-acquired infection. The clinical presentation of the infection is quite variable in children and many symptomatic children do not meet the Centers for Disease Control AIDS case definition, which is based on adult experience. In infants, the number of T-helper cells is not as predictive of prognosis as in adults. This is partly because normal standards for T-helper cell number have not been established for different pediatric age groups. In addition, the progression of the infection tends to be more rapid in infants compared to adults. Most children infected as infants become symptomatic within the first 3 years of life in contrast to adults in whom the estimated incubation period is 7.8 to 11.0 years. Survival times after diagnosis of AIDS are shorter for children infected in the first year of life compared to adults. Advances in understanding this disease and its treatment in infants and young children must come from studies in this age group, since experience in adults is not representative of the infection in children.

These examples of diverse diseases show the types of differences that exist between children and adults in the manifestations of disease processes. Considering these differences, it is no surprise that information derived from research in adults frequently cannot be readily extrapolated to children of various ages and stages of development and that new knowledge about diseases and therapies for children must be sought through research with children.

Lessons Learned from Advances in Childhood Therapeutics

A substantial amount of new information has been accumulated during the past two decades that enhances our understanding of the influence of growth and development on responses to and toxicity of therapeutic agents used to treat illness during childhood. Some of this information has been derived from empirical observations arising out of therapeutic misadventures, but much of it has evolved from well-designed prospective research. The following is an overview of the types of information derived from research that has led to an increased understanding of the interactions between growth, development and therapeutic interventions, and the resulting implications for the care of ill children.

Changes in body composition and functional capacity of the primary organs of elimination that occur during childhood and adolescence alter the distribution and elimination of many drugs used to treat sick infants and children. This process modifies the weight-adjusted doses required in children at different ages to produce the desired effect while avoiding dose-related toxicity.

The respective apparent distribution volumes of the penicillin, aminoglycoside, and cephalosporin antibiotics, which distribute primarily in extracellular water, tend to be greater in infants and decrease during maturation coincident with the progressive relative decrease in extracellular water (Koren, 1988). Maturational changes in tissue binding of a drug also may affect its apparent volume of distribution. For example, the binding of digoxin to the myocardium and red blood cell membranes of infants and children up to thirty-six months of age is two to three times that of adults, resulting in a significantly greater apparent volume of distribution of digoxin in children compared to adults (Andersson, Bertler, and Wettrell, 1975; Park et al., 1982; Gorodischer, Jusko, and Yaffe, 1976).

The capacity to metabolize and excrete drugs changes throughout infancy, childhood, and adolescence. The rate of metabolism and elimination of a drug is important because it determines the dose and dosing interval necessary to provide optimal concentrations of the drug in the body. The ability of the liver to metabolize drugs and of the kidney to excrete drugs is physiologically decreased during the newborn period. As renal and hepatic functions mature during the first year of life, the capacity to eliminate drugs increases. With maturation of hepatic and renal function, the clearance of many drugs in young children older than one year of age equals or exceeds that in adults when corrected for body surface area (Kauffman, 1991). Typically, the greatest capacity to metabolize and eliminate drugs is in prepubescent children. During puberty the clearance of many drugs decreases to adult levels. The physiologic decline in drug metabolism during puberty appears to be related, in part, to hormonal changes associated with puberty (Levitsky et al., 1989).

In some instances, the dominant pathway by which a drug is metabolized changes during maturation. The metabolic pathway may alter the risk of adverse effects of a drug. For example, caffeine accumulates to pharmacologically active concentrations in infants who are receiving theophylline for more than ten days because infants metabolize theophylline to caffeine and then are unable to efficiently eliminate the caffeine (Aranda et al., 1984). Accumulated caffeine adds to the pharmacologic effect of theophylline and may contribute to risk of theophylline toxicity. At approximately six months of age, the oxidative pathways by which the methylxanthines are metabolized mature; metabolism to caffeine becomes a minor metabolic pathway for theophylline, clearance of caffeine increases, and caffeine accumulation no longer occurs.

The metabolic profile of acetaminophen also differs in children compared to adults (Miller, Roberts, and Fischer, 1976). The dominant pathway in infants and prepubescent children is sulfate conjugation. During puberty the major pathway shifts to glucuronidation and remains so during late adolescence and adulthood. In contrast to caffeine, the difference in acetaminophen metabolism between children and adults appears to decrease the risk of acetaminophen toxicity in children relative to adults (Lieh-Lai et al., 1984).

The age-related doses of many drugs reflect the developmental changes in drug metabolism and elimination. Typically, smaller doses, adjusted for body weight, are required in infants. It is frequently assumed this is the case throughout childhood. However, the highest weight-adjusted doses are required in prepubescent children, and dose requirements are reduced to adult levels during puberty. For example, the maintenance dose of digoxin for premature infants is 5 μg/kg; for full-term newborns, 8–10 μg/kg; for infants less than two years, 10–12 μg/kg; for prepubescent children greater than two years, 8–10 μg/kg; and for adults, 3–4 μg/kg (Park, 1986). Recommended theophylline intravenous infusion rates to maintain therapeutic concentrations are 0.3–0.6 mg/kg/hr for infants less than twelve months; 0.8–1.0 mg/kg/hr for children one to nine years; 0.7 mg/kg for children nine to twelve years; and 0.5 mg/kg/hr for nonsmoking adults (Hendeles and Weinberger, 1983). The weight-adjusted dose of aminoglycoside antibiotics required to achieve equivalent plasma concentrations in children are 50–100 percent greater than in adult patients (Vogelstein, Kowarski, and Lietman, 1977).

The complex processes involved in growth and development also influence the vulnerability of the child to toxicity from medications. In some instances, children are more susceptible to toxicity and in others they are less susceptible. Numerous examples of toxicities are unique to children and would not be predicted from studies in adult subjects.

Tetracycline antibiotics are not recommended for use by children less than nine years of age because they cause enamel dysplasia in developing teeth (Stewart, 1973). Likewise, the fluoroquinolone antibiotics are contraindicated in children because they induce dysplasia of growing cartilage (Muszynski, Christenson, and Scribner, 1988).

Metoclopramide and prochlorperazine are commonly used to reduce vomiting associated with chemotherapy. Both these drugs can cause acute dystonic reactions due to their stimulation of dopamine-2 receptors in the central nervous system. Younger children are more susceptible to this adverse effect, possibly because of greater concentration of dopamine-2 receptors in the immature brain (Wong et al., 1984).

Infants and young children are more prone to hyperpyrexia caused by anticholinergic drugs such as atropine and scopolamine. Cases have been described in which toxicity occurred following topical ocular administration of these drugs (Morton, 1939).

Verapamil is a calcium channel blocking drug that is a medication of choice to treat supraventricular arrhythmias in older children and adults. However, infants with supraventricular tachyarrhythmias are at increased risk of sudden cardiac arrest when verapamil is administered (Garson, 1987). Because of this, verapamil is not recommended for use in infants less than one year of age.

Valproic acid, a commonly used anticonvulsant drug, can cause acute hyperammonemia associated with hepatoencephalopathy in rare instances. Children under five years of age are at greatest risk for this life-threatening adverse reaction (American Academy of Pediatrics Committee on Drugs, 1982).

Desflurane, a new inhalation anesthetic, provides rapid, smooth, and safe induction of anesthesia in adult patients. However, in pediatric patients it causes an unacceptable incidence of laryngospasm, breath-holding, and hypersecretion when used as an induction agent (Zwass et al., 1992). It does provide safe anesthesia once induction is accomplished and the patient is intubated.

Immaturity does not invariably predispose to greater toxicity. Some types of toxicity are decreased in the immature individual. Infants and young children appear to be less susceptible to ototoxicity and renal toxicity from aminoglycoside antibiotics compared to older patients (McCracken, 1986). This may be due, in part, to reduced ability to concentrate the drugs intracellularly in renal tubular epithelial cells (Hermann, 1983).

Children tend to experience relatively mild liver toxicity from acute acetaminophen overdoses compared to adults. Evidence indicates that this is due to a greater capacity to metabolize acetaminophen by nontoxic pathways (Lieh-Lai et al., 1984).

Hepatotoxicity from the general anesthetic, halothane, is relatively rare in children, even following multiple anesthetic exposures, whereas it is not uncommon in adult patients (Warner, et al., 1984). Similarly, the risk of isoniazid-induced hepatitis is age-related. The incidence of hepatitis is negligible in patients less than twenty years of age whereas the reported incidence is 23 per 1000 in patients fifty to sixty-five years old (Food and Drug Administration, 1978).

The central lessons to be derived from the foregoing overview are (1) that responses to therapeutic agents change in fundamental ways during maturation; and (2) that new knowledge and understanding of the interrelationships between development and response to medications must be gained from research involving children at various stages of development.

Major Future Directions for Biomedical Research with Children

The past three decades have been marked by major advances in the development of new medications, primarily through synthetic chemistry. During the next decade, the most innovative and beneficial new therapeutic agents will be developed through biotechnology involving the use of genetically engineered organisms, recombinant DNA, and continuous cell lines. Several products produced with this technology currently are available, including human insulin, human growth hormone, erythropoietin, colony stimulating factors, rabies vaccine grown in human diploid cells, antibody to gram negative bacterial endotoxin, and genetically engineered clotting factors. A recent survey of biotechnology products in development revealed a 60-percent increase in the number of new biotechnology medications under study during the four years preceding the survey and 132 therapeutic products in various phases of testing at the time of the survey (Pharmaceutical Manufacturers' Association, 1991). These include clotting factors, colony stimulating factors, dismutases, interferons, interleukins, monoclonal antibodies, peptides, tissue plasminogen activators, tumor necrosis factors, vaccines, and antiretroviral agents. As these new therapies come into clinical testing, their respective roles in the treatment of diseases affecting children will need to be assessed and appropriate research in pediatric patients carried out.

Gene therapy, an exciting new area of therapeutics still in its infancy, recently was reviewed by Croghan (1991). This new therapeutic modality involves the introduction of exogenous genetic material into host cells to code for the expression of a protein not normally produced by the host. This procedure may be used to replace a defective gene in an individual with a genetic abnormality or to produce a therapeutic biological agent in a target tissue. Early human experiments with gene therapy have demonstrated the feasibility of this technology. One of the earliest attempts at gene therapy involved infusing T lymphocytes transfected with a retroviral vector containing the coding sequence for adenosine deaminase into a patient with inherited adenosine deaminase deficiency. Adenosine deaminase deficiency typically becomes apparent during infancy as a severe combined immune deficiency that predisposes the infant to life-threatening infections. No accepted treatment exists, and replacement of the defective gene offers the promise of a cure. The transfected T cells are transfused in the hope that they will produce sufficient adenosine deaminase to correct the patient's deficiency. In another gene therapy trial, two patients with malignant melanoma were given tumor-infiltrating lymphocytes transfected with the gene coding for tumor necrosis factor. The hypothesis was that these cells would migrate to the tumor where they produce high concentrations of tumor necrosis factor leading to lysis of the melanoma. Yet another proposed approach is to treat skin cancer by administering tumor-infiltrating lymphocytes containing the genes for interleukin-2 and interleukin-4 in the hope that the interleukins will stimulate anticancer reactive cells in the patient. Examples of other future potential applications include treatment of atherosclerosis, rheumatic diseases, inherited clotting disorders, hemoglobinopathies, cystic fibrosis, and a host of other inherited diseases that result from deficiency of a protein or production of an abnormal protein. This is a technology that not only promises great benefit but undoubtedly will also present us with ethical issues with which we have not previously been confronted.

Summary

Biomedical research has brought numerous advances in the diagnosis and treatment of disease during the past forty years. The next forty years promise even greater progress along with enormous challenges. Much of the clinical research on the horizon will address diseases that have their expression during fetal life, infancy, and childhood. It is imperative that investigators working with children always design, conduct, and interpret their research in the context of the dramatic and complex changes that take place during the process of growth and development.

References

American Academy of Pediatrics Committee on Drugs (1982). Valproic acid: Benefits and risks. *Pediatrics 70:*316–319.
American Academy of Pediatrics Committee on Fetus and Newborn (1991). Surfactant replacement therapy for respiratory distress syndrome. *Pediatrics 87:*946–947.
Andersson, K. E., Bertler, A., and Wettrell, G. (1975). Post-mortem distribution and tissue concentrations of digoxin in infants and adults. *Acta Paediatrica Scandinavica 64:*497–504.
Aranda, J. V., Scalais, E., Papageorgiou, A., et al. (1984). Ontogeny of human caffeine and theophylline metabolism. *Developmental Pharmacology and Therapeutics 7*(suppl. 1):18–25.

Bancalari, E., and Gerhardt, T. (1986). Bronchopulmonary dysplasia. *Pediatric Clinics of North America 33:*1–23.

Baron, J. C., Roeda, D., Munari, C., et al. (1983). Brain regional pharmacokinetics of [11]c-labeled diphenylhydantoin: positron emission tomography in humans. *Neurology 33:*580–585.

Caldwell, M. B., and Rogers, M. F. (1991). Epidemiology of pediatric HIV infection. *Pediatric Clinics of North America 38:*1–16.

Centers for Disease Control (1991). *Preventing Lead Poisoning in Young Children.* Atlanta, Ga.: Department of Health and Human Services, Public Health Service, Centers for Disease Control.

Croghan, T. W. (1991). Advances in gene therapy. *Hospital Formulary 26:*880–884.

Cryotherapy for Retinopathy of Prematurity Cooperative Group (1988). Multicenter trial of cryotherapy for retinopathy of prematurity. *Archives of Ophthalmology 106:*471.

Food and Drug Administration (1978). *FDA Drug Bulletin 8:*11.

Garson, A., Jr. (1987). Medicolegal problems in the management of cardiac arrhythmias in children. *Pediatrics 79:*84–88.

Gorodischer, R., Jusko, W. J., and Yaffe, S. J. (1976). Tissue and erythrocyte distribution of digoxin in infants. *Clinical Pharmacology and Therapeutics 19:*256–263.

Hendeles, L., and Weinberger, M. (1983). Theophylline: A state of the art review. *Pharmacotherapy 3:*2–44.

Hermann, G. (1983). Renal toxicity of aminoglycosides in the neonatal period. *Pediatric Pharmacology 3:*251–254.

Hoffman, J. I. E. (1990). Congenital heart disease. *Pediatric Clinics of North America 37:*25–43.

Hoyt, C. S., Good, W., and Petersen, R. (1991). Disorders of the eye. In *Diseases of the Newborn,* 6th ed., ed. H. W. Taeusch, R. A. Ballard, and M. E. Avery. Philadelphia: W. B. Saunders, pp. 1015–1017.

Kauffman, R. E. (1991). Drug therapeutics in the infant and child. In *Pediatric Pharmacology, Therapeutic Principles in Practice,* 2nd ed., ed. S. J. Yaffe and J. V. Aranda. Philadelphia: W. B. Saunders, pp. 212–219.

Kauffman, R. E., and Kearns, G. L. (1992). Pharmacokinetic studies in pediatric patients, clinical and ethical considerations. *Clinical Pharmacokinetics 23*(1):1–20.

Kearns, G. L., and Reed, M. D. (1989). Clinical pharmacokinetics in infants and children: A reappraisal. *Clinical Pharmacokinetics 17*(suppl. 1):29–67.

Koren, G. (1988). Clinical pharmacology of antimicrobial drugs during development: How are infants and children different? In *Antimicrobial Therapy in Infants and Children,* ed. G. Koren, C. G. Prober, and R. Gold. New York: Marcel Dekker, pp. 47–52.

Lambert, G. H., Schoeller, D. A., Kotake, A. N., et al. (1986). The effect of age, gender, and sexual maturation on the caffeine breath test. *Developmental Pharmacology and Therapeutics 9:*375–388.

Leventhal, B. G. (1992). Neoplasms and neoplasm-like structures. In *Nelson Textbook of Pediatrics,* 14th ed., ed. R. E. Behrman, R. M. Kiegman, W. E. Nelson, and V. C. Vaughan III. Philadelphia: W. B. Saunders, pp. 1291–1322.

Levitsky, L. L., Schoeller, D. A., Lambert, G. H., et al. (1989). Effect of growth hormone therapy in growth hormone-deficient children on cytochrome p-450–dependent 3-n-demethylation of caffeine as measured by the caffeine $^{13}CO_2$ breath test. *Developmental Pharmacology and Therapeutics 12:*90–95.

Lieh-lai, M. W., Sarnaik, A. P., Newton, J. F., et al. (1984). Metabolism and pharmacokinetics of acetaminophen in a severely poisoned young child. *Journal of Pediatrics 105:*125–128.

Long, W., Thompson, T., Sundell, H., et al. (1991). Effects of two rescue doses of a synthetic surfactant on mortality rate and survival without bronchopulmonary dysplasia in 700– to 1350–gram infants with respiratory distress syndrome. *Journal of Pediatrics 118:*595–605.

McCracken, G. H., Jr. (1986). Aminoglycoside toxicity in infants and children. *American Journal of Medicine 8:*172–175.

Malet-Martino, M.-C. and Martino, R. (1991). Uses and limitations of nuclear magnetic resonance (NMR) spectroscopy in clinical pharmacokinetics. *Clinical Pharmacokinetics 20:*337–349.

Maxwell, G. M. (1984). *Principles of Paediatric Pharmacology.* New York: Oxford University Press.

Miller, R. P., Roberts, R. J., Fischer, L. J. (1976). Acetaminophen elimination kinetics in neonates, children and adults. *Clinical Pharmacology and Therapeutics 19:*284–294.

Morton, H. G. (1939). Atropine intoxication: Its manifestations in infants and children. *Journal of Pediatrics 14:*755–760.

Muszynski, M. J., Christenson, J. C., and Scribner, R. K. (1988). DNA-Gyrase inhibitors: Nalidixic acid, quinolones, and novobiocin. In *Antimicrobial Therapy in Infants and Children,* ed. G. Koren, C. G. Prober, and R. Gold. New York: Marcel Dekker, pp. 433–463.

Park, M. K. (1986). Use of digoxin in infants and children with specific emphasis on dosage. *Journal of Pediatrics 108:*871–877.

Park, M. K., Ludden, T., Arom, K. V., et al. (1982). Myocardial vs serum digoxin concentrations in infants and adults. *American Journal of Diseases of Children 136:*418–420.

Peltola, H., Kayhty, H., Sivonen, A., et al. (1977). Haemophilus influenzae type b capsular polysaccharide vaccine in children: A double-blind field study of 100,000 vaccinees 3 months to 5 years of age in Finland. *Pediatrics 60:*730–735.

Pharmaceutical Manufacturers' Association (1991). 1991 Survey report, 132 biotechnology medicines in testing represent a 63% increase over 4 years. In *Development: Biotechnology Medicines.* Washington, D.C.: Pharmaceutical Manufacturer's Association.

Shapiro, E. D. (1990). New vaccines against *Haemophilus influenzae* type b. *Pediatric Clinics of North America 37:*567–583.

Spino, M. (1985). Pediatric dosing rules and nomograms. In *Textbook of Pediatric Clinical Pharmacology,* ed. S. M. MacLeod and I. C. Radde. Littleton, Mass.: PSG, pp. 118–128.

Stewart, D. J. (1973). Prevalence of tetracyclines in children's teeth—study II: Resurvey after five years. *British Medical Journal 3:*320–322.

Vogelstein, B., Kowarski, A., and Lietman, P. S. (1977). The pharmacokinetics of amikacin in children. *Journal Pediatrics 91:*333–339.

Wagner, H. N., Jr. (1991). Clinical PET: Its time has come. *Journal of Nuclear Medicine 32:*561–564.

Warner, L. O., Beach, T. P., and Garvin, J. P. (1984). Halothane and children. The first quarter century. *Anesthesia Analgesics 63:*838–842.

Wichmann, H. M., Rind, H., and Gladtke, E. (1968). Die elimination von bromsul-
phalein beim kind. *Zeitschrift Kinderheilk.* *103:*262–276.

Wong, D. F., Wagner, H. N., Dannals, R. F., et al. (1984). Effects of age on dopa-
mine and seratonin receptors measured by positron tomography of the living human
brain. *Science 226:*1393.

Zwass, M. S., Welborn, L. G., Cote', C. J., et al. (1992). Clinical pharmacology of
anesthesia with desflurane and nitrous oxide in infants and children. *Anesthesiol-
ogy 76:*373–378.

2

Scientific Issues in Psychosocial and Educational Research with Children

GERALD P. KOOCHER
PATRICIA KEITH-SPIEGEL

It is no secret that we begin life as small, defenseless, egocentric beings, largely unaware of our own capabilities and without verbally based interpersonal relationships. We progress through stages in physical, social, intellectual, and emotional development. Along the way, we pass through critical periods of vulnerability and opportunity. Although these phenomena are worth studying and lead to valuable and helpful information, the events that make children interesting also present unique risks and challenges to the social science investigator.

Developmental Differences

Social development focuses successively on self-exploration and then interaction in the family, peer group, and ultimately in society as a whole. Through

This chapter is adapted from Chapters 5 and 6 of G. P. Koocher and P. Keith-Spiegel (1990) *Children, Ethics, and the Law*, University of Nebraska Press.

this process we learn about the world and are "socialized," or taught about various societal roles by our families and social institutions. The "terrible twos" and "rebellious adolescent years" are well-known social concepts that present the adult perception that it is difficult to deal with children who challenge or question authority. The point to be made here is that the process of socialization presents considerable pressure for children to conform or acquiesce to adults' wishes. As a result of these pressures, it is likely that offers to exercise various rights (e.g., the right to decline participation in a research project) will not be recognized or acted on by many children. Likewise, oppositional responses sometimes may occur more as a function of developmental stage than of reasoned choice.

The role of cognitive development is well illustrated by the evolution of time perspective. Ask a child, "Do you want a little candy bar today, or a big one next week?" To the four year old for whom next week may seem a decade away, immediate gratification is the obvious choice. A child's ability to go beyond the present and conceptualize the future, including hypothetical or potential outcomes, is closely linked to stages of cognitive development. One must be mindful of this when asking children to participate in decisions involving a recognition and assessment of potential or future outcomes.

Time perspective becomes critically important whenever a decision involves being able to weigh its short- versus long-term consequences. It is also an important consideration when developmental level predisposes children to choose immediate gratification, while ignoring or failing to weigh their longer-term best interests.

Availability

Children are often more readily available as research participants than are adults. Minors are found in bunches at schools, day care centers, hospitals, agencies, and so on, which makes them attractive to anyone attempting to locate an easy-access sample. Captive populations tend to minimize logistical complications which may invite more risk-taking by investigators (Rae and Fournier, 1986).

Investigator Competence

Ideally, all investigators studying children should possess competencies in research methodology, statistics, developmental psychology, family studies, and child/adolescent mental health. Some do, but many are weak in one or more of these areas. Traditional institutions training developmental psychologists emphasize experimental and research methodology skills and deemphasize or neglect altogether clinical skill training, and vice versa for clinical psychologists and other mental health professionals.

Ethical Implications of Investigators' Theoretical Perspectives

Theories of development vary with regards to such factors as the role of biological and genetic bases versus experience and the role of learning, the scope of the theory (e.g., holistic versus specific area of development) and so on. The research design usually mirrors the theoretical orientation, values, and the interpretation of the results. Ethical issues that may compromise the integrity of the research design and interpretation of the results are ever present, often without the full awareness of the investigator. For example, if an investigator's theory holds that the mother is the key to the family dysfunction that leads to sexual abuse of the children by the father, and if an interview schedule focuses exclusively on mother issues, disconfirming data may not emerge simply because there was no built-in possibility for that outcome (de Chesnay, 1984).

Ethical dilemmas also can arise when the investigator's theory of human development heavily influences risk assessment. For example, if one adheres to a theory that children are tough and resilient, techniques may be proposed that an investigator holding a more vulnerable view of immaturity would never consider. For example, one investigator may believe that lowering children's self-esteem or manipulating a failure experience for research purposes poses no problems in very young children because they will have forgotten about the whole thing by the next day. Another investigator, holding a theory that young children are very vulnerable to long-term effects of early negative experiences, would be unlikely to use such techniques in the first place or would attempt to assure that any negative effects were removed before the child left the room.

Practical Problems Affecting Data Validity with Children

Children, particularly younger ones, pose some practical problems that must be taken into consideration when planning research. Their limited vocabularies and potential for misunderstanding verbal instructions, coupled with the experimenter's possible misinterpretation of the meaning intended by the minor's verbal responses, may create "noise" in the communications. Children's variable moods (e.g., silliness, anxiety, or shyness around strangers) and their often limited attention spans can affect data quality. Situational variables, such as experimenter's physical appearance, personality style, or the setting in which the data are collected, may be even more influential on performances for children than for adults and should be carefully considered and controlled at the onset.

Sampling Bias and Dropouts

Fussiness, fatigue, and short attention span are conditions that frequently plague experimental trials involving young children. Even if a very sleepy or anxious participant persists to the end, the validity of the data is in doubt. In many cases these conditions make it necessary to terminate the trial prior to its conclusion. Data analysis generally excludes these "drop outs." For example, in studies of infant perception, it has been estimated that between 25 percent and 70 percent of the participants cannot maintain an alert or nonfussy state long enough to complete the experimental sessions (Caron, Caron, and Caldwell, 1971).

Therapeutic versus Nontherapeutic Research

During the deliberations of the National Commission for the Protection of Human Subjects of Biomedical and Behavioral Research work in the late 1970s, the distinction between *therapeutic* and *nontherapeutic* research that was earlier popularized by many commentators was carefully reevaluated. Basically, the notion was that research proposals designed to directly benefit those with some illness or other problem might be evaluated very differently in terms of what could ethically be "done to" children (including how consent was to be obtained and the acceptable level of potential risk), as compared to research conducted for the sole purpose of obtaining generalizable knowledge about children.

Opinions about conditions under which children could, or whether they should ever, be enrolled in *nontherapeutic* research have varied markedly, often in the form of lively debate (e.g., Ackerman, 1979; Campbell, 1974; Comiskey, 1978; Cooke, 1977; Gaylin and Macklin, 1982; Glantz, Annas, and Katz, 1977; Langer, 1985; Lowe, Alexander, and Mishkin, 1974; McCormick, 1974, 1976; and Ramsey, 1976). Here the usual assumption that parents know what is best for their children, and thus may "consent" for them, is inapplicable because there is no *direct* beneficial intent to begin with. Is it ethical to use children for the "social good," even if parents give their permission? The issue is not resolved easily, because research application is a process that tracks across time, with findings overlaid upon each other as the knowledge stockpile grows. No one can say for certain what information ultimately will be beneficial regardless of the initial intent.

Use of the terms *therapeutic* research and *nontherapeutic* research ultimately was abandoned by the National Commission and replaced with a conceptualization of levels of acceptable risks depending on the potential benefits accruing to the participants or to others.

Allowable Risks with Child Research Participants

The Department of Health and Human Services (HHS) (1983) guidelines place considerable responsibility for risk-level assessment and approval in the hands of the institutional review boards (IRBs). So long as a proposed research project involving minors poses "no greater than minimal risk," HHS-sponsored research can be deemed acceptable even if *no* benefit to the child participants or to children in general is anticipated.

As for the definition of "minimal risk," HHS (1983) offers us only the following:

> Minimal Risk means that the risks of harm anticipated in the proposed research are not greater, considering probability and magnitude, than those ordinarily encountered in daily life or during the performance of routine physical or psychological examinations or tests.

Although the National Commission for the Protection of Human Participants in Research (1977) offers examples of minimal risk techniques (which include questionnaires, psychological tests, and puzzles), the definition remains ambiguous. It even lends itself to the possible interpretation that a research protocol may include risks as *great* as the sort that a child might encounter in an average day (Furlow, 1980), which could include being run down by a car or sexually molested on the way home from school. The loose definition also leaves room for the disturbing interpretation that the standards of risk can be adjusted up or down depending on the life situation of the population under investigation. That is to say, one might attempt to justify the use of more risky procedures under a "minimal risk" standard if the child participants live in dangerous families or neighborhoods. The HHS definition could benefit from clarification, although we assume that the standard level to be used implicitly envisions a relatively safe and caring home and environmental context. Thus, in our estimation, an example of a "minimal risk" study with those risks actually manifesting themselves, would look something like this:

One hundred children in several age groups were compared in a reaction-time experiment. They were asked to push a button as fast as they could every time a blue light appeared on a panel. All went well except for one nine-year-old who complained of a sore finger after he slammed the button vigorously, and a six-year-old who started to cry upon becoming confused about when she was supposed to push the button.

These two children's temporarily sore digit and stress would seem to fall into the realm of children's "everyday" risks, similar to tripping over a toy or feeling upset after a failed attempt to get juice into a cup. As such, this study would very likely be judged in the "minimal risk" category.

Research involving greater than minimal risk but presenting the prospect of direct benefit to the child participants is also appropriate according to the HHS guidelines, as long as the IRB determines that the risk is justified by the antici-pated direct benefits and that the anticipated risk/benefit ratio is at least as favorable as that of other available procedures or approaches. Research involv-ing "greater than minimal risk" but which holds out *no* prospect of direct benefit to the child participants also may be appropriate if: the risk is judged to be a "minor increase over minimal risk"; the intervention or procedures experienced by the children are reasonably commensurate with those "inherent in their actual or expected medical, dental, psychological, social, or educa-tional situations"; the intervention or procedure is "likely to yield generaliz-able knowledge about the subject's disorder or condition which is of vital im-portance for the understanding or amelioration of the subject's disorder or condition." Ambiguous terms persist, however, not only in the definition of what is a "minor increase over minimal risk," but also with respect to what comprises "direct benefit," important "generalizable knowledge," or even what constitutes a "disorder" or "condition" that requires alleviation that the "direct benefit" may provide. In social or behavioral research, such concepts are not easily operationalized, and opinions among professionals may clash. If the child learned something or felt good about being a research participant, is that sufficient to claim that a "direct benefit" has resulted? Some would sup-port that argument (e.g., Bower and de Gasparis, 1978). If the child becomes nervous when taking school exams, is this a "condition" or a normal (albeit troublesome) human characteristic? Where lines are drawn becomes critical in the assessment of research protocols because allowable risk varies accordingly.

A fourth category in the HHS guidelines allows the possibility of "research not otherwise approvable" to be conducted if it provides a reasonable opportu-nity to understand, prevent or alleviate a serious problem affecting the health or welfare of children, such as a rapidly spreading and dangerous virus. How-ever, far more rigorous external review, including the opportunity for public review, is mandated in such instances. It is unlikely that a social or behavioral science study would ever appropriately fit into this category.

Risks to Children in Psychosocial and Educational Research

Psychosocial and educational research does not typically present the more serious consequences to participants, such as pain or a worsening of a physical condition, that can arise in biomedical research. In fact, the risks in psychosocial and educational research often appear trivial. Yet such risks are also difficult to define, detect, and assess for long-term impact.

Among the less significant risks for children in the experimental setting itself are tedium or boredom, confusion, inconvenience, temporary anxiety due to the presence of strangers or the novelty of the situation, and disruption of normal routine. Such risks are often much like other "downside" aspects of a child's average day.

Risks that may present more disturbing experiences for children include induced anxiety or stress, fear of failure, a lowering of self-esteem, reactions to intrusions of privacy, conflict or guilt caused by opportunities or temptations to behave counter to values or expected rules of conduct, embarrassment, physical discomfort, and adverse reactions to the investigator or to the true purpose of a deception experience upon being "debriefed."

Other risks of participation in psychosocial and educational research can manifest themselves over the longer term. Many of these may harm children significantly. Withholding or delaying needed interventions, breaches of confidentiality, "social injury," "labeling" that unfairly stereotypes or stigmatizes the participants, and loss of trust in adults as a result of investigators' thoughtlessness or upon learning that one was lied to or manipulated are among the more troublesome risks. The effects may linger long after the study has been completed, allowing no opportunity for the investigator to ameliorate the problem or to even become aware that a harm had materialized.

Although the risks noted above are potentially operative in psychosocial and educational research with any population, including competent adult humans, the vulnerabilities inherent in minor status place additional responsibilities on investigators. We have much to learn about children. Yet current knowledge allows for the assumption that traumatic or emotionally upsetting experiences are problematic for one whose tender age and accompanying immaturities preclude a full understanding of causes and dynamics related to events. Assessment and coping strategies are less fully developed in children than in adults. What experiences trigger negative reactions or what factors determine their intensity may vary as a function of age alone.

It must also be kept in mind that most minors who are sought out as research participants often possess vulnerabilities beyond those imposed by age. Disadvantaged background, emotional disturbance, developmental disability, mental or physical illness, stressed, judged "at risk" for school failure or other problem, school dropout, and criminal or acting-out behavior are among the relatively common criteria for minors conscripted into research activities. Unfortunately, more vulnerable research target populations also tend to be subjected to more risks (Wells and Sametz, 1985). As Fisher and Tryon (1988) have noted, "nonnormal" participants are more likely to be exposed to more deficit-oriented stimuli that may be more uncomfortable (thus, more risky) than stimuli used with "normal participants." For example, research on aversive conditioning techniques is difficult to justify using "normal" children, but their use with autistic children is often viewed differently.

Individual Differences Among Risk Assessors

A given design can often be evaluated for risk differently depending on the values and perspectives of those empowered to make such assessments. For example, in a survey of pediatricians, Janofsky and Starfield (1981) found remarkable variability in risk assessment levels assigned to very common and routine pediatric procedures. Three cases, presented below, illustrate how individual differences in risk assessments may arise among psychosocial and educational researchers.

> Investigators studied the relationship between children's first names and their popularity with peers. Children were asked, in private, which three classmates they liked the best and which three they disliked the most. Each child's sociometric choice was compared to his or her name category, such as "common," "old-fashioned," "odd," or "trendy."

It is not readily apparent how this study could benefit the children involved, and the project also seems a bit trivial. Some risk is attendant, at least for the less preferred children who were made more salient in the other children's minds and may have been teased or gossiped about (e.g., "Who did you say you didn't like?"). However, some have contended that less popular children are not placed at any additional disadvantage by participating in a sociometric procedure, (e.g., Hayvren and Hymel, 1984). It can also be argued that the results of such a study may benefit children in the future, if certain types of given names are consistently linked to more or less peer acceptance, by sharing the findings with prospective parents.

> A group of children identified as mildly shy and "quiet" by teachers were enrolled in an experimental program designed to build assertiveness, enhance

self-esteem, and teach the children how to stand up for themselves and defend their points of view.

Benefits for the children appear potentially substantial and no risks are readily apparent. However, it could be argued that children who reach the program goals could be put at risk at school or at home since some teachers and parents may label the children's newly emerged behavior as "stubborn," "arrogant," "rebellious," or "disrespectful." Thus, such children could conceivably face censure and punishment as a direct result of successful participation in a program with beneficial intent.

A group of parents whose unborn child was identified through amniocentesis as showing the XYY genotype were selected for an intensive educational, child-management class. This experimental program was designed to better prepare the parents to cope with any behavioral disorders that might materialize.

Such a program may well assist parents in approaching their genetically different child from an informed and sensible perspective. At the same time, however, some untoward effects are possible as well. Critics of this program contended that these "educated" parents may become unnecessarily alarmed, especially if they also familiarize themselves with the flashier "criminal gene" literature. Parents may even create a self-fulfilling prophecy by interpreting normal child outbursts as ominous and menacing, reacting inappropriately, and in turn create an abnormal upbringing that could foster the development of a behavior disorder in the child (adapted from Dickens, 1984).

One can hope that when clashing views on risk presence and intensity emerge during IRB review, the same diversity that led to the differences of opinion also assures the ultimate protection of the participants. The more conservative or protective points of view deserve to be heard and should be carefully considered before rejecting them as unnecessarily stifling.

Developmental and Individual Differences in Children's Responsivity

Risks must be viewed from a developmental perspective because minors—ranging from those with tiny incompetent bodies and nearly content-free minds to large, highly skilled, and competent beings—can vary in many areas with respect to the impact of manifested risks. The infant and young child, for example, may be distressed by unfamiliar surroundings, strangers, and the absence of a primary caretaker whereas adolescents often seek novel experiences and prefer that their caretakers are nowhere to be found. However, younger children are generally less aware of and affected by confidentiality breaches, and thus less susceptible to embarrassment that may ensue as compared with adolescents who are more sensitive to what others know and may be talking about. Developmentally based analyses of risks will not completely predict the impact on minors of different ages because individual differences among children of the same age can be marked (Thompson, 1992).

Consider this example. In a study of startle response patterns, eight-year-old children were asked to open several jack-in-the-box type containers. Objects inside of the boxes included a curly wig, a plastic spider, a rabbit's foot, and a live lizard. Some children remained nonplussed or even amused with these stimuli, whereas others flinched. A few were frightened or repulsed.

Another similar example involves a study of children's reactions to "strange" dogs. Responses of six-year-olds to the introduction of a small, unleashed, friendly, and harmless terrier into a playroom situation were observed. Although actual risk may be nil, an occasional child may experience extreme terror and thereby be at risk as a direct result of the experimental manipulation. When it is possible that sensitivity or past events may elicit discomfort or fear, prescreening is recommended. Fortunately, the parental permission-seeking phase should accomplish this goal much of the time, as, for example, when a parent would know that her child is terrified of lizards or any kind of dog.

When the minor participants are vulnerable in other ways, research procedures that would be comfortable for the "average" child may be distressing to those with special characteristics (Fisher and Tryon, 1988). For example, a questionnaire concerning family lineage may be uncomfortable for the adopted child. Or a study involving aggression modeling may be experienced far differently by the child who is being physically abused at home. Thus, special characteristics should be ascertained whenever possible before proceeding, and the research procedures evaluated and amended accordingly.

How to Reduce Risks

Before undertaking any research activity, investigators would be wise to carefully analyze every feature of their proposal relative to its risk potential. Hopefully most researchers will not have to go to the impressive extremes detailed in Hyers and Scoggin's (1979) remarkable account of the safeguards instituted prior to running a high-risk-to-benefit-ratio study involving minors. Yet simply to assume that "all will go fine" or "the chances of a problem are too small to worry about" betrays professional responsibility. As Pearn (1981, p.115) declared, "The unexpected is more likely to happen with children than with adult subjects."

Generally, the investigator should evaluate risk potential from several vantage points such as those proposed by Levine (1978). What does common sense reveal about the potential for harm at various developmental stages? What does the investigator's experience with similar interventions or procedures contribute to an understanding of the proposed risks in this particular study? What is the situation of the proposed participants? That is, what might be vulnerable about this specific group?

Other basic considerations involve an honest assessment of questions about the importance of the research. If no knowledge that would benefit humankind and/or generalize and integrate into the knowledge stockpile is likely to emerge, the research project (regardless of risk level) cannot be justified.

The literature also should be thoroughly searched to learn what has already been contributed and what has been learned about risky procedures and their sequelae. It has never been easier to accomplish such searches, thanks to computerized abstract banks.

If risk effects are not expected but are conceivably possible, or if risk effects are simply unknown, one should consider running a small pilot sample comprised of the least vulnerable but appropriate sample to check out risk elements before proceeding. For planned risks, that is when procedures to be used are known or expected to put the children at some degree of risk, every effort should be made to assure that these are as noninvasive and mild as possible without compromising ethics or data validity.

All experimental equipment should be assessed for safety from the "child's eye" view. The physical environment in which the study is to take place should be appropriate to the age and size of the children for reasons of comfort as well as safety. For example, electrical outlets may require safety covers; child-sized furniture is desirable; and sharp, easily breakable objects, or those that might be swallowed should be removed. In a well-publicized incident at a large university, electrical equipment used with children was alleged to have faulty and exposed wiring that posed a potentially fatal hazard.

Unfortunately it is not uncommon to find incidental risks materializing when investigators fail to be sensitive to the possibilities and/or put convenience ahead of participant welfare. For example, in one study school children were pulled out of their classes on several occasions for assessments by an unfamiliar investigator wearing a white lab coat. Rumors quickly circulated among the other children that the "dumb, bad kids were getting shock treatments."

Another effort to remove incidental risks involves a consideration of unintended and/or unnecessary psychological harm. For example, if the data collection involves any discomfort, departure from routine, extended duration, or involves very young children, the presence of a parent (or another person known or trusted by the child) should be considered an ethical necessity in most cases. Investigators must be mindful that the younger child's sphere of social comfort is usually far more narrow than that of adults, and that even routine events can cause wariness and uneasiness in unfamiliar surroundings.

Simulation Issues

A difficult dilemma arises when a fully competent researcher faces a conflict between ideal methodology and ethical considerations. For example, investigators who were interested in the effects of expressions of pain by an aggressed-upon target on grade school children in aggressive and nonaggressive settings devised a box with a large padded button. The box was painted with expressionless eyes and the button was placed where a nose would be. The box was wired to "respond" to being "hit in the nose" by producing cries of pain (e.g., "ouch," "that hurts," and "ow"). This design, only partially described above, is adapted from a study by Dubanoski and Tokioka (1981). It was rejected for publication by the editor of one journal because the reviewers did not believe that striking an inanimate object could be termed aggression, or that the indicators of pain were meaningful to the children, or that the results could be generalized to children's behavior in response to hitting a person. However, the researchers had purposely chosen their methods to minimize any psychological stress or mental discomfort by using an inanimate object rather than a real or more lifelike victim. Dubanoski, who felt caught in a "Catch-22" situation, asks the chilling question, "Does one conduct possibly unethical research in hope of publication or ethical research in fear of nonpublication?" (1978, p. 8). This dilemma of "good science" versus "participant welfare" is most evident in research involving control groups and randomized assignment to conditions.

Control Group Issues

Fetterman (1982) presents a case illustrating more profoundly how a control group of youngsters, in this case high school dropouts, were used as a "negative treatment group," thus biasing the meaning of the results. Teenagers who expressed interest in an experimental "second-chance" educational program funded by the government went through an elaborate screening program. Through a lottery process, one-fourth were not admitted to the experimental conditions. Fetterman cogently argues that this group of youngsters, who now felt resentful and demoralized, did not comprise a nonbiased group with which to compare treatment groups.

When a control group is necessary, its members should normally be exposed to whatever treatment or resources are already available. However, "no treatment" control groups can be ethically justified under some conditions. For example, if the research does not involve participants in need of benefit relative to the experimental topic area, and the consignment of those not to be exposed to the experimental variable causes them no risk or loss, a baseline control group can be ethically justified. Another acceptable example occurs when participants in research intended to be beneficial agree to be placed into a no-treatment control group and are, as a result, put at no additional risk. This practice can be justified so long as consent was properly obtained and the participants understood and fully agreed to this assignment. Finally, there may be times when investigators can justify a no-treatment control when resources limit services to fewer than the available participants, no other options or resources are available to participants, participants realize and accept from the beginning that not everyone can be enrolled in the treatment, the treatment has not been proven effective, and assignments to the treatment are made equitably (adapted from Conner, 1982). Staggered treatment, dose response controls, and other innovative designs that may help reduce ethical conflicts should be considered (e.g., DiTomasso and McDermott, 1981; Garfield, 1987; Veatch, 1987).

Randomization

The ethical issues embedded in the use of randomization in assigning participants to experimental and control groups, varying only the independent variable(s), are discussed most frequently relative to biomedical research, usually in the field of oncology. This fact is not surprising, because the consequences to at least some participants could prove lifesaving or fatal. However, the same general issues apply to social and behavioral research despite the fact that the outcomes for participants in any assigned group do not often involve the potential for any physical disability or deterioration.

Under two conditions randomized designs pose few if any ethical complications. In the first instance, a *nontherapeutic* no-risk or minimal-risk study usually causes no harm to participants since they are not chosen on the basis of need and the study itself carries virtually no risk to them. The second instance in which randomized designs pose few ethical complications occurs when research intended to benefit children in need, even when risk may be present, involves an *honest* null hypothesis. That is to say, it is absolutely unclear and unknown whether one treatment or procedure is any better than any other (or possibly even any better than no treatment or procedure that would acceptably allow for a no treatment or placebo group as well). However, this seemingly ethical-problem-free situation rarely occurs. Usually an investigator has some pilot data or a data-based trend or some other reason to suspect that one treatment may be superior to the alternatives.

Randomized designs present ethical dilemmas for researchers when the participants have some problem that requires amelioration, the methods of treating or dealing with it either do not exist or are not fully satisfactory or efficacious, and some degree of risk (often unknown) is inherent in placing participants in one or more of the experimental groups. By its very nature, randomized designs do not allow for "selective placement," that is, the investigator's careful considerations of which group assignment might be the best for each particular participant. To meet the full scientific requirements of a randomized design, the study should normally be allowed to run its full course until all relevant outcome data are collected. To determine placement in a study by flipping a coin, however, runs counter to one's role as a caring advocate for a particular participant (Marquis, 1983; Schafer, 1982, 1984).

Longitudinal and Other Research Designs

Whether the participants are adults or children, the quality of a research design is itself an ethical issue (Edsall, 1969; Rutstein, 1969). Poorly designed studies yield uninterpretable, easily misinterpreted, or useless findings. Participants have at best wasted their time and at worst were needlessly put at risk or harmed. Future consumers also may be harmed if the findings are generalized and applied. Overall, the scientific knowledge stockpile has been contaminated.

Longitudinal designs, whereby the investigator collects repeated data sets on the same participants over time, provide a valuable tool for studying developmental changes. Thus, children are often the participants in longitudinal studies. Despite the logistical problems (e.g., expense, following whereabouts of participants, dropout bias, contamination effects), this valuable design is the only one to result in a "true" developmental curve.

Ethical issues that may accompany the use of the longitudinal technique are often related to the fact that the participant-experimenter relationship exists for an extended period of time, often many years. Identifying information must be maintained, yet kept secure. Participants or their families who decide to discontinue their involvement in the project pose a major disappointment for investigators since it is not possible to simply insert new replacements. Thus, an attempt to clarify any misunderstandings or to check back to assure that the desire to disengage was not due to a momentary mood state is understandable, but heavy-handed coercion must be avoided.

The longitudinal design sometimes involves the creation of dependencies, and the investigator must be sensitive to this situation when the data gathering phase has been completed. For example, if participants and their families were given special counseling or educational experiences, as may occur in long-term educational/intervention projects, the time frame for terminating the services and the participants' needs may not coincide. To abandon these families, who had come to rely on such interventions over a period of time, may cause them even more hardship than had they been left alone all along to their own coping strategies.

Other designs where participants serve as their own control, such as the baseline comparison technique, can raise profound ethical dilemmas when risk is associated with participants being in the baseline condition (Noonan and Bickel, 1981). For example, investigators at a large state hospital facility designed an experimental technique to reduce the frequency of self-injurious behavior in autistic children. In order to assess the effectiveness of their experimental technique, it was necessary to gain information about each child's rate of self-injurious behavior. Each child was observed and videotaped individually for one hour without any intervention unless it was judged that the child was engaging in a behavior that would cause permanent injury. Instances and time sequences were recorded.

The development of a minimally restricting method of reducing self-injurious behavior in psychotic children is a worthy challenge, and assessing the technique's advantage over the child's baseline behavior is methodologically important. Alternatives to observing the child in a potentially dangerous state should always be considered and may include approximations of baseline behavior available in records or from hospital staff observations. It may also be possible to use the current method of controlling injurious behavior as the baseline (if it is other than restraint). If only a baseline recording period is feasible, it should be as short as possible. For a child who is actively self-injurious, an hour is obviously too long.

Hazards of Deception

The inherent potential for harms and wrongs in the use of deception techniques are found in two aspects of its use, and these are often interrelated. First, the deception manipulation itself may be stressful or humiliating, as when participants are told they did poorly on an intelligence test (when in fact they did very well, or the test itself was not an intelligence test, or the test was not even scored). Second, even though the deception itself may not have elicited any reaction (or it may have been experienced as positive as in cases when bogus feedback about performance was highly flattering), a negative reaction may occur upon the "debriefing" when the participant learns of the deception manipulation. Sometimes debriefing may bring forth feelings of relief, but, the "inflicted insight" (as Baumrind, 1976, calls it) can also be painful or unwelcome. Negative consequences for adults of either facet of deception have been described in the literature and include feelings of degradation, loss of self-esteem, embarrassment, anger, disillusionment, anxiety and mistrust (Baumrind, 1976, 1977, 1985; Cupples and Gochnauer, 1985; Kelman, 1967; Seeman, 1969; Stricker, 1967; Warwick, 1975; Weinrach and Ivey, 1975).

Because there are no solid data on child-specific risks of deception, our comments must be considered speculative. Many children are extremely sensitive and suggestible. Because of their less-mature capabilities of processing information and still-emerging self-concepts, children may be more vulnerable than are adults to manipulations involving deflation of self-esteem, negative false feedback, induced anxiety or stress, or the berating of cherished attitudes, values, beliefs, people or institutions. The following case illustrates how children, in particular, may feel unsettled as a result of being deceived.

> In a study of the reactions of eight-year-olds to "failure to live up to a responsibility," children were asked to stay alone to watch over a box of four live kittens for a five-minute period. They were admonished to assure that the kittens stayed safe and in the box. During the second minute a buzzer was set off directly behind the child, causing a reflexive orienting response. While the child's eyes were diverted, an investigator's confederate slipped his hand through a slot in the wall and removed one of the kittens. For the next five minutes, the child's reactions to the missing kitten were observed through a one-way window. When the investigator returned, he listened to the child's story about what happened and told the child that "the kitten would show up and couldn't have gotten very far." He then thanked and excused the child.

It may be useful for us to know more about how failure to live up to adult standards feels to children and what impact it has on them. A structured and controlled laboratory approach to the matter is potentially more useful than are anecdotal or clinical reports. Nevertheless, this study method raises several ethical questions. The children were put in a position that may have caused near-panic in the more sensitive ones, and the problem was dismissed but not resolved at the end of each child's participation. Many children may have worried about the kitten's safety for a very long time, and the guilt could be potentially harmful. The acceptability of this design could be markedly enhanced by altering the "failure" experience to something more emotionally neutral, collapsing the "failure observation" time to a minimum, and either fully debriefing the children (running the risk here of reinforcing the notion that adults pull mean tricks on little kids) or, at the very least, assuring that the problem is completely resolved (i.e., finding the kitten, perhaps with the child's assistance).

Upon debriefing (or "dehoaxing" as Holmes [1976a, 1976b] calls it), the mere reassurance that things were not as they seemed may not fully (if at all) "disabuse" or "desensitize" the participants or restore them to their "former sense of self." This is especially true if the participants were "set up" to behave in ways that would make them feel ashamed, embarrassed, or guilty, upon learning that they were manipulated or observed. Because of the more vulnerable status of children, it seems reasonable to suspect that the failure of debriefing to resolve any emotional residue is more likely and profound than for adults.

Another case illustrates how the socialization process could be influenced by participation in a deception study. A child confederate of the investigator tells several other children a contrived "secret." The child confederate also elicits promises that the secret will remain unshared. Later a teacher's aide (also a confederate) asks each child individually if they know anything about a specific "secret related" matter. Secret content was varied to see if children would break their promises more readily when a secret involved a misdeed (i.e., stealing another child's toy) as opposed to a personal matter in the sharer's life (i.e., parents were getting a divorce).

Even if proper permission was obtained from parents, and some useful information about children's promise-keeping behavior emerged, and the children were all told later about the true purpose of the study, ethical concerns persist. Upon debriefing, children may have felt guilty about tattling on their friend, and this may be difficult to desensitize easily. Impressions that adults (including one of their own teachers) misled them may cause resentment, not to mention the poor role modeling.

An example of a child's "honesty assessment" (many of which, ironically, use deception) also illustrates other insidious debriefing risks. A child is asked to look for one minute at a diagram of an extremely complicated maze. Then, with pencil placed in the start box, the child is asked to close her eyes "real tight" and to negotiate through the maze "without any peeking allowed." The maze itself is purposely so complex that an adequate performance would be possible only if one disobeys the rule and peeks.

Debriefing children who peeked may well cause some emotional reaction such as guilt or embarrassment and shame upon learning that they were found out. A decision not to debrief in this instance (even if it were ethically justifiable) creates unfortunate effects as well. That a good performance can be achieved by cheating is reinforced in the "peekers," and honesty is punished by a poor performance.

The shift in realities that emerges during debriefing may be especially confusing to younger children. They agreed to do one thing under one set of expectations and then are told, in effect, "that is what you thought happened, but it isn't really what happened." Rather than emerging enlightened, children may emerge feeling confused, tricked, unsure of themselves, or stupid.

The American Psychological Association's (APA) ethics code (1992) does specify that debriefing should be done "as early as feasible." Although the allowable time lag may be interpreted variously, the general ethic is that research participants should not hold misconceptions for an extended period. This is especially important, of course, if the misconception affected the participant negatively. As noted in at the beginning of this chapter, children's sense of time is subjectively different than that of adults. A lack of timely feedback to children could exacerbate or intensify any negative aftereffects. The next case is illustrative.

> A study of the effects of negative feedback of ability on classroom behavior and attitudes towards school involved selecting one group of students who normally performed very well academically. The children were told that they scored poorly on an "important abilities test." A month later, teachers were given rating scales focusing on the assessment of changes in the students' behavior since "failing" the test. The children were given the same rating scale that was administered two months earlier about their attitudes towards school. Afterwards, children were told that a mistake had been made in calculating their test scores and were given honest performance feedback.

Certainly there are better ways of studying the impact of school evaluations than resorting to ethically objectionable tactics. Children who take pride in their school abilities would likely be devastated upon being evaluated as "dumb." The inordinate amount of time that the children were forced to carry around false beliefs about themselves, however, is particularly abhorrent. A month's experience in the life of a child and the unfortunate shifts in self-concept that could have germinated may not so easily be undone by the less-than-honest declaration that a mere scoring error was later discovered.

Alternatives to Deception

Alternatives to the use of deception should always be carefully explored before proceeding. Critics have argued that deception techniques have often provided a quick, noncreative and undesirable shortcut to more ethical and scientifically sound experimentation. Role-playing and other simulation alternatives have been developed (e.g., Diener and Crandall, 1978; Geller, 1982) that may be appropriate for use with older children. Alternatives do present new methodological problems, but they diffuse the ethical ones to a great extent.

Forewarning deception techniques (see Sieber, 1982a) or partial disclosure methods during assent also may alleviate many of the potential risks of total deception. In this scenario, participants are informed at the onset that full disclosure about the study will be offered after their participation is completed. Thus, permission or assent to be deceived is obtained at the onset. Or, if several different manipulations are involved, participants may be given complete information about all conditions, but are informed that the one they are in will not be disclosed to them until later.

An effective use of partial disclosure with child research participants is adapted from Baumrind (1976) in the following case.

A graduate student planned a study using a modified "prisoner's dilemma" game, played by two children at computer terminals. Baseline cooperative data were to be gathered by using a standard sequence of computerized plays followed by a series of actual interactive plays with the human partner. The investigator wanted the children to assume that the "partner" was always a real person rather than a computer. To diminish deceiving the children, while at the same time maintaining the integrity of the study purpose, the children were told that part of the time they would be playing a computer and part of the time they would be playing their human partner, but that they would not know when they were playing each.

In this study the children knew at the onset that something would remain unknown. The dilemma of the use of misinformation regarding their peer's cooperative and competitive strategies was completely avoided. Later the children were told that the first 125 plays were with a computer and the last 75 with their human partner, but this information did not conflict with the information given at the time of obtaining assent.

Participant Privacy and Data Confidentiality

Two trends in society continue to emerge: a tendency to retreat from the position that parents or others have an *absolute* right to know anything and everything about minor children (especially teenagers) and an increasing recognition of a minor's rights to privacy. The concept of obtaining a minor's assent acknowledges the child's right to know that she is a subject of a research study and has the right to accept or reject this opportunity to be intruded upon.

Generally, ethics codes and federal policy admonish investigators to protect the privacy of their participants and to maintain the confidentiality of data. With child participants, however, complications can arise. The parents may have a strong desire for feedback and/or believe that they have a right to know the details of their child's study behavior or performance. School personnel, other agencies, or other second-order permission granters may pressure investigators for access to data. The researchers believe that they have discovered findings about specific and identifiable children that should be shared with others, usually for the child's own welfare. A quick answer might appear to be to seek permission from a child to share data. However, questions arise about minors' capabilities to give true "voluntary and informed consent" to allow the data they contribute to be shared with others.

Sharing Research Data with Parents

When parents give permission for their children to participate in research, it is not uncommon for the parents to request or expect detailed feedback, especially if the study topic involves an area of specific interest or concern to the parents. Under what conditions, if any, is it ethically acceptable to share a specific child's data with that child's parents?

The APA ethics code (1992) allows for the sharing of any information originally gained in confidence as long as the person or the person's legal representative gives consent. This principle offers a guideline about sharing data with people other than the parent (i.e., consent from the parent must be obtained) but does not address the question of keeping any data from the parents. Dealing specifically with research participants, the ethics code admonishes investigators to keep data confidential "unless agreed upon in advance." In the APA (1982) elaboration of that principle, it is noted that instances may arise when data sharing with parents, teachers, or therapists could greatly benefit the participant, but also notes that this should not be done without the participants' "free and informed permission."

Even assuming that an investigator can meet the "informed" test by explaining the situation to a child in a way that can be fully understood, the child is likely to be placed in an intensely difficult situation when it comes to "voluntariness." If the parents are demanding data feedback, and the child refused or expressed a desire for his parents not to be informed, how does the investigator share the child's reluctance with the parents in a way that protects the child from pressure or even possible censure? Abused children may be particularly at risk in these situations (Kinard, 1985).

Children's potential for exercising their right to dissent from having data shared with their parents is greatly limited by parental role power. This situation is not easily resolvable. The investigator may attempt to avoid the conflict by agreeing to lie to the parents, although such a tactic raises other ethical issues. Another more appropriate resolution that may be useful in some situations is for the investigator to excuse the child who exhibits considerable conflict, explaining to the parents that their child did not meet study criteria. This action may be justified on ethical grounds because investigators are generally encouraged to excuse any participant who appears stressed or upset and would presumably wish to withdraw. Any irritation the parents may feel is diverted to the investigator, thus protecting the child from parental punishment.

Here is another common problem that usually can be avoided. After their ten-year-old daughter completed a series of achievement and personality tests as part of a cross-sectional study, the parents came to the researcher's office requesting detailed feedback on their daughter's performance. They reminded the investigator that during the permission phase she offered to answer any questions about the study.

The investigator was initially vague about the boundaries of her offer, and this came back to haunt her later. If the researcher wished to keep the data confidential, she initially could have said something like, "While we do not share the findings on any particular child with others, including the parents, we will supply you with a summary of the overall findings and will answer any questions you may have about our results."

Ground rules for data sharing should be established clearly at the outset, with both the parents and the child participants (if they are competent to give assent). This way the parents either agree to not being informed, or the minors realize before they contribute data that their parents will receive information about their performance. This allows the children a chance to protect their privacy, either by withholding assent or by choosing or attempting to alter their performance or to restrict their answers to questions.

Investigators also must be prepared to face another type of parental ploy, illustrated by the following anecdote. Parents informed the investigator that they would permit their seven-year-old daughter to participate in a research project if, and only if, they were given detailed feedback and interpretation of information obtained during her study trial.

These parents are essentially holding their permission hostage. Researchers should not feel comfortable with this ploy and many would not enroll the child into the study at all. Others may promise parents a copy of the final report, based on aggregate data, in the hopes that this would be acceptable as an alternative.

Certainly in those instances when a child may be at risk for some problem, and the research purpose involves—at least in part—assessing that risk, it typically would be inappropriate to withhold any findings from those who could be of assistance in alleviating the problem or to inform others that there is no need for concern. This situation usually can be handled very effectively by making it clear to all parties during the consent phase that such information will be shared as soon as it is available.

Protecting Confidentiality from Access by Other Than the Children's Legal Guardians

Ethics codes and policies involving data access by people other than parents are straightforward. Whereas the child participant, if appropriate, should still be informed at the outset about who will have access to any individualized data (e.g., the school or a therapist), consent must also be obtained from the parents before information about their minor child can be shared with others.

When multiple data sets are collected on minors over a period of time, as is frequently done with longitudinal research, the identity of specific individual's data must be kept for an extended period of time. Here identities should be coded in the data file with the master file available only to the principal investigators. Parents and their children, if appropriate, should be informed at the outset of the procedures for maintaining confidentiality and any foreseeable limitations of such procedures (e.g., the possibility of a subpoena).

Rapidly growing technology allows for the possibility that information that may be potentially damaging, and that could be used to a participant's disadvantage, could be stored in data banks that do not include proper safeguards. APA (1982) suggests that investigators may not wish to contribute data in such instances because of the possibility that the data may be accessed by people who cannot or will not interpret them accurately. This situation may be especially problematic with regard to information contributed by minors because such data more rapidly reach obsolescence, yet could be used to the participants' disadvantage at some later date.

On occasion, an investigator's data may be of great interest to other agencies seeking the identity of the participants or the information the participants supplied to the investigators. With child participants, examples of sought-after data may include drug dealing or use, gang activity, ongoing sexual or physical abuse by adults, sexual activity with peers, or any research data collected on children who are a party to litigation. Investigators working in sensitive or controversial areas should strongly consider applying for confidentiality certificates from the Public Health Service (see Gray and Melton, 1985; Melton, 1988a, 1988b; Melton and Gray, 1988; Reatig, 1979). These certificates are intended to provide immunity from subpoena and offer the best protection of data confidentiality currently available. It is important to note that the certificates do not provide an absolute guarantee that data cannot be accessed by others. Names and other identifying information are protected, not the data. Therefore, if somebody already knows the identification of participants, say in a study of abused children, it is not clear whether a subpoena of the data provided by particular participants would be enforceable. It is also unclear whether reporting laws are abrogated by the certificates. Melton (personal communication, 1988) recommends that when litigants may know who is in a study, a certificate of confidentiality and a protective order or memorandum from the presiding judge should be obtained in advance of any issue or threat of subpoena.

Investigators also should be aware that statutory privileges are preempted in cases of conflict with a constitutional right. Say, for example, a criminal defendant alleges that the data are relevant to the case at hand, and that to deny access to them would deprive the defendant of due process. In such an instance Melton (personal communication, 1989) recommends that the investigator attempt to have discovery limited by *in camera* review of the data for relevancy and necessity. Other helpful sources of data protection techniques include APA, 1982; Boruch and Cecil, 1982 and 1983; Carroll, 1973; and Knerr, 1982.

Published case studies of children tend to be about very unusual or exceptional ones or involve specific details of the process of psychotherapy or treatment. Here it is always possible that a child (and the parents) can be identified by at least some readers. Again, any risks of potential identification should be shared with the relevant parties in advance. Attempts to disguise the individuals or to delete sensitive material should be done to the extent possible without jeopardizing the integrity of the work (APA, 1982).

Third-Party Contacts

Some types of research require contact with others for the purpose of gaining information about children. Parents, teachers, school counselors, therapists, classmates, neighbors, or other family members may be involved. Two risks are present in this situation. First, these parties may reveal information about the child that the child would not want told to an outsider (i.e., the investigators). Second, in the course of interviewing, sensitive and previously unknown facts about the child participant (e.g., that the study is on sexually abused boys or friendless teenagers) may be revealed to interviewees (APA, 1982). Although one should obtain the participants' assent to solicit third-party information, children may not fully understand the ramifications of such an invasion of privacy. APA (1982) suggests that, for this type of research, especially when older children are being studied, the investigator should proceed only after a careful analysis of the ethical problems and with outside consultation to assure that the project merits the potentially serious ethical hazards.

Disclosure of Research Data Without Permission

Researchers may be included by most states under the statutory categories that mandate reporting of specific circumstances or conditions. These categories are not necessarily limited to mental health issues. In this age of concern regarding Acquired Immune Deficiency Syndrome, investigators should also thoroughly familiarize themselves with public health reporting laws. The ethical responsibilities of researchers are similar to those of applied mental health professionals. APA (1982) notes that researchers are not excluded from the requirement to disclose information to avoid harm to a research participant or to protect others from a participant. Further, the participant (and the parents if appropriate) should be informed that information may have to be disclosed and the rationale for it, and should be counseled about the limits of confidentiality.

When the study purpose and techniques are benign and the study population has not been selected because its members are "at risk," elaborate limits of confidentiality procedures are not necessary. In such instances the likelihood of the need to disclose is infinitesimally low, and one runs the risk of needlessly scaring away potential participants. However, if it is known in advance that certain sensitive information may emerge, verbal children can be informed about confidentiality limitations at the onset. For example, in a study of depressed children, or highly aggressive acting-out children, the investigator should reasonably suspect that revelations of contemplated danger to self or others may be discovered. In their survey of researchers who studied childhood depression using self-report inventories in community (nonclinical) samples, Burbach, Farha, and Thorpe (1986) found that about 25 percent of the investigators had not even considered the possibility of actually locating seriously depressed or suicidal children. More than two-thirds of the sample either made no plans in advance should such children be identified, or planned not to intervene at all. More than one-third of the investigators ultimately did experience a need to intervene directly on a child's behalf although their efforts were often not thoroughly thought through.

Consider this case. Identified teenagers were administered a widely used and standardized self-report depression scale as part of a larger battery of assessments. One young man's test indicated such an elevated score that the researcher was seriously concerned about his welfare.

Because the young man was identifiable, the researcher should seriously consider taking action, after consultation with an assessments expert if needed and without revealing the participant's identity at this point. With teenagers, a direct conference may be appropriate to assess the matter including learning if the minor is already receiving therapy, if the parents are aware of and dealing with the depression, if the school's professional staff has knowledge and is involved, etc. Given the dynamics in a particular instance, the investigator may assist in providing resources or make contact on the participant's behalf. If the conference leaves the investigator unsatisfied, additional consultation with experts and other avenues of action should be immediately explored.

Suppose the assessments as described above were taken anonymously and, at the bottom of the answer sheet the young person also wrote, "These items are like I feel all of the time and I'm going to do away with myself. I mean it!!!" As Burbach, et al. (1986) put it, here is a time when ignorance is not bliss. Would the researchers have any duty to attempt to locate the individual from the total pool of anonymous participants? Such a note may be an attempt at adolescent black humor or sarcasm, but it may also be a cry for help to someone the youngster perceives as a professional, and as such should be taken seriously. If the data are collected in such a way as to prevent identification of the individual who wrote the note, the investigators should consider extending general invitations for "the person who wrote us a note to get in touch with us for more information."

When research participants threaten harm to another, researchers are not excluded from the potential obligation to take protective action, if the victim is identifiable. If there is no specific victim (e.g., an adolescent research participant says, "I hate girls and I intend to tear up as many of 'em as I can"), then one must attempt to assess the significance of the threat and possible risks and seek consultation.

Naturalistic Observation

Observing children's behavior in their everyday environment has advantages. The behavior is natural, unstilted, and therefore potentially more generalizable than is the frequent affected, inhibited or withdrawn behavior that can occur in the unfamiliar setting of a laboratory. However, issues of invasion of privacy can arise, particularly if the children are unaware of the investigators' presence and "mission."

The HHS guidelines (1983) allow for observations in public settings without permission or assent so long as there is no interference or manipulation of the situation. Yet, the meaning of *public* is not clear-cut. Sieber (1982b, 1982c) defines public behavior as activity that others may freely observe. Yet *private* behavior (that intended not to be observed) often occurs in public settings, as the next case illustrates.

The researcher's assistant sat in a booth in a restaurant known to be a teen hangout. He surreptitiously took notes on the customers' conversations and antics as part of a study of contemporary adolescent social behavior. Overheard topics dealt with problems with parents, experimentation with drugs and sex, various plottings to gain the attention of admired peers, and considerable unflattering gossip about classmates.

Even though the teens were personally unknown to the research assistant, and therefore unidentified except for their sex and general physical description, the young people were most certainly under the assumption that they were not being monitored. Since minors are probably less aware of and concerned than are adults about their immediate surroundings, except for their immediate focus of attention, their privacy is easier to invade. However, their reactions to learning of the eavesdropper would likely be intensely negative.

Another case illustrates a situation where no problems were foreseen. While collecting crayon drawings for a benign cross-sectional study of school age children's artistic creations, an educational psychologist noted that an eight-year-old boy drew pictures at a startling variance with the array of houses with chimney smoke, trees, animals, happy people, and suns produced by the other children. One showed a blood-soaked, dismembered, male adult figure. Another was of a man hanging by a rope from a tree with a large dagger in his chest.

The educational psychologist was a bit shaken with the boy's drawings, and very uncertain about what, if anything, she should do. Some past course work on children's drawings alerted her to the possible pathology, but she had no significant expertise in this type of assessment. She did not know the boy at all, and for all she knew he was reflecting some morbid recollections from a movie or news broadcast.

Investigators working from a strictly experimental model only have permission (and the minors' assent, if appropriate) to collect data and do not typically obtain in advance any consents to further intrude into the participant's private lives. The educational psychologist could opt to ignore the discrepant drawings, although this may cause her lingering concern. A first course of action would be to share the materials (without identifying the artist) with a colleague who is an expert in the area of clinical assessment of·children's drawings. At this point she may get a better understanding of what the drawings could mean and what other options are available to her. If the consultant also expresses concern, the investigator may opt to share the information with the school psychologist or some other appropriate person who may be in a position to advocate or protect the boy. We do not recommend, in this instance, going initially to the parents because the drawings could indicate a negative or abusive home situation that could place the child in further danger. However, in other types of instances the parents could be informed of a potential problem, such as when a participant performs in such a way to indicate a possible perceptual dysfunction, and suggests further evaluation.

The general rule of thumb here is to make a decision based on the child's overall best interests as carefully weighed against any agreements about data confidentiality. It also is strongly recommended that if the child is old enough to understand, an explanation for the investigator's actions should be offered (Kinard, 1985).

Prevention/Educational Intervention Research Program Risks

Many research programs designed to avert risk of harm or to remediate preexisting damage involve children as the primary target group. Educational, psychotherapeutic, and coping or other skill building techniques are frequently used intervention strategies. The research component usually involves assessing the efficacy of different approaches and/or evaluating the outcome of the intervention and comparing it to the status quo. Direct benefit to the participants in the experimental group is virtually always intended. Therefore, prevention/ educational intervention research has generally been regarded as humanitarian, socially relevant, and an unlikely candidate for ethical pitfalls or criticism. As Gray (1971) put it, "It was taken for granted that a program with clear implications for human welfare was rooted in positive motives and intent" (p. 80). Indeed, the need for prevention and early intervention programs seems more critical today than ever before. Drug abuse, family and gang violence, high teenage pregnancy rates, environmental damage, and AIDS are among the many woes within our borders that threaten the very fabric of our society.

The focus of this brief discussion will be on the more common type of prevention/intervention project that involves participants judged to be at risk for the manifestation or worsening of some malady, educational failure, disadvantage, or other negative consequence should the individual remain on an unaltered life course. Sometimes the children are judged to be at risk primarily because they live in risky families or environments (e.g., with substance-abusing parents, a stressed single parent, divorcing parents, a mentally ill parent, or in a poor neighborhood). At other times, children may be judged to be at risk because of indicators already observable in the children's behavior, performance or physical state that suggest likely adverse consequences should interventions not occur. Examples here include poor school performance, hanging out around gangs, membership in some social group that is often victimized by discrimination, being overweight, or frequent fighting with other children.

The usual child target study populations for prevention and intervention research are often vulnerable in more ways than simply tender age. The children are often from ethnic minority groups and/or underprivileged families. The children's parents are often a factor in the children's deficit condition; people who may be unable to properly nurture or provide for their offspring. While such children are most certainly in need of supportive resources, they and their proxies are often at a distinct disadvantage when it comes to negotiating the traditional requirements for voluntary and informed consent, avoiding even subtle coercion from a seemingly helping hand or authority figure, and assessing research risks in the context of perhaps an even riskier everyday life.

The fact that the children and families under study are often unlike those of the research team creates the potential for insensitivity to, ignoring of, or even the disparagement or destruction of the cultural traditions or values of the study population. Sometimes whatever it is that is to be prevented reflects the political or value orientation of the programmers, and these may run counter to the welfare of the participants or deprive them of their civil rights. The ethical investigator in this line of work should become thoroughly familiar with—and respectful towards—the study community, its values, and its traditions. The study also should include consultants from the community during all phases of the project.

Although all researchers may have some direct or indirect political implications, this fact is most obvious in prevention and intervention work. As Kessler and Albee (1975) have noted, political, social, and ethical implications accrue whenever things are done to large groups of people. Because change is the goal, and this type of work usually takes place in the community and is often focussed on more vulnerable and powerless groups, it comes under the scrutiny of many eyes. Who has the right or the power to decide what should be prevented or interfered with? Is one person's notion of prevention another's notion of the loss of self-determination or choice? How does one balance the benefits of intrusion into people's lives against their civil rights? Do the target populations have clear rights and/or the capability to withhold consent from being intervened upon? Can any prevention or early intervention program be truly effective without first abolishing injustice and poverty?

Intervention work with children, as Melton (1987) has discussed, poses special confusions. On the one hand there has been an increasing recognition of children's rights ("child advocacy") while on the other an increasing justification for coercive intervention in the lives of children and their families as social problems become redefined as public health problems ("child saving"). Those who become involved in intervention work with children can expect to confront a number of clashing policy perspectives and values.

Powerful people often are interested in the results of prevention–intervention work and often favor a particular outcome. Sometimes the reason is as simple as wanting to maintain a job or position and sometimes it is more insidious, such as a desire to support a preconceived belief (e.g., unfounded beliefs that black children are inherently more aggressive than white children or lesbians make bad mothers). Investigators must be sensitive to their own biases and vigilant to any attempt by others to pressure or coerce. Investigators who are able to specify data ownership and procedures for the dissemination of results clearly and in advance are less likely to face political pressures to suppress their findings.

Prevention–intervention research is often expensive, which means that it must be funded by some private foundation or governmental agency source. Another political agenda can arise here in that the source of the funds is often in a position to determine what could or should be "prevented" or "remediated." Considerable agreement often exists about these decisions (e.g., the acceptability of programs designed to prevent drug use among teenagers, or intervention programs for children who have been the victims of sexual abuse). Yet, across-the-board agreement is not always the case. Sometimes the offensive condition is reflective of value judgments about which rational people vary widely (e.g., "masculinizing" boys with traditionally feminine interests, providing easy-access abortions to unwed teenagers, or the early tracking of young school children into academic or trade school pathways).

Prevention–intervention research is rarely conducted in a laboratory, but rather in a community or the schools where the target population resides. Scientific control is usually compromised to some extent, which bruises the validity of the data to an often unknown extent. People other than the investigators themselves often are involved, and assuring their competence and adherence to the program is difficult to monitor. The variables being measured and the program being administered are often complicated and difficult to operationalize (e.g., building self-esteem) resulting in, as Cowen (1982) described it, a rhetoric and conceptual field that is far ahead of its data base.

Prevention–intervention programs run considerable risk of stigmatizing the participants through labeling because the focus often is on some presumed or potential deficit rather than on what strengths the individual also possesses. Since people other than the investigators may know or learn of the project and its purpose, participants may become generally known as "those underachievers," "delinquents," "dummies," and so on. It may not matter that, as in primary prevention work, the labels are not accurate because the problem has not even manifested itself. That the child is at possible risk, say for a mental disorder, may be sufficient to lead others to label her as already afflicted. Negative labels can affect the children's self-esteem and even possibly lead to a self-fulfilling prophecy. In some cases, the procedure for conscripting participants into the program may itself cause them to label themselves, as when the previously unaware child is told she is at risk for a future unwanted pregnancy. Attempts to camouflage the study purpose by referring to such programs by acronyms (e.g., KIP for Kindergarten Intervention Project) or using upbeat names (e.g., the Sunshine Club) may be only partially successful in combatting the tendency of others to label the children. Since this problem may be difficult to avoid, and most certainly involves an ethical problem, investigators should consider whether the potential for averting the risk outweighs the consequences of labeling.

In addition to the problem of protecting the participants' confidentiality by overt revelation or unintended leaks about the study, other privacy issues arise in prevention and intervention research. What criteria should be used to determine whether an intrusion into the life of a child and her family is justifiable, particularly if the study poses risks to the children and the potential benefits accrue to society rather than to the participants? Much of this kind of work is highly sensitive and requires the disclosure of extremely personal matters that might embarrass or upset participants. Primary prevention research presents an additional unusual twist in that the participants are judged to be ''at risk'' for a problem that has not yet manifested itself. Can any degree of coercion or invasion of privacy, however slight, be ethically justified under this circumstance? Certainly one obvious condition must be a thoroughly adequate consent phase and yet, target populations involved are often the very ones who will have the greatest difficulties protecting their own welfare.

Sometimes prevention–intervention work creates dependencies in the participants that must be handled carefully and compassionately upon completion of the formal research project. Contemporary ethical standards would not allow for abandonment of participants simply because all data of interest to the investigative team have been collected. The assumption that the children and their families are at least as well off as they were when they were conscripted into the study may not be a valid one, especially for long-term support projects that may leave participants more resourceless than they would have been left to cope on their own all along.

Conclusion

Research with children is far more complicated than simplifying procedures used with adults or adapting equipment ''down to size.'' If there is one thing we have learned during the relatively brief history of child study and developmental psychology, it is that children are neither the most intricate of animals nor smaller-sized versions of adult humans. Childhood and youth have cognitive and other qualities that are unique and, as such, pose special challenges to psychosocial and educational researchers.

Investigators must always be aware of the special vulnerable qualities of their study sample by carefully assessing risks and minimizing them to the greatest extent possible.

The emerging and rapidly changing developmental status of children poses special considerations for psychosocial and educational researchers. When studies involve a span of time, for example, a training program or longitudinal design, there is no second chance to try it again with the same sample if the results were not as expected or if there were any negative effects.

Finally, investigators must negotiate and navigate among an array of people and policies in order to advance knowledge about children. Although these hurdles are meant to be safeguards rather than barriers, often they pose delays, confusion, and other frustrations. Investigators must be patient and resist temptations to circumvent consent and other mandated procedures.

References

Ackerman, T. F. (1979). Fooling ourselves with child autonomy and assent in nontherapeutic clinical research. *Clinical Research 27:*345–348.

American Psychological Association (1992). Ethical principles of psychologists. *American Psychologist 47:*1597–1611.

American Psychological Association (1982). *Ethical Principles in the Conduct of Research with Human Participants.* Washington, D.C.: American Psychological Association.

Baumrind, D. (1976). Nature and definition of informed consent in research involving deception. Paper prepared for the National Commission for the Protection of Human Subjects of Biomedical and Behavioral Research, Department of Health, Education, and Welfare, Washington, D.C.

Baumrind, D. (1977). Informed consent and deceit in research with children and their parents. Paper presented at the biennial meeting of the Society for Research in Child Development.

Baumrind, D. (1985). Research using intentional deception: Ethical issues revisited. *American Psychologist 40:*165–174.

Boruch, R. F., and Cecil, J. S. (1982). Statistical strategies for preserving privacy in direct inquiry. In *The Ethics of Social Research: Surveys and Experiments,* ed. J. E. Sieber. New York: Springer-Verlag, pp. 207–232.

Boruch, R. F. and Cecil, J. S., ed. (1983). *Solutions to Ethical and Legal Problems in Social Research.* New York: Academic Press.

Bower, R. T., and de Gasparis, P. (1978). *Ethics in Social Research.* New York: Praeger.

Burbach, D. J., Farha, J. G., and Thorpe, J. S. (1986). Assessing depression in community samples of children using self-report inventories: Ethical considerations. *Journal of Abnormal Child Psychology 14:*579–589.

Campbell, A. G. M. (1974). Infants, children, and informed consent. *British Medical Journal 3:*334–338.

Caron, R. F., Caron, A. J., and Caldwell, R. C. (1971). Satiation of visual reinforcement in young infants. *Developmental Psychology 5:*279–289.

Carroll, J. D. (1973). Confidentiality of social science research sources and data: The Popkin case. *PS (American Political Science Association) 6:*268–280.

Comiskey, R. J. (1978). The use of children for medical research: Opposite views examined. *Child Welfare 57:*321–324.

Conner, R. F. (1982). Random assignment of clients in social experimentation. In *The Ethics of Social Research: Surveys and Experiments,* ed. J. E. Sieber. New York: Springer-Verlag, pp. 57–78.

Cooke, R. E. (1977). An ethical and procedural basis for research on children. *Journal of Pediatrics 90:*681–682.

Cowen, E. (1982). Primary prevention research: Barriers, needs, and opportunities. *Journal of Primary Prevention 2:*131–137.

Cupples, B., and Gochnauer, M. (1985). The investigator's duty not to deceive. *IRB: A Review of Human Subjects Research 7:*1–6.

deChesnay, M. (1984). Father-daughter incest: Issues in treatment and research. *Journal of Psychosocial Nursing and Mental Health Services 22:*9–16.

Department of Health and Human Services. (1983, March 8). Protection of human subjects. 45 *CFR* 46.

Dickens, B. M. (1984). Interests of parents in pediatric laboratory medicine—ethical and legal. *Clinical Biochemistry 17:*60–63.

Diener, E., and Crandall, R. (1978). *Ethics in Social and Behavioral Research.* Chicago: University of Chicago Press.

DiTomasso, R. A., and McDermott, P. A. (1981). Dilemma of the untreated control group in applied research: A proposed solution. *Psychological Reports 49:*823–828.

Dubanoski, R. A. (1978). The Catch-22 of ethical research. *SRCD Newsletter 3:*8.

Dubanoski, R. A., and Tokioka, A. B. (1981). The effects of verbal pain stimuli on the behavior of children. *Social Behavior and Personality 9:*159–162.

Edsall, G. A. (1969). A positive approach to the problem of human experimentation. *Daedalus 98:*463–479.

Fetterman, D. M. (1982). Ibsen's baths: Reactivity and insensitivity—a misapplication of the treatment-control design in a national evaluation. *Educational Evaluation and Policy Analysis 4:*261–279.

Fisher, C. B., and Tryon, W. W. (1988). Ethical issues in the research and practice of applied developmental psychology. *Journal of Applied Developmental Psychology 9:*27–39.

Furlow, T. G. (1980). Consent for minors to participate in nontherapeutic research. *Legal Medicine Annual,* pp. 261–273.

Garfield, S. L. (1987). Ethical issues in research on psychotherapy. *Counseling and Values 31:*115–125.

Gaylin, W., and Macklin, R., ed. (1982). *Who Speaks for the Child: The Problems of Proxy Consent.* New York: Plenum.

Geller, D. M. (1982). Alternatives to deception: Why, what, and how? In *The Ethics of Social Research: Surveys and Experiments,* ed. J. E. Sieber. New York: Springer-Verlag, pp. 39–56.

Glantz, L. H., Annas, G. J., and Katz, B. F. (1977). Scientific research with children: Legal incapacity and proxy consent. *Family Law Quarterly 9:*253–295.

Gray, J. N., and Melton, G. B. (1985). The law and ethics of psychosocial research on AIDS. *Nebraska Law Review 64*:637–688.

Gray, S. W. (1971). Ethical issues in research in early childhood intervention. *Children 18*:83–89.

Hayvren, M., and Hymel, S. (1984). Ethical issues in sociometric testing: Impact of sociometric measures on interaction behavior. *Developmental Psychology 20*:844–849.

Holmes, D. S. (1976a). Debriefing after psychological experiments. I. Effectiveness of post-deception dehoaxing. *American Psychologist 31*:858–867.

Holmes, D. S. (1976b). Debriefing after psychological experiments. II. Effectiveness of post-experimental desensitizing. *American Psychologist 31*:868–875.

Hyers, T. M., and Scoggin, C. H. (1979). Ethical and practical problems of a high risk to benefit ratio study in children. *Clinical Research 24*:293–296.

Janofsky, J., and Starfield, B. (1981). Assessment of risk in research on children. *Journal of Pediatrics 98*:842–846.

Kelman, H. C. (1967). Human use of human subjects: The problem of deception in social psychological experiments. *Psychological Bulletin 67*:1–11.

Kessler, M., and Albee, G. W. (1975). Primary prevention. *Annual Review of Psychology 26*:557–591.

Kinard, E. M. (1985). Ethical issues in research with abused children. *Child Abuse and Neglect 9*:301–311.

Knerr, C. R. (1982). What to do before and after a subpoena of data arrives. In *The Ethics of Social Research: Surveys and Experiments,* ed. J. E. Sieber. New York: Springer-Verlag, pp. 191–206.

Langer, D. H. (1985). Child psychiatry and the law. *Journal of the American Academy of Child Psychiatry 24*:653–662.

Levine, R. J. (1978). Research involving children: The National Commission's report. *Clinical Research 26*:61–66.

Lowe, C. U., Alexander, D., and Mishkin, B. (1974). Nontherapeutic research on children: An ethical dilemma. *Journal of Pediatrics 84*:468–472.

McCormick, R. (1974). Proxy consent in the experimentation situation. *Perspectives in Biology and Medicine 18*:1–20.

McCormick, R. A. (1976). Experimentation in children: Sharing in sociality. *Hastings Center Report 6*:41–46.

Marquis, D. (1983). Randomized clinical trials: Leaving therapy to chance. *Hastings Center Report 13*:40–47.

Melton, G. B. (1987). The clashing of symbols: Prelude to child and family policy. *American Psychologist 42*:345–354.

Melton, G. B. (1988a). When scientists are adversaries do participants lose? *Law and Human Behavior 12*:191–198.

Melton, G. B. (1988b). Ethical and legal issues in research and intervention. Paper presented at National Institute of Mental Health workshop, Washington, D.C.

Melton, G. B., and Gray, J. (1988). Ethical dilemmas in AIDS research. *American Psychologist 43*:60–64.

National Commission for the Protection of Human Subjects of Biomedical and Behavioral Research (1977). *Report and Recommendations: Research Involving Children.* HEW Publication [OS] 77–0004. Washington, D.C. U. S. Government Printing Office.

Noonan, M. J., and Bickel, W. K. (1981). The ethics of experimental design. *Mental Retardation 19:*271–274.

Pearn, J. H. (1981). The child and clinical research. *The Lancet 2:* 510–512.

Rae, W. A., and Fournier, C. J. (1986). Ethical issues in pediatric research: Preserving psychosocial care in scientific inquiry. *Children Health Care 14:*242–248.

Ramsey, P. (1976). The enforcement of morals: Nontherapeutic research on children. *Hastings Center Report 6:*21–30.

Reatig, N. (1981). DHHS internal policies for reviewing research involving children. *IRB: A Review of Human Subjects Research 3:*1–4.

Rutstein, D. R. (1969). The ethical design of human experiments. *Daedalus 98:*523–541.

Schafer, A. (1982). The ethics of the randomized clinical trial. *The New England Journal of Medicine 307*(12):719–724.

Schafer, A. (1984). The randomized clinical trial: For whose benefit? *IRB: A Review of Human Subjects Research 7:*4–6.

Seeman, J. (1969). Deception in psychological research. *American Psychologist 24:*1025–1028.

Sieber, J. E. (1982a). Deception in social research: I. Kinds of deception and the wrongs they may involve. *IRB: A Review of Human Subjects Research 4:*1–6.

Sieber, J. E. (1982b). Deception in social research: II. Evaluating the potential for harm or wrong. *IRB: A Review of Human Subjects Research 5:*1–6.

Sieber, J. E. (1982c). Deception in social research: III. The nature and limits of debriefing. *IRB: A Review of Human Subjects Research 6:*1–6.

Striker, L. J. (1967). The true deceiver. *Psychological Bulletin 68:*13–20.

Thompson, R. A. (1992). Developmental changes in research risk and benefit: A changing calculus of concerns. In *Social Research on Children and Adolescents,* ed. B. Stanley and J. E. Sieber. Newbury Park, Calif.: Sage.

Veatch, R. M. (1987). *The Patient as Partner.* Bloomington, Ind.: Indiana University Press.

Warwick, D. P. (1975). Deceptive research: Social scientists ought to stop lying. *Psychology Today 10:*38–40.

Weinrach, S. G., and Ivey, A. E. (1975). Science, psychology, and deception. *Bulletin of the British Psychological Society 28:*263–267.

Wells, K., and Sametz, L. (1985). Involvement of institutionalized children in social science research: Some issues and proposed guidelines. *Journal of Clinical Child Psychology 14:*245–251.

3

Ethical Issues in Exposing Children to Risks in Research

DAN W. BROCK

A widespread consensus exists in our society that competent individuals should not be used in research without their informed and voluntary consent. This consensus is expressed in a number of authoritative documents such as the Nuremberg Code (see Appendix B) and the Helsinki Declaration (see Appendix C), in the bioethics and legal literature, as well as in federal regulations governing all parties receiving federal funds for research. Institutional Review Boards within health care institutions monitor compliance with this requirement. Children, on the other hand, are presumed to be incompetent to consent or refuse to participate in research, and so if they are to participate in research they must be protected by means other than their own consent. This chapter explores some of the ethical issues raised by the participation, and more specifically the placing at risk, of children in medical and other research.

In medical therapy, competence to give consent to treatment is a legal status. Adults are presumed competent to give consent to their own treatment while minors (persons below the age of eighteen) are presumed not to be competent to decide about their treatment. In each case, the presumption of competence or incompetence should be understood as rebuttable in some cases. Adults' decision-making capacities often are impaired by the effects of injury or disease, of medications and other treatments, and from a host of other causes, but in most cases these are impairments of their usual decision-making capacities and follow a period of competence. In the case of children, limited decision-making capacity in the great majority of cases results from developmental limitations, does not follow a period of competence, and will be overcome in the natural course of the child's development. The focus here will be on minors who lack the capacity to decide for themselves and whose participation in research could not be justified by their own consent.

As an ethical matter, many older minors do have adequate decision-making capacities to make at least some health care decisions and to make an informed and voluntary decision about participation in research (Brock, 1989). In the case of medical therapy and treatment, the law in most states recognizes this capacity of many minors in three ways (Capron, 1982).

First, specific statuses of the minor patient such as being married, a mother, a member of the armed forces, or living on one's own emancipate minors for the purposes of deciding about their medical treatment. Second, for specific treatments, such as treatments for sexually transmitted diseases or substance abuse, and prenatal care, minors can obtain treatment without the consent of their parents or guardians. Third, for minors who are capable of understanding their medical condition and the alternative treatments for it with their attendant risks and benefits, and of then making an informed decision about treatment, so-called "mature minor" rules permit them to give or refuse consent to their own treatment without the necessity for parental consent. Plausible ethical justifications can be offered for at least some version of each of these three kinds of legal exception to the general incompetence, and lack of legal authority, of minors to make their own health care decisions.

An ethical case could be made for extending at least some or all of these exceptions to minors' incompetence to decide about their treatment in the research context as well. However, current federal regulations generally have not extended these exceptions to the general presumption of minors' incompetence to consent in the research context. In addressing the issue of exposing children to risk without their consent, there are two significantly different interpretations of the class of children—on the one hand, those lacking legal authority to consent (generally all minors) or, on the other hand, those lacking the capacities required by the most plausible ethical analysis of competence to consent. A different way of putting this point is that there is a class of minors that lacks legal authority to consent to research participation, but that does have adequate decision-making capacities to ground an ethical right to make such decisions. For these minors, the same arguments that ground the legal authority of competent adults to consent or refuse to participate in research will ground the minors' ethical rights to do so as well, though the law now fails to recognize fully those ethical rights. The concern in this chapter is not with minors who have the capacities to give or refuse valid consent to participate as human subjects in research, but only with those minors who lack these capacities. The relevant capacities necessary for children to be competent to make decisions about participation in research are discussed in chapter 5 of this volume.

There are two general ethical issues raised by the participation in research of children who lack the capacity to give their own consent to participate. Who should have authority to decide about children's participation in research? What standards should those deciding about children's research participation use for those decisions? These are the same general questions that arise regarding all incompetent persons and their medical treatment as well as research.

In the two decades following World War II, participation in research was commonly thought to be substantially the same as participation in medical treatment (Rothman, 1991). The researcher–subject relation was viewed as very similar to the physician–patient relation in medical therapy. Perhaps the signal event in changing this assimilation of research to therapy was the publication in 1966 of Henry Beecher's paper describing twenty-two instances of ethically problematic use of human subjects in research (Beecher, 1966).

There followed a growing recognition of the fundamental conflict of interest between researchers and their research subjects. Unlike medical therapy, in which professional traditions and norms require the physician to promote the well-being of his or her patient, the fundamental aim of research is the advancement of generalizable knowledge. With the recognition of serious abuses of the interests of human subjects in research, special rules and procedures were adopted by the federal government to regulate the protection of human subjects in research. Both the ethical and legal responses to the conflict of interest between researcher and subject, and to human subject abuses generally, focused on the importance and necessity of obtaining the informed consent of human subjects in research.

Use of informed consent as the principal means of protecting research subjects, however, and of determining the risks to which subjects can be exposed, was not available in the case of children unable to give valid consent. In the case of some other populations who had suffered serious human-subject abuses and who also are unable to give valid consent to their own participation—for example prisoners, for whom the central problem is the questionable voluntariness of their consent, not their lack of decision-making capacities, or the mentally retarded—their participation in research was by and large stopped. The same has not happened with children, and this chapter, in examining the justification for exposing children to risk in research, explores why. For children, despite this important difference between medical therapy and research, it is instructive to look first at medical therapy where there has been considerable attention to the two questions of who should decide for incompetents unable to consent for themselves and by what standards. This will provide a touchstone against which the different research settings can be evaluated.

Decision Making for Children in Medical Therapy

Answers to the ethical questions of who should make medical treatment decisions for incompetent persons and by what standards can be thought of as an ethical framework for such decision making. In work done elsewhere with Allen Buchanan, I have argued that the answer to the question of who should decide for incompetents is that there is a presumption that the family of the incompetent individual should be the decision maker (Buchanan and Brock, 1989).

The important general point here is that the family's authority to decide for an incompetent family member should be understood as presumptive—that authority can be rebutted in some instances, for example, where the family member also is incompetent or where there is a serious conflict of interest between the family member and the incompetent person that affects the decision in question. But without specific reasons that disqualify the family member from acting as surrogate for the incompetent individual, the presumption for the family as surrogate will hold. I address in the following the general reasons for the family to act as surrogate for an incompetent individual, and the special reasons for the parents to be the decision makers for their children. However, the case of children is not essentially different from that of other incompetent individuals—if anything, the case is stronger regarding children—in the presumption that the family is the appropriate surrogate, and the case of research is not essentially different from that of therapy in who should act as surrogate for an incompetent child.

The standards to be used by family members acting as surrogates for incompetent patients may be thought of as guidance principles for that decision making. In the case of guidance principles for decision making by surrogates for incompetent children, however, the appropriate principles are not the same as for incompetent adults. In the case of incompetent adults, it is widely agreed that there are three ordered guidance principles for surrogates' decision-making: Advance Directives, Substituted Judgment, and Best Interests. These are an ordered set of principles in the sense that, if possible, the first principle is used, if that is not possible then the second, and if that is also not possible then the third. The Advance Directives principle directs the surrogate to decide in accordance with a valid advance directive, given by the patient while still competent and which applies to the decision at hand. The Substituted Judgment principle directs the surrogate to use his or her knowledge of the patient, and the patient's aims and values, to attempt to decide as the patient would have decided in the circumstances, if the patient were competent. Finally, the Best Interests principle directs the surrogate to make a decision that best promotes the incompetent individual's interests. Since the Best Interests principle should only be employed when the surrogate lacks the knowledge of the patient's aims and values necessary to apply the Substituted Judgment principle, employing Best Interests will amount to asking how most reasonable persons would decide in the circumstances. This is appropriate because when the Best Interests principle is used, the surrogate lacks knowledge of how the incompetent person's aims and values differ from most persons.

It is an oversimplification to think of these principles as strictly ordered in the way I have suggested, since evidence of the incompetent individual's aims and values that have bearing on the decision in question is often neither fully decisive nor fully absent. In practice, that evidence comes on a wide continuum in its strength and decisiveness for a particular choice. The stronger that evidence, the more important substituted-judgment reasoning should be; the less decisive that evidence, the more important the role of best-interests reasoning. In many decisions, the surrogate appropriately employs both forms of reasoning.

This ethical framework for decision-making is justified by two fundamental values—patient self-determination and patient well-being. Medical treatment offered by a physician for a patient, whether competent or incompetent, should be for the well-being of that patient. One central reason for the presumption for family members to be the surrogate is that the decision of family members will usually promote the patient's well-being more than would the use of other persons as surrogates (although other reasons for parents to be surrogates for their children will be discussed below). The three guidance principles ensure that the decisions promote the patient's well-being, as that well-being would be understood by the patient.

The exercise of self-determination typically has two components—making important decisions about one's life for oneself and according to one's own aims and values. While an incompetent person's self-determination cannot be promoted by the person making treatment decisions for him- or herself, it can be promoted by attempting to have the patient's aims and values guide the decisions of others. That is what the first two principles do. Where the patient's judgment of what treatment is best for him or her is in conflict with the judgment of others, the first two guidance principles reflect the view that the patient's self-determination and own view, when competent, of his or her well-being override the views of others.

The distinction between and ordering of these principles makes clear an important difference between children (as well as other incompetent individuals who have never previously been competent) and most incompetent adults. For most incompetent adults, it is usually possible to use either the Advance Directives principle or the Substituted Judgment principle; adults' prior period of competence makes it possible for them to have issued a valid advance directive or, if they have not done so, at least to have formed aims and values that can now guide the surrogate's decision.

Young children who have never had the decision-making capacities necessary for competence cannot have issued a valid advance directive, nor have they developed sufficiently mature aims and values to limit their surrogate's choice. With older children who are not yet competent to make decisions, the more mature and well-developed their decision-making capacities, the more their aims and values should influence their surrogates' choices. Unlike that of adults, children's principal interest in self-determination interest is neither in making the decision for themselves (even if this is sometimes what they most want) nor in having the decision made by another according to the child's current aims and values. Instead, children's self-determination interest consists in having their capacity to develop into autonomous adults protected and promoted by present choices. This means that for the most part the Best Interests guidance principle will apply to surrogate decision making for children in medical therapy. How can this ethical framework apply to decision-making regarding children in research, and how must it be changed to fit the research context?

Reasons Ethically Justifying Children in Research

Medical Benefit to the Child

When the research in question is so-called therapeutic research, the ethical framework for treatment decision making for incompetent patients can be applied directly to children in research. The child's participation then represents a potentially therapeutic alternative to treatment of the child's medical problem. The central value served by this form of research participation is the child's well-being, and the choice to participate can be guided by, or will amount to, application of the Best Interests principle. Research promising potential therapeutic benefit to the child can vary substantially in at least two ethically important dimensions—the degree or amount of potential benefit to the child's well-being and the degree or seriousness of attendant risks to the child's well-being.

Just as the degree of risk to which it is reasonable for competent adults to expose themselves depends on the degree of potential benefit they will gain in doing so, so it is with children. With adults, however, the high value given in

American culture, law, and bioethics to individual self-determination generally prevents society or public policy from objectively balancing the degree of risk that might be warranted by potential benefit. Instead, individual self-determination can justify the balancing that adult patients or research subjects do concerning risks and benefits.

The doctrine of informed consent, as it has developed within medical ethics and the law, requires that the free and informed decision of a competent adult about either treatment or participation in research be accepted. We thereby defer over a wide range to the particular risk/benefit weighting of the patient or research subject in question. With children, who are not competent to make their own risk/benefit judgments, we cannot solve the problem of acceptable exposure to risk in the same way that we do with adults.

For children, both researchers and parents (or other guardians) should attempt to decide whether the degree of risk is warranted by the potential benefit to the child. Whether the risk is very high (including substantial risk of death) or to varying degrees lower, the question is whether the risk is excessive in light of the potential benefits of the therapeutic research. This determination is often controversial for both empirical and normative reasons. Empirical disagreement can occur over the beneficial or harmful consequences for the child from his or her participation in the research, and over the probabilities of these consequences occurring. Evaluative disagreement can occur over the relative importance or seriousness of a particular benefit or risk, or even in some cases whether a particular consequence is a benefit or risk at all.

It is the researcher's responsibility to present, and help the parents to understand, the potential beneficial and harmful consequences, together with their likelihood, for the child from participation in the research. As with medical therapy, comparable information also should be provided about reasonable alternatives for the child, whether of a therapeutic or research nature. Relevant information for the parents should include disclosure of significant professional uncertainty or disagreement regarding the potential consequences to subjects of the research. It is the researcher's responsibility to help the parents evaluate the relative importance of benefits and risks and to offer his or her recommendation regarding the child's participation in the research. It is not the researcher's responsibility to impose his or her own evaluation of the benefits and risks when they are in conflict with the parents' evaluation and when the parents' evaluation is within a reasonable range of parental discretion.

In a later section I evaluate the reasons for, and degree of, discretion properly accorded to parents or other guardians who act as surrogates in deciding about children's research participation. In the case of what is usually called "minimal risk," however, there is a justification for exposure of children independent of the case for parental discretion. It is a banal truism that all of us are continually exposed to a myriad of risks in the course of everyday life without any explicit consent to these risks. When the activities are both unusual, and so only engaged in by relatively few individuals, and also carry substantial risks, such as auto racing and hang gliding, then we often are consciously aware of these risks. However, in the case of the activities of everyday life— driving cars, using home appliances, taking showers, and so on—that carry more limited risks and are judged by nearly all people as clearly outweighing the risks of the activity, we are usually not even conscious of the risks. These are roughly what the federal Office for the Protection from Research Risks regulations call "minimal risks." Though adults often are consciously unaware of these minimal risks, the justification for their exposing themselves is in part that in the past they were aware of these risks and chose to shoulder them in order to pursue their everyday lives. Or that if asked to consent to these risks, they would do so as a reasonable and unavoidable cost of pursuing their daily activities.

But just because often no explicit consent is given, a part of that justification is an assessment—largely according to shared, communal judgments of the relative importance of benefits and risks—that the benefits of these activities clearly outweigh their minimal risks. This same assessment can justify exposing children to these, or other comparable, minimal risks of everyday life in the absence of their being able to give consent to that exposure. This justification can have more weight with children than adults because the alternative justification with adults that appeals to their actual or hypothetical consent is not possible for children. In the case of adults, unusual aims or values could lead some individuals to refuse to consent to some particular minimal risks of or comparable to the risks of daily life. Just as there is a strong prima facie case for respecting individuals' unusual aims and values, so there is a strong case for respecting their choices based on those aims and values. In such cases the shared communal judgment that these minimal risks are clearly justified is overridden by the judgment of the particular individual that they are not justified.

In the case of children, and especially young children, there are no well-informed and well-considered unusual aims and values to override the communal assessment. Thus, virtually any significant degree of potential therapeutic benefit from research participation, in comparison with standard therapy, could justify exposure of the child to minimal risks. I shall examine below reasons for still requiring parental permission even to exposure of children to minimal risks, but therapeutic benefit to the child will justify that exposure unless parental permission is refused.

Nonmedical Benefit to the Child

In discussing research that promises potential therapeutic benefit to a participating child, I have assumed that the benefit is from the treatment itself, which we hope will improve the child's medical condition; for example, experimental chemotherapy to treat the child's cancer. There are other arguments that propose some benefit to the child from participating in the research that is not a direct benefit of any condition or treatment being studied. There are many possible versions of this argument and I shall cite only one example in which research participation is claimed to be a valuable part of a child's socialization into his or her community and growth as a responsible moral being and citizen. An important communal value, a value of being a member of a community, is the shared sense of responsibility that members have and feel towards other members of the community. This benefits individuals in the obvious respect that they can count on the aid of other community members in circumstances in which they may need that aid, although it also imposes on them an obligation to provide similar aid to other community members in need. But an equally important benefit is satisfying common human needs to belong to a group in which one has a variety of close ties with its members, including ties of mutual responsibility; such communal ties enlarge and deepen our concerns and our lives. Children benefit by becoming members of such communities in which all members have some mutual ties of responsibility to each other. They learn responsibilities by seeing that others in the families and communities in which they are raised accept such responsibilities to, and expect such responsibilities from, other community members. They learn their own status as community members when they learn that such altruistic actions are expected by others of them.

Thus, when parents teach their children that they should be willing to participate in medical research designed to benefit others, this is a small, though not inconsequential, respect in which they are helped to become moral beings, with a concern for the well-being of others besides themselves and their close relations and friends; the potential beneficiaries of medical research are to a significant extent persons unnamed and as yet unknown. Willard Gaylin cites the example of a father who orders his son to give a small sample of blood for research purposes after the son has refused to do so because it would hurt a little. The father explained that this was

> his moral obligation to teach his child that there are certain things one does, even if it causes a small amount of pain, to the service or benefit of others. "This is my child. I was less concerned with the research involved than with the kind of boy that I was raising. I'll be damned if I was going to allow my child, because

of some idiotic concept of children's rights, to assume that he was entitled to be a selfish, narcissistic little bastard.'' (Gaylin, 1982)

The benefit to the child, in a nutshell, is the larger process of becoming a social and moral being, tied by social and moral responsibilities to a broader community of persons.

Benefit to Others

I turn now to research that does not hold out the promise of benefit to the children participating in it. The fundamental goal of all research—the advancement of knowledge—is the most obvious and important ground that might justify placing children at some risk in these circumstances. Here, it is useful to distinguish research that requires the participation of children from research that might be conducted with adult subjects. In the former, what is sought is knowledge of the special effects of treatments on children, different from the effects of comparable treatments on adults. Without knowledge of how potential treatments will affect children, we will not be able to tailor treatments to the special needs and circumstances of children. The potentially different effects of treatments on children distinguishes children from other groups receiving special protection in federal regulations, such as prisoners and the institutionalized mentally retarded. The special status of these other groups is usually not related to unique treatment needs or special features that affect what is appropriate treatment for them, as is commonly the case when treatment should be varied for children.

If the child subject is not expected to benefit from research participation, that participation will involve putting an individual at risk without his or her consent for the benefit of others. Some commentators have argued that this is never, or virtually never, justified (Ramsey, 1970).

But the central and most plausible ethical reason usually given for requiring consent for research participation from those capable of giving consent is to respect their status as persons, entitled to decide whether to shoulder burdens or risks for the benefit of others. Because children are not yet capable of giving or withholding consent to participate, enrolling them in research without their consent does not fail to respect them as persons in the sense of ignoring their right to decide for themselves whether to participate. They lack the requisite ability for having that right. However, if the research will impair, or seriously risk impairing, their future development of the capacities needed for responsible choice as persons, then it can fail to respect the child's self-determination interest in becoming a responsible agent and adult.

This argument that seeking knowledge specifically about children, although the research holds out no promise of benefit to the subjects, can justify selecting children for research participation instead of others who are capable of consenting. What is sought in the research is knowledge about the effects of treatments (or of not treating) on a class of persons whose special character makes them incapable of giving or withholding consent. Absent this feature of children as research subjects, there would be strong reason to seek subjects from among persons capable of giving consent, as is now done with adults. This argument does not justify exposing children to unlimited risks, and the degree of risk it would warrant is obviously not independent of the potential benefits to others of the research. A rough guide to reasonable risks on this ground would be the risks that competent adults are commonly willing to undertake for the benefit of others who bear no special relation to them beyond also being adults. However, while a few competent adults might consent to exposing themselves to very substantial research risks for the benefit of others, the degree of risk to which anyone is justified in exposing children for the benefit of others is substantially more limited. The appeal to the ethical importance of individual self-determination can justify the former but does not apply to the latter.

The argument for children's research participation in the absence of benefit to them in order to obtain knowledge about the special effects of treatments on children is related to a distinct but far more controversial argument for nonbeneficial participation. This argument purports to establish not simply the ethical permissibility of children's participation in research not expected to benefit them, but an ethical obligation to do so. Others have made this argument with regard to adults, but it is adaptable to the case of children as well (Ramsey, 1970).

Children today benefit from the past participation of both adults and other children in research that put those others at risk. Children today benefit from the medical knowledge accumulated from prior research. Sometimes the benefit is direct, as when a child today receives a treatment that would not have been available without that past research. Even if a child today never needs such treatment, that child benefits from the availability of the treatment and the assurance that should the child need it, it would be available. This benefit to children is claimed to be the basis for their obligation to assume the burdens of research participation.

The argument appeals to a notion of fairness applied across generations rather than to the more usual case of cooperating contemporaries. There are, however, some special problems in applying it to nonconsenting children. The argument relies on an appeal to a principle stating a duty of fair play along the following lines:

If one has freely participated in and accepted the benefits of a practice in which others have freely assumed burdens required by the practice for the benefit of others besides themselves, then one has a duty of fairness to do one's part by assuming similar burdens when one's turn comes in the practice to do so.

Now the main difficulty in applying this argument to children is obvious—children are incapable of making a free choice to accept this benefit of others' past participation in research and the medical knowledge that was gained. This is so in at least two respects, one of which holds for adults as well. For adults or children today, there was never a choice to accept the benefits of past medical research or to reject it—it is simply a part of the social conditions in which we now find ourselves that medicine has and uses this knowledge. It would not be feasible or sensible to ask our physicians to treat us without using any knowledge that came from the past use of human subjects in research. But for children in particular, there is also no free choice, in the relevant sense of a free responsible choice, for the consequences of which one could be reasonably held accountable. Adults are capable of such a choice, while children are not.

The argument can be reformulated to apply to children while retaining its plausible ethical appeal to fairness and reciprocity. Here, too, the distinction between persons capable of consenting but who refuse that consent and persons incapable of consenting is of crucial importance. Any free choice to participate in and accept the benefits of the practice in the case of children will have to be a hypothetical choice, although I believe no general and problematic appeal to proxy consent for them by others is needed. Even assuming that contemporary persons choose whether to participate in the practice of using children in medical research while under a Rawlsian veil of ignorance that prevents them from knowing how they will be affected has obvious difficulties; merely knowing that one already exists tells one that the self-interested choice is to refuse to participate in the practice, since one possesses the benefits of past research and can have them without accepting research risks for oneself (Rawls, 1971).

This is an instance of the general problem of applying contract arguments across generations. So the veil of ignorance has to be stretched so that one does not know to which generation one belongs—past, present, or future—when one decides whether to accept and to participate in a practice in which children, though unable to give or withhold consent, participate in research potentially beneficial to other children. Assuming that the expected benefits of such research over time exceeded its burdens, and if this is not the case then no justification of it should be possible, individuals under this veil of ignorance should be willing to participate. It is important to underline that this argument, if sound, establishes not just that it is ethically permissible for children to participate in research not expected to be of benefit to them but that it is ethically obligatory for them to do so. We may still prefer as a matter of public policy not to enforce this obligation through legal or other coercive means, and not to volunteer children for research that is not expected to benefit them without their parents' consent as a way of respecting parents' interest in making decisions importantly affecting their children. But doing this will not be because the parents' permission is all that could make the children's research participation ethically justified. Indeed, this hypothetical consent argument could be reformulated not in terms of children's participation, but in terms of the practice of parents volunteering their children to participate. The moral obligation or duty of fair play would then be on parents to consent to or volunteer their children's participation.

These are the main ethical grounds for children's participation in research, whether research is beneficial to the child or to others. The role of parents or guardians must now be brought into the picture for at least two reasons. First, parents are commonly thought to have a right to make important decisions about their children, which plausibly can include giving or withholding permission for their research participation. Second, if they have some such right, it is important to determine the degree of discretion they should be accorded in such decisions, especially with respect to deciding which benefit/risk ratios justify their permitting their children's research participation. Even if the ethical grounds for children's participation in research are those I have spelled out above, what are the grounds for parents having the authority to give or withhold consent for their children's research participation?

Parents' or Guardians' Interest in Making Decisions Concerning Their Children

Parents' (or guardians') rights to give consent to their children's research participation presumably derive from the more general justification for parents making decisions about their children. I believe that there are several different and sound reasons that support the interest of parents in making decisions for their children, and these reasons support different degrees of parental discretion in their decisions for their children. (There are representative philosophical discussions of this issue in W. Aiken and H. La Follette, eds., *Whose Child? Children's Rights, Parental Authority, and State Power,* Totowa, N.J.: Littlefield, Adams & Co., 1980) In the case of entering the child into a research protocol in which the experimental treatment is considered to promise benefit to the child equal to the best standard treatment (if there is a standard treatment, or if the research is at least comparable to no treatment when there is no alternative treatment), then the reasons for parental decision-making authority should not differ from the more familiar case of medical treatment for the child. After considering the general reasons for parental decision-making authority in this case, we can then consider how the case for parental authority changes when there are less or no expected benefits to the child from participation.

The first reason for parents' decision-making authority is based simply on the incapacity of children to decide for themselves, the consequent need for someone else to decide for them, and a general presumption that parents will usually do a better job of deciding than anyone else who could do so instead. Because in most cases parents both care deeply about the welfare of their children and know them and their needs better than others do, they will be more concerned, as well as better able, than anyone else to ensure that the decisions made serve their children's welfare. Of course, with infants and very young children this claim that parents know the needs of their children best is less persuasive. The fact that parents' legal authority does not vary substantially with the child's age suggests that more than this first argument undergirds parents' legal authority to make health care decisions for their children. This argument will justify no independent interest or right of parents to decide for their children and to enforce their choice when it may not best serve their children's welfare. Instead, it makes the parents' claim to decide dependent on their deciding most in accordance with their children's welfare. This is essentially one of the standard arguments for family members serving as surrogate decisionmakers for incompetent adults; there, too, the surrogate has no independent right to make a choice that serves the surrogate's interests or wishes as opposed to the wishes or interests of the incompetent patient.

The second reason appeals to the fact that parents must bear the consequences of treatment choices for their dependent children and so should have at least some control of and discretion over those choices. In some form, this is part of the basis for competent persons' authority to make their own treatment decisions—they will bear, and have to live with, the consequences of the decisions. While the costs of the treatment provided in a research protocol are typically not borne or fully borne by parents, the parents do bear many of the longer-term consequences, financial and other, of the choices made. As a result, it may be thought unfair to force them to bear the consequences of the decision that their child will be a research subject while denying them any input. Even if this argument is accepted, it would establish only an interest of the parents in having some input into and control over the decision, but certainly not unlimited discretion. The child in nearly all instances bears the principal consequences of the choice, and so on this line of reasoning the child's interests should principally determine the decision.

A third reason claims a right of parents, at least within some limits, to raise their children according to the parents' own standards and values and to seek to transmit those standards and values to their children. Virtually no one today believes that children are simply their parents' property, to be done with as the parents wish. Rather, proponents of this line of argument typically claim that children begin life as a *tabula rasa* without aims and values and only through a process of socialization and development acquire their own aims and values, together with sufficient experience and powers of judgment to be able to make choices that warrant others' respect. In this respect, the case for parents' discretion in treatment choices for their children who have not yet acquired stable and mature values of their own is more persuasive than the analogous case for family members deciding for now incompetent but once competent adults; previously competent adults, unlike young children, once did have their own values and goals that should be respected and that can now guide others' choices for them. In the case of young children, someone must inevitably shape their acquisition of their own goals and values. Since, for a variety of reasons, we assign childrearing responsibilities in our society largely to the family, it seems reasonable to accord to the family some significant discretion in imparting its values to the children within it. This discretion should be limited, however, by the child's basic interests in life, well-being, and the functional capacities necessary for the child to develop into an independent adult with a reasonable range of opportunities to pursue a life on his or her own.

A related, but distinct, fourth line of argument draws on various respects in which the family is a valuable social institution, such as its role in fostering intimacy and providing privacy. In most societies, the family provides both the most significant source of intimate relations for many adults as well as the context in which children's own capacities for intimacy are developed. The family is also the principal context in which privacy needs of individuals to be free from the observation, scrutiny, and evaluation of others are satisfied. The family must have significant freedom from oversight, control, and intrusion to achieve intimacy, and one aspect of this freedom or privacy is the right, at least within some limits, to make important decisions about the welfare of its incompetent members.

Finally, a fifth argument in support of parents' rights to decide for their children appeals to the fact that usually it is the parents whom the child would or does want to decide for him or her. In the case of incompetent, but previously competent, adults, this is probably the most important moral basis for family members to serve as surrogate decision makers. In the case of never-competent children, it has substantially less weight because the children have never possessed the decision-making capacities that would warrant reliance on their wishes.

The first of these five reasons would entitle parents only to make the best choice for their children, but even it alone can justify some parental decision-making discretion. Since a practice of giving decision-making authority to someone besides parents, for example a court appointed guardian, would also result in more nonoptimal decisions as measured by the child's welfare, a higher standard should not be insisted on for parents. Cumbersome, expensive, and intrusive review procedures for parental decisions, just as in the case of interventions for child abuse and neglect, should not be invoked unless the parents' decision is seriously in conflict with the child's interests, even if only the first reason is accepted for parental decision-making authority. Elsewhere, Allen Buchanan and I have distinguished between guidance principles, whose purpose is to guide surrogates' decisions for incompetent persons, authority principles, whose purpose is to locate presumptive decision-making authority for incompetent persons, and intervention principles, whose purpose is to specify when others should intervene to attempt to remove decision-making authority from the presumptive surrogate (Buchanan and Brock, 1989, ch. 2).

While Best Interests is generally the appropriate guidance principle for surrogates deciding for children, it is not an appropriate intervention principle in this context. Failure to select the course of action that best promotes their child's interest does not warrant intervention, for example by the state, in parents' decision making for their children, whether in decisions about medical care for the child or in decisions in many other areas, such as schooling. This first reason for parental decision-making authority provides a practical or instrumental reason for according parents some discretion in decision making for their children.

The other four reasons for parental decision-making authority provide a principled, not just a practical, basis for limited parental discretion. Some reasonable disagreement about the proper scope of that discretion results from reasonable disagreement about the relative weight to be accorded these last four reasons, or perhaps even from disagreement about whether all four are sound reasons. There is no specific limitation of parental discretion that is not subject to reasonable dispute, much less to unreasonable controversy. Nevertheless, when research participation promises reasonable benefit to the child in comparison with available treatment outside the research context or with no treatment, there are sound reasons for accepting parents' decisions to enroll their children in research protocols.

These arguments for parents' decision-making authority about their children justify significant parental discretion in making risk/benefit assessments concerning participation for their children. But none of those arguments, in my view, carry the weight we rightly accord to individual self-determination when competent adults make choices about their own treatment or research participation. The appropriate discretion of parents in making risk/benefit assessments about their children is substantially narrower than the comparable discretion competent adult patients or research subjects are rightly accorded. Therefore, it is considerably more important with children to have independent standards and/or procedures for assessing acceptable levels of risk that can be assumed for particular levels of potential benefit.

Procedures for Determining Acceptable Levels of Risk for Children

The procedures now used to determine the level of research risk to which children can be exposed are complex and involve different assessments, at several different points, by different persons in different institutional roles with different institutional responsibilities. I believe these procedures can be understood as a way of balancing the imposition of some community standards of protection regarding the risks to which children can be exposed with the accordance of a reasonable degree of discretion to parents in deciding about acceptable risks for their children. Understood in this way, this complex of procedures can be seen as a reasonable accommodation to the ethical case developed here for exposure of children to research risks.

The first assessment of risk exposure to subjects is made by the principal investigator(s) of the research project, often together with his or her research associates, who develop the project and make a judgment that the project is sufficiently promising in its potential benefits to subjects and/or knowledge to warrant exposing participating research subjects to its risks. Since the researchers' principal commitment should be to the furtherance of knowledge that, in the research in question here, requires the use of children as human subjects, there is a potential conflict of interest between the researchers and the research subjects; other less noble motivations of many researchers, such as furtherance of their own careers and financial remuneration, only exacerbate the potential conflicts. Consequently, the researchers' assessment of the benefits and risks of the research would not be sufficient. The research abuses that led to the current process of regulation gives empirical and historical confirmation of the inadequacy of sole reliance on the judgment of the researchers.

One important component of independent evaluation of the potential significance of the research is the process of evaluation of the grant proposal when the research is to be externally funded, as the great bulk of research employing human subjects is today. In this process, typically, committees of peers in study sections evaluate and rank the relative promise of the research in comparison with competing proposals. This process probably focuses more on the potential medical and scientific significance of the research than on the risks to subjects, though flagrant abuses would likely be identified at this stage. Institutional review boards within individual institutions are also charged with evaluating whether the potential benefits of the research warrant its risks to subjects, although since they are usually not composed of experts in the particular area of research, they are much less well-placed to evaluate the potential signifi- cance of the research than are grant-making bodies that draw on the evaluations of experts in the particular area of the research. Institutional review boards are, on the other hand, charged to concentrate especially on the risks to human subjects, in particular whether subjects are adequately protected from undue risks and whether appropriate consent procedures are followed.

Thus, the individual researchers, the peer reviewers, the funding agency, and the institutional review board each are charged with evaluating, and are more or less well-placed to evaluate, whether a particular research program should proceed and in what form participation in it will be offered to any subjects. Each of these evaluations will generally employ shared, communal standards of risks and benefits, and their relative importance, though some potential for bias towards the importance of new knowledge and downplaying of risks to subjects cannot be eliminated. This use of community standards is appropriate for a community enterprise like medical research, and is inevitable in any case at this stage of evaluation.

Before any individual child participates in a research project, however, an additional evaluation must follow the determination of whether the project will go forward and participation be offered to any human subjects. This evaluation is made from the perspective of the particular subject and his or her interests as they will be affected by participation. The parent or guardian, the person generally responsible for the child's welfare, must consent to the child's partici- pation in the research. When the child is old enough and mature enough to do so, the child's assent (signifying his or her agreement to participate, although lack of authority to consent to doing so) to participate must also be secured. At this second stage, any special needs or concerns of the child different from those of most children or persons should be considered.

For understanding our present practice of determining who can expose a child to research risk, it is crucial to distinguish among these stages of the process, the different parties taking part at those stages, and their roles and responsibilities. Before any child can participate in a research project, the proj- ect itself must be evaluated by general community standards for whether the risks it poses to human subjects are warranted by the potential new knowledge and/or benefits to subjects it promises. Then the child's participation must be evaluated from his or her perspective by those responsible for the child's wel- fare, including the child to the extent possible. This mix of communal and individual evaluation by those standards is well suited to combine judgments about what research risks a community will tolerate with what risks are reasonable from the perspective of the child and those responsible for his or her welfare.

The Special Case of Using Children as Research Subjects Without Parental Consent

The reasons discussed above for requiring parental consent are compelling. However, just as there are exceptions to the requirement of parental consent for medical therapy for children, there might also be similar exceptions in the case of research involving children. The difference between therapy and research is important when discussing whether there should be exceptions to the requirement of parental consent. In the case of therapy, public policy empowers the courts and child-welfare authorities to intervene, usually under neglect and abuse statutes, and requires treatment against parents' wishes when that treatment is of fundamental importance to the child's well-being. Thus, for example, the courts generally have not permitted Jehovah's Witness parents to refuse blood products for their children when doing so would threaten the child's life. Are there comparable benefits in the case of research that might justify forcing children's participation against the wishes of their parents?

In the case of therapeutic research, the fact that therapy must take place in a research context implies that no comparably large and well-established benefit to the child can be secured outside of a research context; if it could be, then the context would be therapy, not research. While in many cases parents do consent to therapeutic research for their children as holding the best chance of benefit to their child, the uncertainty regarding outcomes in research means that the benefit of participation to the child will not be sufficiently important and well-established to force the child's participation over the parents' objection.

When the expected benefit of the research is principally medical or scientific knowledge, then the case for requiring parental consent means that children should not be used as subjects without their parents' consent when there is the alternative of finding other research subjects for whom parental consent can be obtained. But might there be research for which parental consent would likely be systematically refused and which was of sufficient importance in the knowledge it promised, though not promising significant benefits to subjects in the research, to warrant use of children without their parents' consent? At most, there will be very few cases of this sort. However, it might be that the nature of the research was threatening to the parents, although of little risk to the children who participate, and important in the knowledge it promises to generate. The most common examples are collection of epidemiological data about children that reflects badly on the parents or children; for example, research about child abuse done on abused children where the children have not been removed from the parents' home and so remain in their parents' custody. In such a case, the grounds for parents' decision-making authority regarding their children also would be substantially weakened by their past abuse of their children. In theory at least, it might seem very likely that the research could lead to preventing similar abuse of other children in the future.

The possibility cannot be ruled out in advance that the benefit of the research to others might be sufficiently great, the risk to the children who are subjects sufficiently small, and the claim of parents to decide for their children sufficiently attenuated that it was deemed ethically permissible to use children in the research without their parents' consent. Nevertheless, as a matter of public policy we should be extremely cautious about authorizing deception or coercion of parents who retain custody of their children in order to enroll their children in research for the benefit of others and against the parents' wishes. Granting such an authority would threaten important values involving the family and family privacy, and be subject to serious well-intentioned misuse and/or ill-intentioned abuse. If such research is ever permitted, it should only be after special, publicly accountable review bodies at a national level (in the United States, probably best located within the Department of Health and Human Services) have determined that the research should be undertaken. At present, I believe it has not been established that there is sufficient research of compelling importance to children that cannot now be done because of the requirement of parental consent to warrant making exceptions to that requirement.

Conclusion

We have seen that an understanding of the ethical issues in exposing children to risks in research can build on an ethical framework for decision making about children's treatment in therapeutic contexts. The ethical framework for the research context will take account of the differences the research context introduces, such as the additional uncertainty regarding benefit to the child and the additional nonpatient-centered goal of generalizable knowledge. It is important to distinguish three kinds of benefits that can justify exposing children to research risks—therapeutic benefits to the child, nonmedical benefits to the child, and benefits to others from the knowledge gained in the research.

We have also seen that there are several distinct grounds of parents' authority to make decisions regarding their children, including decisions to expose them to research risks. These grounds support significant, though not unlimited, discretion for parents in making these decisions. The complex institutional processes, involving different parties in different social or legal roles and with different responsibilities, that authorize children's research participation can be understood as an attempt to balance communal standards limiting risks to which children can be exposed with appropriate parental discretion in making decisions about their children.

References

Beecher, H. K. (1966). Ethics and clinical research. *New England Journal of Medicine 74:*1354–1360.

Brock, D. W. (1989). Children's competence for health care decisionmaking. In *Children and Health Care: Moral and Social Issues,* ed. J. Moskup and L. D. Koppelman. Dordrecht, Holland, and Boston, Mass.: Reidel Publishing.

Buchanan, A. E., and Brock, D. W. (1989). *Deciding for Others: The Ethics of Surrogate Decision Making.* Cambridge: Cambridge University Press.

Caplan, A. L. (1984). Is there a duty to serve as a subject in biomedical research? *IRB* 6:5 (Sept./Oct.), pp. 1–5.

Capron, A. C. (1982). The competence of children as self-deciders in biomedical interventions. In *Who Speaks for the Child: The Problems of Proxy Consent,* ed. W. Gaylin and R. Macklin. New York: Plenum Press, pp. 57–114.

Gaylin, W. (1982). Competence: No longer all or none. In *Who Speaks for the Child: The Problems of Proxy Consent,* ed. W. Gaylin and R. Macklin. New York: Plenum Press, pp. 27–54.

Ramsey, P. (1970). *The Patient as Person.* New Haven: Yale University Press.

Rawls, J. (1971). *A Theory of Justice.* Cambridge, Mass.: Harvard University Press.

Rothman, D. J. (1991). *Strangers at the Bedside: A History of How Law and Bioethics Transformed Medical Decision Making.* New York: Basic Books.

4

The Law of Human Experimentation with Children

LEONARD H. GLANTZ

There is a long history of research on children (see Chapter 1) but a relatively short history of legal control of this activity (Annas, Glantz, and Katz, 1977). There are a number of reasons for this. Legal restraints on research in general were virtually nonexistent until the promulgation of the Nuremberg Code in 1947, and even that document does not mention research with children (Grodin, 1992). Furthermore, the idea that children might have rights in and of themselves is a concept that was largely ignored until the last half of the twentieth century. Until then children were usually seen as extensions of their parents who could make all decisions on behalf of their children (Rodham, 1973). Indeed, even today there is still a substantial question about how much the state should and may control a parent's authority over a child. In general, parents have broad discretion in making important decisions on behalf of their children, and until these decisions are found to be abusive or neglectful, the state generally may not intervene in parental decisions about their children.

In recent years, however, children, particularly older children, have come to be seen as persons with their own rights, civil and human, separate from their parents' rights (*Tinker v. Des Moines Independent Community School District,* 1969). This circumstance produces some tensions over what parents can decide for their children, what children can decide for themselves, and how much the state can regulate these matters. This complex tripartite authority for overseeing children's rights and welfare is evident in the questions raised concerning the legal controls on research with children. The major legal questions that such research present are:

1. May parents, who are supposed to be the protectors of their children, permit their children to be research subjects?
2. Do children have the right to consent to being, or refuse to be, a research subject?
3. Are there research activities that the state may prohibit children from participating in regardless of the consent of the parent or the child?

Because of the lack of legal rules or guidelines that directly answer these questions, this chapter discusses situations and issues that are closely analogous to the issues presented by research with children. It then analyzes the only specific legal rules in the United States that exist in this area—the federal regulations on research with children.

The Authority of Parents to Consent to Medical Care

Cases for Parental Power

As a general rule parents, as the natural guardians of their children, have the authority, and even the duty, to consent to medical care on behalf of their children. Until the 1960s it was often held by courts that the only person who could consent to the care of a child was its parent. Even close relatives, such as adult sisters, were held not to be able to consent to necessary medical care for a child (*Moss v. Rishworth*, 1920). There are two bases for this rule. The first is that parents are best able to determine what is in their child's best interest, and this should not be interfered with by someone else, no matter how well intended. The second reason is less noble. Since parents are liable for the support and maintenance of their children, and are also entitled to the child's services, some courts have noted that parental consent is required because the parents' liability for support and maintenance may be increased and the value of a child's services decreased by an unfortunate outcome (*Lacey v. Laird*, 1956). This, of course, comports with the old notion of the child as chattel of its parents. The parents' consent is required because something they own is at risk of being broken.

For the most part, parents have been given broad discretion in deciding whether or not to consent to medical care on behalf of their children. In the absence of life-threatening circumstances, courts tend not to interfere in parental health-care decisions. Thus, a parental decision to not permit an operation on a fourteen-year-old boy to repair a hairlip and cleft palate was upheld by a court although physicians and social workers claimed it was important to the child's well-being to undergo this procedure (*In re Seiferth,* 1955). Similarly, there is a case involving a seventeen-year-old boy who suffered from severe spinal degeneration. Doctors recommended a spinal fusion that would enable the boy to continue to be able to sit up. Without the operation the boy would become a bed patient. His mother's refusal to consent to the procedure was upheld by a court (*In re Green,* 1972).

In an unusual case, a court ordered cosmetic surgery for a fifteen-year-old boy who had a "massive deformity" on one side of his face. As a result of this deformity the boy was socially isolated, did not attend school, and suffered serious psychological harm. The court ordered the surgery over his mother's objections (*In re Sampson,* 1970). This case is quite unusual since it did not involve treatment for a life-threatening condition and has rarely been followed.

When a child's life is endangered by a parental refusal to consent to ordinary medical care, the courts uniformly order treatment. The best known and most often decided cases of this type involve children of Jehovah's Witnesses who have religious objections to blood transfusions (Holder, 1985). No court has ever permitted parents to withhold such ordinary and simple care necessary to save the life of a child. Courts have also ordered treatments such as chemotherapy for children with leukemia where the treatment had a good likelihood of success and withholding treatment meant certain death (*Custody of a Minor,* 1978). However, there is at least one court that upheld a parent's decision to withhold life-saving heart surgery from a twelve-year-old boy with Down syndrome, a case that was later overturned in a separate proceeding (*In re Phillip B.,* 1979). In that case there was evidence that the child's condition would deteriorate over time and that without the surgery the child might live twenty years. However, the surgical mortality rate was estimated to be between five to ten percent. Given these facts the trial court held that there was no clear and convincing evidence that the child was being deprived of the "necessities of life" and, therefore, was not neglected.

These are all cases in which a parent refuses to permit a child to undergo recommended medical treatment. The courts give great deference to parental decisions in such situations, and are hesitant to authorize the state to violate a child's body against parental wishes. This is because there is a powerful presumption that parents are best suited to decide what is in the best interests of their children, even when such decisions do not comport with what a majority of parents are likely to do in a similar situation, or with what medical experts recommend. Courts are very reluctant to take away what should be parental decisions from parents and give them to the state. It is only in the most extreme circumstances, such as when a child will die without clearly beneficial treatment, that courts rule that there is no way they can find that parents are acting in the child's best interest.

Limits on Parental Power

The fact that parents have broad discretion in refusing recommended medical treatment does not mean that parental power is unlimited. States do have the authority to protect the interests of the child. For example, mandatory education laws and child-labor laws are state restrictions on parental power. Similarly, while parents may corporally punish their children, there are limits on how severely they may use such punishment. Parents can use "reasonable force," but not force designed to cause a substantial risk of "death, serious bodily injury, disfigurement or extreme pain . . ." (Mnookin and Weissberg, 1988). Crossing these boundaries constitutes child abuse for which state intervention and even criminal action may be taken.

In terms of health care, there are some unusual cases in which parental consent, while necessary, may not be sufficient to authorize the invasion of the child's body. Parents have broad authority to make medical decisions for children because, as mentioned above, it is presumed that parents act in the child's interest. However, relatively recent medical innovations have created circumstances in which there is a willingness to subject a child to the risk of bodily invasions without physical benefit to the child. These are cases in which a healthy child could be the organ donor for a sick sibling or relative. In these cases a child (or an incompetent adult, which raises similar issues) is subjected to the risks of surgery for the benefit of another. The question is, does the law permit this use of a child?

The first case of this type was brought in Massachusetts in 1957 when organ transplantation was in its infancy. The case involved nineteen-year-old twins at a time when the age of adulthood was twenty-one (*Masden v. Harrison,* 1957). The healthy twin, Leonard, and his parents consented to the removal and use of his kidney to treat his sick brother, Leon. Since there was uncertainty as to whether the parents could legally consent to an operation on a healthy child for the purpose of removing a healthy organ to benefit another child, a court was petitioned to resolve this issue. Psychiatric testimony was produced to demonstrate that Leon's death would have a "grave emotional impact" on Leonard. The court found that the operation was necessary to save Leon's life and that Leonard had been fully informed and understood the consequences of the procedure and had consented to it. Instead of simply finding that the consent of the parents and the nineteen-year-old "child" was sufficient to authorize the operation, the court went on to find that because of the negative psychological impact Leon's death would have on Leonard that the operation was "necessary for the continued good health and future well-being of Leonard and that in performing the operation the defendants are conferring a benefit upon Leonard as well as upon Leon."

By finding that Leonard "benefitted" by having his healthy kidney removed, the court was able to avoid the difficult issue of the validity of parental consent to a nonbeneficial procedure. The same court handed down two more rulings that year in which it found that fourteen-year-old twins would benefit from the removal of their kidneys for transplantation into their sick siblings (*Huskey v. Harrison,* 1957; *Foster v. Harrison,* 1957). As in the first case, the court found that the fourteen-year-olds understood the consequences of the procedure and freely gave their consent. In these three cases the court found that in circumstances in which the parents and minors consent, and there is "psychological benefit" to the donor, such procedures may be lawfully performed.

A 1969 Kentucky case involved a potential donor, Jerry Strunk, who was not a minor but a twenty-seven-year-old with an I.Q. of thirty-five and a mental age of six, who lived in a state institution (*Strunk v. Strunk,* 1969). Tommy Strunk, Jerry's brother, was twenty-eight years old, married, employed and a part-time student who suffered from a fatal kidney disease. No other member of the family qualified as a donor. A case was brought by Jerry's mother to obtain court approval for the organ removal procedure. A guardian *ad litem* was appointed to protect Jerry's interests. The guardian opposed the procedure. The Department of Mental Health, in whose facility Jerry resided, argued in favor of the procedure. In its report, the department said that Tom's life was "vital to the continuity of Jerry's improvement," that Jerry makes constant inquiries about Tom's coming to see him, and that Tom is Jerry's only sibling and upon the death of their parents Tom's presence will be necessary to Jerry's stability and optimal functioning. A psychiatrist testified that Tom's death would have "an extremely traumatic effect" upon Jerry. The court also found that the operative risk to Jerry was small, about 0.05 percent. The trial court found that Jerry's well-being would be more severely jeopardized by the death of his brother than by the removal of his kidney. The appeals court, using the doctrine of "substituted judgment," found that if Jerry were competent, he would consent to the procedure, and so affirmed the trial court's authorization of the procedure.

This was a very close case, decided by a four-to-three vote. In a strongly worded dissent, Judge Steinfield argued that guardians must act to "protect and maintain the ward." He was unimpressed by the prediction of psychological trauma, which he called "at best most nebulous." The dissenters firmly stated that the ability to fully understand and consent should be a prerequisite to the donation of an organ and feared the "dire results" the majority opinion could lead to.

This is the first case in which a healthy organ was removed from a person who could not give consent because of his mental condition. Although in the earlier Massachusetts cases the minors could not give a legally binding consent, the courts found that they had freely and knowingly given their consent in fact. Also, in *Strunk,* the court never held that guardians could consent to organ removal, but that the state's courts had the authority to approve such organ removal. In this regard it did not bestow upon parents or guardians the discretion to unilaterally make this type of decision on behalf of children or wards.

In 1972, a Connecticut superior court permitted a kidney transplant from a seven-year-old to her twin sister. (*Hart v. Brown,* 1972). In that case the guardian *ad litem* supported the procedure as did the family's clergyman who felt the decision was morally and ethically sound. A psychiatrist testified that the procedure would be of "immense benefit to the donor in that the donor would be better off in a family that was happy than in a family that was distressed. . . ." The court was less impressed than previous courts with the psychiatric testimony, finding that the procedure would be of "some benefit" to the donor.

In concluding the court found:

> [I]t would appear that the natural parents would be able to substitute their consent for that of their minor children after a close, independent and objective investigation of their motivation and reasoning. This has been accomplished in this matter by the participation of a clergyman, the defendant physicians, and attorney guardian *ad litem* for the donee, and indeed, this court itself. . . .
>
> Natural parents of a minor should have the right to give their consent to an isograft kidney transplantation procedure when their motivation and reasoning are favorably reviewed by a community representation which includes a court of equity.

It should be noted that, once again, the court did not give parents the same authority to consent to this type of procedure as they would have had to consent to purely beneficial procedures. Here the parents were given a limited power to consent, subject to review by "community representation."

To a large degree, courts continue to authorize the removal of kidneys from incompetent persons based on the psychological benefit theory (*Little v. Little,* 1979). But some courts have taken a more direct approach. In one Massachusetts case involving bone marrow donation from a six-year-old to her ten-year-old brother, the court that invented the psychological benefit justification called it into question. In that case the court said

[T]o require a finding of benefit to the donor, and particularly to accept a psychological benefit as sufficient, often seems to invite testimony conjured to satisfy the requirement by words but not by substance. . . .

It is the court's opinion that a better approach to the issue involved in this case is to consider that the primary right and responsibility for deciding the delicate question of whether bone marrow should be taken from Toni and transplanted into William is that of the parents with reference to both children. (*Nathan v. Farinelli*, 1974)

The court in this instance simply found that, based on all the facts, the parents' decision to permit the bone marrow donation from their six-year-old was "fair and reasonable" and based its approval on that finding. While the court seems to have relaxed its review of parental decisionmaking, compared to the kidney transplant cases, this may be because the court viewed bone marrow donation to be less risky and less permanent than kidney donation. Bone marrow donation, while painful, does not involve a surgical procedure, and bone marrow, unlike kidneys, regenerates so that there is no permanent loss.

But courts have not given universal approval to the removal of kidneys from incompetent potential donors. In a Louisiana case, *In re Richardson* (1973), the court prohibited the removal of a kidney from a seventeen-year-old mentally retarded boy, Roy, which was to be transplanted into his sister Beverly (*In re Richardson*, 1973). The court found that the transplant was not immediately necessary to save Beverly's life since she could be sustained indefinitely by hemodialysis. It also found that while Roy was the best donor, since there would be a 3–5 percent chance of rejection of his kidneys, other donors were available who could donate with a 70–80 percent chance of success. The court also rejected the argument that Roy would benefit because Beverly could care for him after their parents' deaths as "highly speculative . . . and highly unlikely." But the court also held that permitting such a procedure would not conform to the state's legal mandate to "promote and protect the ultimate best interests of the minor."

In a Wisconsin case, *In re Pescinski* (1975), a petition was filed asking permission to transplant a kidney from Richard, a thirty-nine-year-old schizophrenic with a mental age of twelve who had been institutionalized for sixteen years, into his thirty-eight-year-old sister, a mother of six minor children. The transplant surgeon said he would not consider using Beverly's parents who were sixty-seven and seventy-years-old as donors as matter of personal principle, or any of her children as a matter of his "own moral conviction." Another forty-three-year-old brother refused to be a donor. The court was clearly suspicious of the motives of the physician and those other healthy donors. The court ruled that since there was no evidence that any interests of Richard would be served by the donation, and guardians must act to protect the best interests of their wards, that it would not approve the removal of his kidney.

While these cases do not directly address the issue of research with minors, they do present the issue of parents' and guardians' authority to subject children and incompetent adults to risks where there seems to be no benefit (at least no direct physical benefit). These cases limit the authority of parents to consent to such physical intrusions on their children. In those cases in which courts authorize organ removal, they do not hold that parents have the same authority to consent to such procedures as they have to consent to ordinary and beneficial medical or surgical procedures. Rather the courts either grant permission using their own authority, as in *Strunk,* or ratify parental consent based on its own review, as in *Hart.* Also, the courts' ongoing struggle to fashion and accept the "psychological benefit" theory demonstrates their reluctance to permit the physical invasion of a child's body where the child does not receive any direct benefit. But most importantly, these courts permit the removal of healthy kidneys from children because it is necessary to save the life of another child within the family. In this sense the courts are recognizing the power of the family to protect its members. The courts seem to be accepting the notion that when a child is sick the family as a unit is permitted to use its resources and make reasonable sacrifices to save the life of a sick child. Judges simply do not want to stand in the way of families who wish to act in this lifesaving manner. Indeed one court says as much. In *Little v. Little* (1979) after authorizing removing the kidney of a fourteen-year-old mentally retarded girl for transplantation into her brother Steven, the court stated "Nothing in this opinion is to be construed as being applicable to a situation where the proposed donee is not a parent or sibling of the incompetent."

It is also worth noting that in the two cases in which courts refused to permit the removal of a kidney, the incompetent donor was living in an institution, not at home. As a result, the courts may have sensed that these potential donors were not truly part of the family unit of which other courts were so protective.

To demonstrate that these cases do not provide authority for the general proposition that parents (or even courts) can authorize the nonbeneficial invasion of a child's body, one can examine this hypothetical case. Assume that researchers are on the verge of curing kidney disease but need healthy kidneys from children to complete their work. The researcher argues that children whose kidneys were removed would receive enormous psychological benefit from knowing that they helped eradicate this terrible disease, and that the risks are minimal as characterized by the courts that have permitted kidney removal in the transplant cases. Since the effects of kidney removal on the child are identical in this and the transplant situation, would courts permit it? The answer is clearly "no." Once one removes the direct lifesaving goal of this procedure, and once the family issues are removed, courts would not find that consent to such procedures would be in the child's best interest.

A similar set of issues is found in the sterilization cases. These cases involve mentally retarded minors, virtually always girls, whose parents wish to have them surgically sterilized either to prevent pregnancy or to simplify menstrual care. Because of the history of sterilization abuse in this and other countries, sterilization of incompetent persons is viewed with appropriate suspicion. This suspicion is reflected in U.S. government policy that refuses to permit the use of Medicaid funds to sterilize institutionalized or incompetent persons (42 *CFR* 441.254) or persons under twenty one years of age (42 *CFR* 50.201–50.206). Sterilization not only is suspect because of its past use for eugenic purposes, but because it deprives individuals of a healthy function, and may infringe on their rights to procreate. It is generally accepted that parents do not have the authority to consent to the sterilization of their minor children. Instead, such decisions are taken to the courts for authorization and the courts are split on deciding under what circumstances sterilization is permissible. Most of the courts require stringent procedural safeguards, and an ultimate finding that sterilization is in the child's best interest. Absent such a finding courts refuse to authorize sterilization (*Matter of Eberhardy*, 1981; *Wentzel v. Montgomery General Hospital*, 1983).

Sterilization is different from nonbeneficial research with minors. The purpose of sterilization is to deprive a person of a normally functioning bodily process, and therefore can be seen as always physically "harmful." However these cases also demonstrate that parental power to consent to medical procedures is not unlimited.

Children's Authority to Consent

There is a widely accepted rule of law that touching without consent is a battery. For a consent to be valid the person giving that consent must have the legal capacity to do so. Because children have historically been considered legally incompetent to give such consent, parents have had to consent to their children's care. It has been legally convenient to have a clear line between minority and adulthood. Thus, when one became eighteen-years-old, and therefore an adult, parental consent was no longer required for medical care, or for all the other activities to which adults consent.

Over the past two decades this rule of a minor's legal incapacity to consent to medical care has been modified through both legislative and judicial actions. It became recognized that there were children who could not, or would not, involve their parents in their medical care and therefore would be denied beneficial medical treatments if parental consent were required. This was, in part, in response to adolescents in the late 1960s and 1970s who were leaving home prior to attaining the age of majority. These children, often labeled "runaways" were outside of their parents' control and sometimes became pregnant, contracted diseases, or had problems with drug use. In response, many states adopted statutes that permit minors to consent to care for specific conditions. These conditions include venereal and contagious diseases, drug abuse and addiction, and pregnancy. The conditions on this list are ones states want to encourage treatment of, and ones minors might not want their parents to be aware of. The reason for relaxing parental consent requirements for these conditions is that such consent requirements were not protecting children, but instead, negatively affecting children's health.

In some states the age at which minors can consent to all medical care has been lowered. In addition courts have come to adopt the "mature minor rule." This means that older minors who have de facto capacity to give an informed consent may give a legally binding consent. For example, when a seventeen-year-old girl consented to a skin graft for the treatment of a badly damaged finger, a court held that lack of parental consent was not adequate grounds upon which to bring a suit, since the minor was mature enough to "understand the nature and consequences and to knowingly consent to the beneficial surgical procedure" (*Younts v. St. Francis Hospital,* 1970). The mature-minor rule is well enough established that one commentator has noted that in the last twenty-five years there is no reported case in which parents have recovered damages for the treatment of a child over the age of fifteen on the grounds of lack of parental consent (Holder, 1988).

Indeed, in the area of abortion the mature minor rule has reached constitutional dimensions. After *Roe v. Wade* (1973) liberalized abortion laws in all states, Missouri passed a law that required minors to obtain parental consent prior to undergoing an abortion. The U.S. Supreme Court ruled that "constitutional rights to do not mature and come into being magically only when one attains the state-defined age of majority. Minors, as well as adults, are protected by the Constitution and possess constitutional rights" (*Planned Parenthood of Missouri v. Danforth,* 1976). The court stated that the right of minors to make the abortion decisions does not suggest that every minor, "regardless of age or maturity," could give effective consent. Rather the court adopted the position of a lower court judge that a minor can give effective consent if she is "sufficiently mature to understand the procedure and to make an intelligent assessment of her circumstances with the advice of her physician.'' In a later case, the court upheld the authority of the state to require a minor to undergo a judicial procedure if she wished to bypass a parental-consent requirement. But the court noted that the judge's task would be to determine if ''she is mature and well-informed enough to make intelligently the abortion decision on her own'' (*Belloti v. Baird,* 1979). Once such a determination was made, the abortion decision was entirely in the hands of the minor woman.

What the mature minor rule has done is to apply the law of competence to minors. Adults are presumed to be competent by law. However, if one can prove that an adult is in fact incompetent to make a treatment decision, which means that the person is mentally incapable of understanding the nature and purpose of a proposed procedure, then that person is no longer able to give a legally binding consent. In such a circumstance a proxy must consent on the incompetent person's behalf. Unlike adults, minors are presumed to be incompetent. But the mature minor rule permits minors to rebut this presumption and to be deemed competent to give a consent when they demonstrate the capacity to do so.

The law increasingly recognizes that the arbitrarily defined the age of majority should not deprive minors of making decisions that affect them, but rather that a case-by-case determination of maturity should be made. For example, when a statute required the consent of the mother to terminate her parental rights in order to place her child for adoption, a court ruled that a fourteen-year-old mother can provide such a consent (*Adoption of Thomas,* 1990).

For the most part, the rules that enable minors to act on their own behalves are designed to assure that minors receive beneficial health services. Thus, the mature-minor rule was adopted so that children could obtain health care that is beneficial and necessary. Rules that prohibited obtaining such services seemed arbitrary and counterproductive. Since such rules were adopted in the context of obtaining beneficial care, it is not clear that they are applicable to all research settings. However, they might well empower minors to refuse to be the subjects of research that might be detrimental to them, or give them a shared voice in making such decisions.

Bonner v. Moran *and Dual Consent*

On its face the Nuremberg Code would appear to prohibit research on infants and children of questionable capacity to consent. The code's first principle states ''the voluntary consent of the human subject is absolutely essential.''

This statement makes no exception for proxy consent. However, the drafters of the code were not discussing the subtleties of human experimentation when they drafted that document. The atrocities that the Nazis called research were performed with the consent of no one, old or young, competent or incompetent. Thus the code's first principle is vitally important, but not necessarily all-inclusive.

The later Declaration of Helsinki of the World Medical Association, a more moderate document, says that research subjects must give their free consent but "if he is legally incompetent the consent of the legal guardian should be procured." This is an ambiguous statement that can be read to mean that the guardian's consent is sufficient, or that the guardian's consent must be in addition to the consent of the incompetent. The Helsinki Declaration uses the term *legally* incompetent, not factually incompetent; thus it is conceivable that the term "incompetent" could pertain to one who could, in fact, give a knowing consent.

There is one United States case, decided in 1941, that addresses this issue (*Bonner v. Moran*, 1941). John Bonner was the fifteen-year-old cousin of Clara Howard, who was a "hopeless cripple" as a result of severe burns. Clara's aunt, who was also John's aunt, took Clara to a hospital that specialized in plastic surgery. It was determined that Clara required a skin graft from a donor of the same blood type. The aunt persuaded Bonner to go to the hospital for a blood test, where it was determined that he was a compatible donor. At that time the surgeon, Dr. Robert Moran, performed the first operation on Bonner's side. Although Bonner lived with his mother she was ill and unaware of the procedure. After the operation he went home and told his mother he had to go back to the hospital to get "fixed up." However, once in the hospital he was not fixed up. Instead, more operations were done in order to cut a "tube of flesh" from his armpit. This tube was then attached to his cousin forming a true flesh and blood bond between them. The procedure was unsuccessful due to poor circulation in the tube of flesh. The tube was severed after Bonner lost so much blood that he needed transfusions himself. From beginning to end he was hospitalized for two months.

Bonner sued Dr. Moran for assault and battery. The trial court adopted the mature-minor rule stating that when a minor is capable of appreciating the nature, extent and consequences of a bodily invasion, he could consent to the invasion. The trial judge then found in favor of the physician, which means he found that Bonner in fact appreciated the nature, extent and consequences of the procedure performed on him.

The appeals court decision noted that as a general rule a minor could not give a binding consent to undergo a medical procedure. The court also recognized, however, that there were exceptions to this rule, including the mature-minor exception employed by the trial court.

> But in all such cases [in which the exceptions apply] the basic consideration is whether the proposed operation is for the benefit of the child and is done with the purpose of saving his life or limb. The circumstances of the instant case are wholly without the compass of any of these exceptions. Here the operation was entirely for the benefit of another and involved sacrifice on the part of the infant of fully two months schooling, in addition to serious pain and possible results affecting his future life. This immature colored boy was subjected several times to treatment involving anesthesia, bloodletting, and the removal of skin from his body with at least some permanent marks of disfigurement.

Thus, the court ruled that in the absence of intended benefit for Bonner, the consent of his parent was necessary. The court said that during his confinement in the hospital his mother may have learned what was transpiring and by not acting to remove her son, may have ratified her son's consent. If this were the case, the physician would not be liable.

At this point the appeals court ruling is unclear. Consent to a bodily invasion must be given prior to the invasion for there to be no battery. Therefore Bonner's mother could not be giving her own consent, which would have happened after the fact. On the other hand the court may be saying that the mother may have known about the second operation where her son was going to get "fixed up" and ratified her son's consent to that procedure. But the court certainly seems to say that if the mother had consented to this nonbeneficial and risky procedure, that her son's case could not succeed.

There is some disagreement among scholars about the holding of this case. Two commentators think it means that nonbeneficial procedures can be performed on minors as long as their parents consent (Curran and Beecher, 1969). Another commentator argues that the case does not give parents independent authority to consent to nonbeneficial procedures (Capron, 1972). Rather, he argues, the case only gives parents the authority to ratify the consent of a minor who also gives his own independent consent. It is this interpretation that is the most likely to be correct, based on the facts of the case. In *Bonner,* the trial court ruled as a matter of fact that Bonner had the capacity to consent and did in fact consent to the bodily invasion. The appeals court never challenged this factual finding. Rather it held that if the mother ratified Bonner's consent, then there was no cause of action. Thus, the only conclusion one can reach with any sense of certainty is that when a minor and a parent both consent, invasive procedures that do not provide the minor with any benefits, and may even be harmful, can lawfully be performed.

The concept that two individuals must consent to validate a decision is not particularly unusual. In the kidney transplantation cases discussed earlier, the courts made it clear that the nineteen- and fourteen-year-olds had all given their consent to the kidney removal even though they were not legally binding consents. If the minors objected to the organ removal, it is unlikely that parental consent could override that decision. Even in the *Hart* case involving a seven-year-old donor, the court felt it useful to note that the donor has been informed of the operation and "insofar as she is capable of understanding desires to donate her kidney . . ." to her sister. Even in the cases where there seems to be no understanding, there is no case in which the donor has expressed even an uninformed refusal.

There is a recent case from another area of law that also discusses the relevance of dual consent involving a parent and child. (*In re E.G.*, 1989). In this case a seventeen-year-old woman was diagnosed as having leukemia, which required treatment including blood transfusions. Both the seventeen-year-old and her mother were Jehovah's Witnesses and both refused the transfusion. The issue confronting the court was whether a seventeen-year-old could refuse lifesaving treatments. The trial court ordered the transfusions but was reversed by the appeals court, which held that the patient was a mature minor and could therefore refuse treatment. The Illinois Supreme Court also held that mature minors can make health care decisions based on both constitutional and common law rights. Although the minor had the right to refuse treatment, such a right is subject to being balanced against the state's interest in abridging the exercise of the right. The court said that the most significant state's interest in this case is "protecting the interests of third parties," namely the parents of the refusing child. The court said

> If a parent or guardian opposes an unemancipated mature minor's refusal to consent to treatment for a life-threatening health problem, this opposition would weigh heavily against the minor's right to refuse. In this case, for example, had E.G. refused the transfusions *against* the wishes of her mother, then the court would have given serious consideration to her mother's desires.

In this case, since both the mother and daughter were in agreement in refusing the blood transfusions, the court affirmed the appellate court and authorized the treatment refusal.

It is worthwhile noting that if the daughter had wanted the transfusion and the mother had refused, there is no doubt, based on previous cases overruling parental refusal of necessary transfusions, that the transfusion would have been ordered. Thus, while dual consent was needed for the treatment refusal decision, the risky and even life-threatening course, a single consent would have been sufficient to authorize the ordinary and recommended medical treatment that could have been lifesaving.

Summary

What can be determined based on the preceding analyses are the following propositions.

> Parents have broad discretion in making treatment decisions for their children when they are at least arguably acting in their children's best interests. It should be noted that even in the early kidney transplant cases which could be viewed as "experimental," no court ever questioned the parent's authority to consent to the procedure for the *recipient* of the organ.

> Older children have been given an increasingly important role in making health care decisions for themselves. Thus, while there remains a presumption that children are not capable of making such decisions, this presumption can be rebutted in the cases of children who are mature enough to understand the nature and consequences of the proposed procedure.

> Courts are very careful, even perhaps reluctant, to permit parents or guardians to consent to procedures that subject children to risk but do not provide benefit. Even courts that permit organ removal or sterilization do not delegate this authority to parents. Rather they require review of such decisions and subject them to close scrutiny.

> The courts seem comfortable with the concept of dual consent when it comes to procedures that may not be seen as benefitting the child.

Given these propositions, the issue was how to incorporate them into a coherent set of rules that researchers, institutions, funding agencies, and subjects could comprehend and apply. Indeed, the larger question was research could be conducted on children, which was seen as producing a social good, and at the same time protect children's rights and welfare, which was seen as a moral imperative.

Balancing Safety and Science

The Development of Federal Regulations

It was ten years from the time the federal government considered regulating research with children until final regulations were promulgated in 1983. This unusually long time frame demonstrates the difficulty of balancing the desire to protect children as research subjects with the recognition that some research is necessary if we are to improve children's health.

On November 16, 1973, the Department of Health, Education and Welfare (later to become the Department of Health and Human Services) issued a "draft working document" on research with children (Draft Working Document on Experimentation with Children, 1973). The proposed rules were largely procedural but subjected proposed research with children to strict substantive review by two boards. The first board was an Agency Ethical Review Board, which would reside in the federal funding agency and be composed of fifteen members from various scientific fields as well as lawyers, ethicists, and public representatives. The function of the committee was to advise the agency as to the societal and ethical acceptability of the proposed research. In so doing the Ethical Review Board was to consider:

> (1) the potential benefit of the proposed activity, (2) the scientific merit and experimental design, (3) whether the proposed activity entails risk of significant harm to the subject, (4) the sufficiency of animal and adult human studies demonstrating safety and clear potential benefit of the proposed procedures and providing sufficient information on which to base an assessment of the risks, and (5) whether the information to be gained may be obtained from further animal and adult human studies.

The second committee, called a "Protection Committee," would be established by the applicant and be composed of at least five members who would be competent to deal with the legal, medical, social, and ethical issues involved in the proposed activity.

The duties of the Protection Committee were to oversee:

> (1) The selection of subjects who may be included in the activity; (2) the monitoring of the subject's continued willingness to participate in the activity; (3) the design of procedures to permit intervention on behalf of one or more of the subjects if conditions warrant; (4) the evaluation of the reasonableness of the parents' consent and (where applicable) the subject's consent; and (5) the procedures for advising the subject and/or the parents concerning the subject's continued partici-

pation in the activity. Each subject and his or her parent or guardian will be informed of the name of a member of the Protection Committee who will be available for consultation concerning the activity.

The proposal also excluded certain children from being research subjects.

A child may not be included as a subject in DHEW activities to which this subpart is applicable if:

(a) the child has no known living parent who is available and capable of participating in the consent process: *Provided,* That this exclusion shall be inapplicable if the child is seriously ill, and the proposed research is designed to substantially alleviate his condition; or

(b) the child has only one known living parent who is available and capable of participating in the consent process, or only one such parent, and that parent has not given consent to the child's participation in the activity; or

(c) Both the child's parents are available and capable of participating in the consent process, but both have not given such consent;

(d) The child is involuntarily confined in an institutional setting pursuant to a court order, whether or not the parents and child have consented to the child's participation in the activity; or

(e) The child has not given consent to his or her participation in the research: *Provided,* That this exclusion shall be inapplicable if the child is 6 years of age or less or if explicitly waived by the DHEW; or

(f) The Protection Committee established under Section 46.26 of this subpart has not reviewed and approved the child's participation in the activity.

These rules are relatively strict. The Ethical Review Board must approve the acceptability of the research by examining the scientific merit of the proposal, determining that there is sufficient potential benefit, and determining that nothing of significance could be learned from further studies with adults or animals. The Protection Committee actively monitors the conduct of research and determines the reasonableness of the parents' consent. The exclusion provisions exclude all children without parents unless the proposed research is designed to substantially alleviate that child's serious medical condition, require both parents to consent to any research, exclude involuntarily institutionalized children, and give all children seven years of age or older the power to veto their participation as research subjects.

The year following the publication of this draft working paper, Congress enacted the National Research Act, which established the National Commission for the Protection of Human Subjects of Biomedical and Behavioral Research (1974). Included in the national commission's charge was the examination of the issue of research with children. Following the most extensive exploration of this issue ever conducted, the commission issued a series of recommendations.

1. The commission found that research with children was important for the health and well-being of children and that such research should be conducted and supported.
2. Research may be conducted or supported if an Institutional Review Board has determined that the research is scientifically sound and significant and "where appropriate" studies have been conducted on animals and adults, then older children, prior to involving infants. Other recommendations involved using the safest procedures possible and protecting the privacy of children and parents.

The commission then divided research into different groups.

1. Research that does not involve greater than minimal risk
2. Research with more than minimal risks but which holds out the prospect of direct benefit to the individual subjects
3. Research with more than minimal risk to the subject that does not hold out the prospect of direct benefit to individual subjects
4. Research that does not fall under any of these categories, that is, it is riskier or less potentially beneficial to individual subjects than denoted in the previous categories. As research is classified as riskier or less beneficial to the subjects, more review or safeguards are provided.

The commission intentionally avoided the term consent in its recommendation. It referred to parental "permission" and the child's "assent." This is because the commission believed that consent is something only an autonomous person can provide for himself, and that children "assent" because they cannot give a legally valid consent. In one of its more controversial positions the commission stated that it believed that the assent of children seven years of age or older "should be required in addition to parental permission." The commission then argued that the objection of a child any age should be binding with some exceptions. The commission says that the objection of a "small child" can be overridden in circumstances when the research might provide "significant benefits" to the child's health or welfare and the intervention is available only in the research context. It would appear that "small child" means a child under seven years old.

The commission also recommended special restrictions on research with children who are wards of the state or who reside in institutions.

The commission engaged in balancing the risks and benefits of research and proposed regulations based on the balancing of these factors. These recommendations, which were largely incorporated into the final rules, are significantly less restrictive than the rules proposed in the earlier HEW draft working document. There are fewer layers of review, the reviews are not as detailed, and much more emphasis is put on the roles of the parent and child as participants in the research decision.

Current Federal Regulations

The federal regulations on children as research subjects are part of a larger body of regulations governing research with human subjects in general (HHS Policy, 1981). Strictly speaking, the federal regulations apply only to research that is funded or conducted by the federal government. However, an institution that wishes to receive funding from the federal government must submit a written assurance that not only assures compliance with the regulations for federally funded research, but which also includes a "statement of principles governing the institution" in regard to protecting the rights and welfare of all human subjects of research "regardless of source of funding." In practice this usually means that all research with human subjects in institutions that receiving federal funding for any research with human subjects is governed by these regulations. This also means that researchers who do not work in such institutions and who do not receive federal funds are not covered by these federal rules, but rather are only subject to the more general restrictions imposed by law or professional guidelines.

The regulations cover "research," defined as "systematic investigation designed to develop or contribute to generalizable knowledge." This means that not everything novel or new is governed by this term. If a new surgical procedure is done for the first time on a patient for the purpose of treating that patient's condition, this does not constitute "research" as defined in the regulations. However, if this were the first of a planned series of procedures in which patients would be observed or followed so that the physician could write or present papers that would add to generalizable knowledge about either the condition or the procedure, it would constitute "research" under these regulations. One of the difficulties in determining whether an activity is "research" is that the definition requires that the intent of the person performing the intervention be apparent. For an activity to constitute research it must be "designed" to contribute to generalizable knowledge. Thus, in the example used above, if the person performing the novel procedure a hundred times is not interested in evaluating the procedure or reporting on it, but simply intends to continue to perform the procedure in the unproven belief that it is beneficial to patients, such a situation does not come under the definition of research. However, this may be very questionable medical practice. Indeed, both physicians and health-care institutions should be wary of the widespread use of unproven medical interventions. Scientific medical practice should be based on formal studies of safety and efficacy and not solely on anecdotal clinical experience.

Before research can be conducted it must be approved by an Institutional Review Board (IRB). Appointments to the IRB are made by the institution covered by the regulations, subject to certain membership requirements imposed by the regulations. Criteria for IRB approval of a proposed research project include its finding that:

- Risks to subjects are minimized
- Risks to subjects are reasonable in relation to anticipated benefits to the subject (if there are any), and the importance of the knowledge that may reasonably be expected to result from the research
- Selection of subjects is equitable
- Informed consent will be obtained and documented from subjects, with certain exceptions to this rule

There are detailed requirements for obtaining and documenting the subjects' informed consent. The investigator must obtain the ''legally effective informed consent of the subject or the subject's legally authorized representative.'' Information must be presented to the subject in language that is understandable to the subject. The information that the investigator presents to the subject must include:

1. A statement that research is being conducted, an explanation of its purpose, the expected duration of the subject's participation, and a description of the procedures to be performed
2. A description of any reasonably foreseeable risks or discomfort to the subject
3. A description of any benefits to the subjects or those that may reasonably be expected from the research
4. A disclosure of appropriate alternative procedures or treatments that might be advantageous to the subject
5. A statement that participation is voluntary and that a refusal to participate or a decision to withdraw from participation will result in no penalty or loss of benefits of any kind

Several other mandatory and optional disclosures are also set forth in the regulations. The regulations also describe the unusual circumstances in which an IRB can alter all or some of the informed consent requirements. The regulations also state that the informed consent requirements do not preempt any state or local laws that may require other information to be disclosed.

There are certain classes of research that are exempt from the federal regulations. These exemptions include research conducted in educational settings involving normal educational practices, such as research on regular or special educational instructional strategies, and research using educational tests if the data derived are recorded in a manner in which subjects cannot be identified. While the regulations exempt such research from review, the institution that sponsors or conducts such research, or in which the research is conducted, may still require review or verification that the research falls within the exempt category. Furthermore, state and local laws and rules would still continue to be applicable.

In addition to these general regulations governing human research, the federal rules contain additional protections for children involved as research subjects (Additional Protections for Children, 1983). The term "children" is defined by the regulations as "persons who have not attained the legal age for consent to treatments or procedures involved in the research, under the applicable law of the jurisdiction in which the research will be conducted." Thus if a state has a statute that permits fifteen-year-olds to consent to a treatment that is part of a research protocol, fifteen-year-olds would not be "children" under these regulations, and therefore would only be protected under the general research rules. If there is judicial recognition of the mature minor rule, the same notion applies.

The federal rules adopt the "sliding scale" approach to regulation proposed by the National Commission. The specificity and restrictiveness of the regulations varies, depending on the amount of risk the child-subject will face, and the amount of benefit that particular child-subject will likely receive from participation. The regulations present four categories of research.

> Category 1: Research not involving greater than minimal risk. Such research is approvable as long as adequate provisions are made for soliciting the assent of the child and the permission of the child's parent or guardian.
>
> Category 2: Research involving greater-than-minimal risk but presenting the prospect of direct benefit to the individual subject. To approve this type of research the IRB must find that the risk is justified by the anticipated benefit to the subjects, that this risk/benefit ratio is at least as favorable to the subjects as available alternative approaches, and that adequate provisions are made for soliciting the child's assent and the parent's permission.

Category 3: Research involving greater than minimal risk and no prospect of direct benefit to individual subjects, but likely to yield generalizable knowledge about the subjects' disease or condition. This category of research is approvable only if the IRB finds the risk represents a "minor increase" over minimal risk; the research procedures are "reasonably commensurate" with those inherent in the subject's actual or expected medical, dental, psychological, social, or education situation; the intervention is likely to yield generalizable knowledge of "vital importance" in understanding and ameliorating the subject's disease or condition; and there is adequate provision for soliciting the subject's consent. Usually *both* parents must give permission for this category of research.

Category 4: Research that does not fall into the other three categories. This type of research is only approvable when the secretary of Health and Human Services, after consultation with an expert panel, finds the research presents a "reasonable opportunity" for the understanding, prevention, or alleviation of a "serious problem" affecting the health or welfare of children, and that the research will be conducted in accordance with "sound ethical principles."

These regulations are very flexible and vague, and a great deal of discretion is left in the hands of IRBs and parents. Of all the proposed rules and regulations on research with children, the final regulations are the least restrictive. For example, unlike earlier proposals, the federal rules do not require the IRB to find that there is some special reason to use children as research subjects for the proposed research, or that appropriate research has been either performed or completed on animal or adult human subjects.

The term *minimal risk* is defined in the general regulations to mean "that the risks of harm anticipated in the proposed research are not greater, considering probability and magnitude, than those already encountered in daily life or during the performance of routine physical or psychological examinations or tests." The term is significant because how research with children is regulated depends in part on whether a risk is "minimal" or "more than minimal." The risks children submit themselves to in daily life can be quite substantial (Kopelman, 1989). Children play high school football, nine-year-olds may ride their bicycles without wearing helmets in heavy traffic, and in some cities, school age children are confronted with the risk of violence from knife- and gun-wielding classmates. Indeed adults, who are more risk-averse than adolescents, may well ordinarily encounter fewer and less significant risks than many adolescents and children. Technically, category 1 research could include sending children out into traffic on their bicycles. A "minor increase over minimal risk'' is not defined at all, and probably could not be. In fact, minimal risk and a "minor increase" over minimal risk have little if any substance in the area of research with children. Rather, these vague terms describe conditions and goals that individual IRBs should try to achieve. Even if riding a bicycle in heavy traffic meets the technical definition of minimal risk, an IRB's common sense approach to this term would make it unlikely to approve such an activity as part of research.

Category 3 research, which involves no benefit to the research subject, is permissible if it presents a minor increase over minimal risk, and the intervention or procedure presents experiences "reasonably commensurate" with those inherent in the child's actual or expected medical treatment. This means that the more that children have done to them as part of their medical treatment, the more that can be done to them as research subjects. One commentator, in discussing this notion, states that it might be "more appropriate to invite a child with leukemia who has had several bone marrow examinations to consider having another for research purposes." He argues that this position reflects the National Commission's judgment that the experience of having undergone such a procedure would make the child familiar with the procedure and its discomfort so that the decision to participate would be more knowledgeable (Levine, 1986). But this provision also justifies such procedures on children who are not capable of making a decision to participate. Indeed, it can well be argued that children who are ill, and are required to undergo invasive or uncomfortable procedures for treatment purposes, should be entitled to more protection from unnecessary and nonbeneficial interventions than are healthy children.

While earlier proposals recommended that the age of assent be placed at seven, the regulations do not adopt this approach. Rather, the IRB is to determine when children are capable of assenting. Since the IRB does not see individual subjects, it must make this decision for the class of subjects proposed by the investigator. However the regulations require the IRB, in determining whether or not children are capable of assenting, to take into account their ages, levels of maturity, and psychological states. While all four categories of research require the IRB to determine that "adequate provisions are made for soliciting the assent of children," a child's assent is not always required. A child's assent is not required when the child's capacity is so limited that he cannot reasonably be consulted. Also, if the research holds out a "prospect of direct benefit" that is important to the child's health or well-being, and is available only in the context of the research project, the absence of the child's assent is not a barrier to participation.

One goal of the federal regulations is to further the ideal of the dual consent rule discussed above. Ideally, a parent and child, or both parents and the child in the instance of research categories three and four, must agree to the child's participation in research. The children's opinion is negated only where they cannot assent or refuse to assent to potentially beneficial procedures. However, it is not clear exactly what it is that constitutes "assent." Assent is defined in the regulations to mean "a child's affirmative agreement to participate in research. Mere failure to object should not, absent affirmative agreement, be construed as assent." It would appear from this and the National Commission's deliberations on which this is based, that the goal is to give children as much of a voice as is possible. It is therefore important for the investigator to explain as much as possible to children about the research in terms they can understand. Children may not be able to understand the subtleties of research, but they do know about needles, pain, hunger, and separation from caregivers. As Weithorn and Scherer discuss in detail in chapter 5, children are capable of participating in the decision to become a research subject to a greater extent than is commonly recognized. The regulations assume that children are capable of making such decisions, and researchers should respect a child's decision unless it can be demonstrated that a child is incapable of such participation.

In rare instances, research can be done without parental permission when seeking such consent is not a "reasonable requirement" to protect the subjects (abused children are given as an example). However, an appropriate mechanism for protecting the child-subjects must be established. Finally, there are more stringent rules for children who are wards of the state.

The federal rules on research with children are not particularly restrictive. A good deal of discretion exists as to the type of research that can be appropriately conducted, and this discretion is lodged primarily with the parents and the local IRBs. Indeed, when the experimental procedure is thought to be "beneficial" there is essentially no restriction on what can be done. The most dramatic example of this is probably the Baby Fae case.

Baby Fae was born on October 12, 1984, suffering from hypoplastic left heart syndrome, a condition where the left side of the heart is too weak to pump blood. The result is usually death. There was a surgical procedure available at the time called the Norwood Procedure that had a forty percent rate of success when performed by its originator, Dr. William Norwood. Heart transplantation was also a possible treatment for this condition. Even when the Norwood Procedure was not totally successful, it could extend a child's life long enough to find a human donor heart. In the Baby Fae case, however, Dr. Leonard Bailey proposed performing a xenograft in which he would transplant a heart from a baboon to the child. The parents agreed to this. Nine days after the procedure Dr. Bailey predicted that Baby Fae might celebrate her twentieth birthday. Baby Fae died eleven days later. Dr. Bailey and his institution received substantial criticism. Commentators questioned whether he had adequately informed the parents about the Norwood Procedure. It appears that a newborn heart was available for transplantation but that Dr. Bailey did not look for a donor heart. Also, the consent form he used was inadequate and possibly misleading (Pence, 1990). For example, the consent form stated that seven years' experience with heart transplants in 150 newborn animals "suggests that long term survival with appropriate growth and development may be possible . . ." (NIH Report, 1986). It does not note, however, that every attempt to use a xenograft in humans has failed.

The Baby Fae proposal passed several institutional review panels including its IRB. A review by the federal Office for the Protection from Research Risks found nothing troubling with this research, with the exception of three short-comings in the consent form: The consent form failed to state whether compensation would be available if an injury occurred as a result of the research, it "appeared" to overstate the potential benefit, and it did not include the possibility of searching for a known heart donor. The criticism was not based on the actual failure to search for a human heart but rather on the failure to include this possibility in the consent form. The review did not suggest that such research should be conducted on consenting adults before doing such research on infants.

This dramatic case illustrates a number of points. Where research can be categorized as "potentially beneficial," especially where a child is fatally ill, what is permissible to do to a child lies within the discretion of the parents and physician. Here the parent is doing something recommended by a doctor to save a child's life. Furthermore, as in the transplant cases discussed above, the family is acting to "save a life" and government stays out of such decisions. Finally such research is not truly regulated by the government—the federal rules make parents the ultimate regulators of research with children in the United States, particularly where there is some potential benefit.

Conclusion

Perhaps the most notable point concerning the legal aspects of research on children is the small role the law has played in this area. There are almost no cases directly on point (*Nielsen v. Regents of the University of California*, 1973), no statutory law, and relatively unrestrictive federal regulations. What the law has done in recent years, however, is set a general tone that indicates that children have some rights that they may exercise on their own behalf, and that parents and institutions have an obligation to protect children and not to exploit them. It is perhaps this more general obligation to protect children that has evolved over time that has served to protect children who become research subjects. Ultimately, what institutions, sponsors, and IRBs permit to be done to children, and what investigators propose to do, is a reflection of how the larger society views children.

There has been an increasing focus on the rights of children. In this regard, there has been much discussion on whether children can consent to their own medical care or "assent" or refuse to be research subjects. As noted earlier, the National Commission recommended that children as young as seven-years-old should assent as a condition to their participation in research. While this notion reflects respect for children as autonomous persons with rights, it also provides legitimization for young children to be used as research subjects. Furthermore, while this assumes that such young children are in a position to protect themselves, it also places a significant burden on young children to make important decisions.

The ultimate "children's right" is the obligation that adults have to protect and nurture children. For example, child labor laws and mandatory education laws are not truly "children's rights" laws. Under the laws children *must* attend school and *may not* engage in certain occupations. Such laws embody paternalistic notions of what is good for children and what is bad for them. What is good is required and what is bad is prohibited. Under such laws the child's consent or assent is irrelevant. While paternalism in regard to competent adults is viewed with suspicion, paternalism as applied to children is both common and desirable. It is the role of adults to ensure that children are not subjected to unnecessary or excessive risks or discomfort. The law is a crude tool for accomplishing this goal. It is able to set forth only minimal standards of behavior that adults must follow in their treatment of children. In a real sense, this is what the federal regulations on research with children do—they set a floor below which adult behavior must not fall. Real protection from research abuses cannot come from the literal application of minimal standards. Rather, such protection can only come from adults who control research with children, who must take seriously their obligation to assure that children are not subjected to harm or exploitation.

References

Additional Protection for Children Involved as Subjects in Research, (March 8, 1983). 48 Federal Register 9818; codified in 46 *CFR* 46, Subpart D.

Adoption of Thomas (1990). 408 Mass. 446.

Annas, G. J., Glantz, L. H., and Katz, B. (1977). *Informed Consent to Human Experimentation: The Subject's Dilemma*. Cambridge, Mass.: Ballinger.

Belloti v. Baird (1979). 443 U.S. 622, 643–44.

Bonner v. Moran (1941). D.C. Cir. 126 F.2d 121.

Capron, A. (1972). Legal considerations affecting clinical pharmacological studies in children. *Clinical Research 21:*141.

Curran, W., and Beecher, H. (1969). Experimentation in children. *Journal of the American Medical Association 210:*77.

Custody of a Minor (1978). 375 Mass. 733.

Draft Working Document on Experimentation with Children (Nov. 16, 1973). *Federal Register 38:*31746.

Foster v. Harrison (Nov. 20, 1957). 68674 Eq., Mass. Sup. Jud. Ct.

Grodin, M. A. (1992). Historical origins of the Nuremberg Code. In *The Nazi Doctors and the Nuremberg Code,* ed. G. J. Annas and M. A. Grodin. New York: Oxford University Press, pp. 121–144.

Hart v. Brown (1972). 29 Conn. Sup. 368, 289 A.2d 386.

Holder, A. R. (1985). *Legal Issues in Pediatrics and Adolescent Medicine,* 2d ed. New Haven, Conn.: Yale University Press, p. 102.

Holder, A. (1988). Disclosure and consent problems in pediatrics. *Law, Medicine and Health Care 16:*219.

HHS Policy for Protection of Human Subjects (1991). 56 *Federal Register* 28003 (June 18), 48 *Federal Register* 9269 (March 4, 1983); codified in 45 *CFR* 46, Subpart A.

Huskey v. Harrison (Aug. 30, 1957). 68666 Eq., Mass. Sup. Jud. Ct.

In re E.G., a minor. (1989). Sup. Ct. 133 Ill. 2d 98, 549 N.E.2d 322.

In re Green (1972). 448 Pa. 338, 292 A.2d 387.

In re Pescinski (1975). 67 Wis. 2d 4, 226 N.W.2d 180.

In re Philip B. (1979). 92 Cal. App. 3d 796, 156 Cal. Rptr. 48; reversed, 139 Cal. App. 3d 407, 188 Cal. Rptr. 781 (1983).

In re Richardson, (1973). 284 S.2d 185 (La. App.).

In re Sampson (1970). 317 N.Y.S.2d 641, affirmed 29 N.Y.2d 900 (1972).

In re Seiferth (1955). 309 N.Y.80, 127 N.E.2d 820.

Kopelman, L. (1989). When is the risk minimal enough for children to be research subjects? In *Children and Health Care: Moral and Social Issues,* ed. L. Kopelman and P. Moskop. Boston–London: Kluwer Academic Public Publishers, pp. 89–92.

Lacey v. Laird (1956). 166 Ohio St. 12, 139 N.E.2d 25.

Levine, R. J. (1986). *Ethics and Regulation of Clinical Research,* 2d ed. Baltimore–Munich: Urban and Schwarzenber, p. 248.

Little v. Little (1979). 576 S.W.2d 493 (Ct. App. Texas 4th Dist.)

Masden v. Harrison (June 12, 1957). No. 68651 Eq., Mass. Sup. Jud. Ct., 1977.

Matter of Eberhardy (1981). 102 Wis. 2d 307, 307 N.W.2d 881.

Mnookin, R. H., and Weissberg, D. K. *Child, Family and State,* 2d ed. Boston: Little Brown, p. 272. (Reprinting ALI Model Penal Code.)

Moss v. Rishworth (1920). 222 S.W. 225, Texas.

Nathan v. Farinelli (July 3, 1974). Civil Action No. 74–87, Mass.

National Commission for the Protection of Human Subjects of Biomedical and Behavioral Research Involving Children (1977). *Report and Recommendations: Research Involving Children.* HEW Publication (OS) 77–0004. Washington, D.C.: U.S. Government Printing Office.

Nielsen v. Regents of the University of California (1973). Civ. No. 665–049 (Super. Ct. San Francisco. Cal., filed Aug. 23.)

NIH Report of Its Review of the Baby Fae Case (1986). *IRB: A Review of Human Subjects Research 8:*1 (March/April).

Pence, G. (1990). *Classic Cases in Medical Ethics.* New York: McGraw-Hill, pp. 251–262.

Planned Parenthood of Missouri v. Danforth (1976). 428 U.S. 52.

Rodham, H. (1973). Children under the law. *Harvard Educational Review 47:*487.

Roe v. Wade (1973). 410 U.S. 113.

Strunk v. Strunk (1969). 445 S.W.2d 145 (KY).

Tinker v. Des Moines Independent Community School District (1969). 393 U.S. 503.

Wentzel v. Montgomery General Hospital (1983). 293 Md. 685, 447 A.2d 1244.

Younts v. St. Francis Hospital (1970). 205 Kan. 292, 301, 469 P.2d 330.

II

Practical Problems

5

Children's Involvement in Research Participation Decisions: Psychological Considerations

LOIS A. WEITHORN
DAVID G. SCHERER

The law has traditionally presumed that children are not capable of meaningful participation in important decisions affecting their own welfare. In the past few decades, however, the law's absolute presumption that children, as a class, are incapable of critical decision making on matters affecting their own welfare has been challenged by policymakers, jurists, scholars, and researchers. At present, legal thinking on the subject is mixed.

Children are different from adults, and these differences must be recognized in legal allocations of decision-making authority. Children are rapidly developing beings whose cognitive and emotional functioning generally has not yet reached adult levels of maturity. Their experiences are qualitatively distinct from and practically more limited than those of adults. Yet the category "children" represents a class that includes neonates and those one day shy of adulthood. For this reason it is not meaningful to talk about children's capacities in general without focusing one's discussion on narrower age spans within this broad class. A growing body of empirical research in developmental psychology indicates that many children are much more capable of participating effectively in important life decisions than the law historically supposed.

In this chapter, we consider children's capacities to take part in decisions about research participation. We examine the nature of the demands that making such decisions places upon an individual's skills and abilities. We then juxtapose those demands with what we know about children's cognitive and emotional functioning. Recognizing that the abilities of children of the same age differ, we also suggest how researchers might assess the capacities of particular children to decide about research participation under specific circumstances. In addition, we discuss how researchers, clinicians, parents, and others can support children in making important participation decisions. But before we embark upon these tasks, we pause to examine a fundamental question: Why involve children in research participation decisions?

Justifications for Children's Involvement in Research Participation Decisions

The simple answer to the question "Why involve children in research participation decisions?" is that such involvement is now mandated by federal regulation. This answer belies the more important fact that the regulations were derived from more complex legal, ethical, and psychological analyses. It is these analyses that give meaning to the regulatory language and guide interpretation of the regulations in the face of ambiguity and discretion.

In addition, the regulations as legal requirements set forth only the minimum acceptable standards for involving children who may participate in research. Within the framework of the regulations, individual IRBs and researchers can choose to provide for even greater levels of involvement, exceeding the minimum legal requirements. It is our position that, with a few exceptions, it is in the interests of children, parents, and researchers to maximize children's involvement in research participation decisions to the greatest extent of which the children are capable.

Psychological Factors

The psychological literature strongly supports the notion that involving children in decisions affecting their own welfare has positive benefits for the children. Furthermore, involving prospective child subjects in research participation decisions is likely to have positive implications for the investigation itself and for any treatment aspects of the research protocol.

First, participation in the decision-making process allows children to obtain needed practice in making important life decisions. In our society, children are often faced with critical choices posed by irresponsible adults or peers (such as whether to use illegal drugs). We should therefore relish any opportunity to give children practice with personal decision making in a supportive context (Rickett and Sheppard, 1988). Such practice can help teach children the skills of responsible decision making (Lewis, et al., 1977; Melton, 1983a; Taylor, Adelman, and Kaser-Boyd, 1985; Weithorn, 1983b).

Second, involving children in important decisions contributes to children's perceptions that they have some control over what happens to them. Psychological theory and research clearly tell us that the perception and the experience of personal control contribute to healthy psychological functioning (Abramson, Seligman, and Teasdale, 1978; Arnkoff and Mahoney, 1979; Averill, 1973; Bastien and Adelman, 1984; Deci, 1980; Frank, 1976; Kendall et al., 1979; Rodin and Langer, 1977; Schulz, 1976; Seligman, 1975; Taylor and Adelman, 1986; Taylor, Adelman, and Kaser-Boyd, 1983; Thoresen and Mahoney, 1974; Weisz and Stipek, 1982; Wilson, 1979) and that they may even promote physical health (Rodin and Langer, 1977; Schulz, 1976). The positive psychological benefits include greater feelings of competence and effectiveness, increased sense of self-esteem, reduced depression, decreased anxiety, and generally less psychopathology. Involving a child in research participation decisions carries the potential for enhancing her sense of herself as an active and responsible determiner of what happens to her in life (Melton, 1983a; Weithorn, 1983b).

Third, a sense of personal control may increase children's commitment to the research endeavor, may improve their performance in the required tasks (including promoting their compliance with treatment regimens), and may lead to an improved treatment outcome (Deci and Ryan, 1987; Devine and Fernald, 1973; Gordon, 1976; Jantzen and Love, 1977; Melton, 1983a; Taylor, Adelman, and Kaser-Boyd, 1985; Weithorn, 1985). For example, where individuals can exercise autonomy related to particular tasks, they demonstrate greater intrinsic motivation for and interest in the tasks (Deci and Ryan, 1987). Furthermore, they reveal "more creativity, more cognitive flexibility, better conceptual learning, a more positive emotional tone, and more persistent behavior change" (Deci and Ryan, 1987, p. 1028). Thus, investigators are likely to obtain greater cooperation if participants are involved in the decision to take part. The importance of such cooperation is most crucial where research protocols involve treatment procedures that require prolonged commitment by participants. In these cases, the benefits of involving children in the decision-making process may make a critical difference in the outcome of the intervention.

Where possible, it is best to make the child a partner in the decision-making process. Where involvement is not possible (such as where a child's capacities preclude such involvement), providing a prospective participant with access to information may sufficiently empower an individual with a sense of personal control (Weithorn and McCabe, 1988; Weithorn, 1983b). Information access serves as a cognitive mediator for personal control, which in turn contributes to participant cooperation, to a positive treatment outcome, and to reducing premature termination (Bastien and Adelman, 1984; Cassileth et al., 1980; Day and Reznikoff, 1980; Kellerman and Katz, 1977; Nannis et al., 1982; Vernick and Karon, 1965). Access to information appears to reduce uncertainty and increase a sense of the environment as a predictable place.

Fourth, if handled properly, decision making may increase children's senses of self-esteem because children may perceive themselves as altruistic. As children age, they experience a more positive sense of themselves as generous and giving when they volunteer themselves for the benefit of others (Froming, Allen, and Jensen, 1985; Perry, Perry, and Weiss, 1986). Obviously, the possibility of such benefits will be undercut or eliminated if the children do not experience themselves as actually choosing to participate.

Finally, involving children in decision making is a statement of respect for children's individuality, autonomy, and privacy. Treating children with dignity by recognizing their separateness as unique persons fosters a positive sense of self (Melton, 1991).

We do not intend to imply that all children should be given autonomy regarding all decisions to participate in research. Individual children's psychological capacities and ages must be considered in light of the task difficulty presented by the decision (Melton, 1983a; Taylor and Adelman, 1986; Weithorn, 1983b). Some decisions may be particularly anxiety provoking for individual children, children of particular ages, or children in particular states of physical or psychological disorder (Weithorn and McCabe, 1988). Institutional Review Boards (IRBs), researchers, clinicians, and parents must remain sensitive to the needs of particular children and the demands of particular research participation decisions. However, IRB members and investigators should be careful not to underestimate children's abilities to cope with emotionally charged information. Children tend to know and handle more than adults expect. Even where adults have refrained from discussing the possibility of death with children who have life-threatening illnesses, the children have demonstrated an awareness of their prognosis (Bluebond-Langer, 1978; Spinetta, 1974; Spinetta, Rigler, and Karon, 1974; Vernick and Karon, 1965). In these cases, the adults' lack of frankness does not serve to protect the children. Instead it tends to isolate them and to deprive them of the opportunity to share thoughts and feelings and to have inaccurate fantasies dispelled. The latter sections of this chapter propose how the children's participation may be maximized in a constructive manner.

Ethical Analyses

Although the law has not always viewed children as persons, we adopt a contemporary perspective and begin with the premise that children are persons (Hart, 1991; Melton, 1983b). Thus, the moral and ethical considerations that apply to adults deciding whether to volunteer their bodies or minds to assist a scientific endeavor also pertain to children, and are qualified only by psychological and situational factors that actually limit children's abilities to decide maturely and freely.

According to the ethical principle of autonomy, individuals have the right to self-govern (Beauchamp and Childress, 1983), and therefore to choose for themselves whether or not to take part in a study. The right of autonomy, however, presupposes that an individual is capable of competent and voluntary decision making.

If incapable individuals are given autonomous decision-making authority, they may make decisions that are not in their own best interests. In agreeing to take part in certain studies, they may subject themselves unwisely to certain risk or harm. In refusing to take part in other studies, they may deprive themselves of needed benefits. These possibilities impose upon others the obligation to intercede to protect those not fully capable from the consequences of unwise decisions. The sometimes conflicting ethical principles of autonomy and beneficence require continual balancing (Beauchamp and Childress, 1983; Faden and Beauchamp, 1986; Levine, 1981).

Children and other classes of persons with uncertain competence should be permitted the maximal level of decision-making autonomy that their capacities permit (National Commission for Protection of Human Subjects of Biomedical and Behavioral Research, 1978). One should never presume that an entire class is incompetent but should evaluate the abilities of each prospective decision maker. This ethical analysis suggests a formula that would permit those of uncertain competence a high level of autonomy while also protecting them. The federal regulations governing research with children, which we will discuss below, set forth such a formula.

Legal Doctrine

Whereas parents in our society generally are empowered to provide consent for their child for most interventions expected to be of direct benefit to that child, parental discretion is limited where the primary purpose of a child's involvement in a procedure is to benefit others, as is the case for many research protocols (Chapter 5; Glantz, Annas, and Katz, 1977). When the proposed research combines investigative and treatment goals, we must balance the complex ethical and legal consent requirements present in "pure" research (research not expected to be of direct benefit to the participants) and "pure" treatment (interventions performed "solely to enhance the well-being of the recipient") (Levine, 1981, p. 2). The more a particular study resembles traditional biomedical or behavioral practice (that is, the more it presents the prospect of direct benefit to subjects necessary to the subjects' health and well-being and the more customary and accepted the practice is), the more we should rely on ethical and legal consent analyses pertaining to treatment contexts. We therefore place greater emphasis on parental discretion, particularly where a child may be of limited competence. The more a particular protocol resembles ordinary research (that is, the less the protocol presents the prospect of necessary benefits to participants and the less accepted or tested a procedure is), the less there is an ethical or legal basis for allowing parents, or anyone, to require a child to take part.

This dichotomy becomes increasingly fuzzy, however, when well-validated and accepted treatments are offered to prospective subjects within the framework of a larger experimental design. Commonly, in studies involving randomized clinical trials, participants agree to the possibility of receiving one of several treatments. Some of those treatments may be well-validated practices, whereas the efficacy and safety of the comparison treatments may not be fully known. In these contexts, where prospective subjects could obtain the hoped-for treatment benefits in a *nonresearch* context if they so chose, ethical and legal doctrines do not support forcing children to participate in the experimental aspects of the protocol. In other words, the ethical mandate permitting adults to require their children to accept needed treatment does not extend to aspects of research protocols that are not essential to the children's well-being.

The governing federal regulations, published in 1983, deal directly with these issues. These regulations (45 *CFR* §§46.401–46.409) augmented preexisting federal regulations relating to the conduct of biomedical and behavioral research and to the authority of IRBs (45 *CFR* §§46.101–46.124). They require capable children's involvement in research participation decisions, although there are exceptions, such as in certain hybrid research-treatment contexts. A key element of the governing regulations is the requirement that researchers solicit the "assent" of those children capable of providing it. The regulations define assent as "a child's affirmative agreement to participate in research. Mere failure to object should not, absent affirmative agreement, be construed as assent"(45 *CFR* § 46.402[b]). In general, the regulations require that where children are capable of providing assent, the assent of the children and the permission of their parents or guardians must be obtained before involving the children in the research (see 45 *CFR* §§46.408[a], 46.404, and 46.405[c]).

The power to determine which children are and are not capable of providing assent lies with the IRB. The IRB is instructed to consider the "ages, maturity, and psychological state of the children involved" (45 *CFR* §46.408[a]). It is empowered to make the determination of capacity "for all children to be involved in research under a particular protocol, or for each child" (45 *CFR* §46.408[a]). And where it determines that the capacities of "some or all of the children" to be involved in the research "is so limited that they cannot reasonably be consulted," it may waive the assent requirement. (46 *CFR* §46.408[a]).

Thus the regulations construct a collateral consent requirement.[1] In theory, the formula allows the child the opportunity to exercise absolute autonomy in refusals. The parental veto also provides for protection against potentially unwise decisions by children to participate. By stacking the decks against participation in many instances, the formula reflects the values of our society where altruism remains voluntary, except in special circumstances.[2] Individuals are not forced to participate in any biomedical or behavioral intervention for the primary benefit of others. Thus, in this context, our society's respect for individual autonomy far outweighs any view that individual citizens have the obligation to give of themselves for the benefit of others. As such, we can certainly expect no more from children than we expect from adults.

The regulations allow the IRB to waive the child-assent requirement where "the research holds out the prospect of direct benefit that is important to the health or well-being of the children *and is available only in the context of the research . . .* " (45 *CFR* §46.408[a]; emphasis added). Yet this provision does not mean that parents are vested with complete discretion for all research that holds out the prospect of some direct benefit to the child participants. Rather, the IRB must determine whether the prospective direct benefit is important to the individual subject's health or well-being and whether the prospective benefit is available only in the research context. If the IRB determines otherwise, the collateral consent formula remains operative. Even if the IRB determines that the prospective benefits are important and/or available only in the research context, the IRB can still require that the prospective subjects play some role in the research participation decision. That role may or may not be one that allows for veto power.

The regulations also provide for an IRB waiver of the parental-permission requirement. The IRB can determine that such permission "is not a reasonable requirement to protect the subjects," and an appropriate consent mechanism can be substituted (45 *CFR* §46.408[c]). Many factors contribute to the determination of what type of substitute consent mechanism is suitable. These include the age, maturity, status, and condition of the prospective subjects, and the level of risk and anticipated benefit of the research protocol. Implied in this section, therefore, is the possibility that mature minors might be permitted to decide autonomously about their research participation in some instances, particularly if the protocol presents no greater than minimal risk. One can envision circumstances when a waiver of the parental permission requirement would be in a child's best interests. For example, many states allow adolescents to seek drug abuse counseling without parental consent because a parental consent requirement might deter adolescents from seeking needed treatment. In such jurisdictions, it makes sense that a researcher investigating the efficacy of drug abuse counseling should also be able to rely solely on the adolescents' agreement to participate. Similarly, where states permit adolescents to provide unilateral consent for abortion, an IRB logically should allow adolescents seeking abortions to provide unilateral consent or refusal for related nonrisky research projects.

In summary, the federal regulations governing children's participation in biomedical and behavioral research employ a flexible model that maximizes children's participation to the extent their capacities reasonably permit. This model is consistent with the most salient ethical considerations. Furthermore, it maximizes the potential positive consequences that participation may have for the subjects' physical and psychological well-being while facilitating subjects' cooperation with and commitment to the research project. The formula implicitly rejects the traditional presumption that, as a class, children are incapable of participating meaningfully in such decisions.

The Legal and Psychological Components of Effective Consent and Assent

Legally Effective Consent for Treatment or Research

In this discussion of the legal and psychological components of consent and assent, we begin with consent. We do so because the legal doctrines, corollary commentary and scholarly analyses, and pertinent behavioral science research focus on consent. Assent is a relatively new concept. Our subsequent discussion of assent flows directly from the analysis of consent.

In general, our contemporary legal system protects each adult's right to determine what will and won't be done with her body and mind (Appelbaum, Lidz, and Meisel, 1987; Meisel, 1979; President's Commission for the Study of Ethical Problems in Medicine and Biomedical and Behavioral Research, 1982 ["President's Commission"]). Thus, health care professionals and researchers generally cannot involve an adult in a biomedical or behavioral procedure without that person's express consent. The law sets up alternative consent mechanisms for those who are judged not to be capable of providing meaningful informed consent. It also permits imposition of certain treatments judged to be necessary to incompetent persons' health or welfare.

To ensure that those who consent are truly exercising autonomy, the doctrine of informed consent requires that legally valid consent be informed, competent, and voluntary (Meisel, Roth, and Lidz, 1977; President's Commission, 1982). The first requirement identifies an obligation of the provider or the researcher seeking the consent. This individual must inform prospective patients or subjects about the proposed procedures and their alternatives so they may consider this information when making a participation decision (Appelbaum, Lidz, and Meisel, 1987; Meisel, Roth, and Lidz, 1977; President's Commission, 1982). The federal regulations (45 *CFR* §46.116[a]) set forth the basic elements of information that must be disclosed in a research setting, including a description of the research procedures, possible risks or discomforts, possible benefits, description of alternative procedures for courses of treatment, and a statement that participation is voluntary.[3] These categories were included to ensure that researchers provide the information necessary to a capable individual's reasoned decision to participate.

The second requirement of the doctrine of informed consent, that of competence, refers to the capacities of individuals to make treatment decisions. More generally, competence (a term sometimes used interchangeably with capacity, intelligence, or—in reference to children—maturity) refers to having certain skills, abilities, knowledge, or experience (Weithorn, 1982, 1983a, 1984). The law is concerned with persons' capacities in a broad range of areas, including abilities to consent to treatment, assent to research, testify in court, or stand trial. Legal competency in one realm does not presume legal competency in another (Weithorn, 1982, 1983a, 1984). This is important to keep in mind. We should not assume that a child who may be incompetent to consent to treatment is also incompetent to assent to research. Before drawing conclusions about competency, we should determine the specific demands of the situation in which competency must be demonstrated. Then we should examine the individuals' ability to meet those specific demands (Grisso, 1986; Weithorn, 1982, 1984).

The law does not provide us with any single, universally accepted definition of what it means to be competent to consent to treatment or research. However, several tests appear in case law, statute, and the legal literature (Appelbaum and Roth, 1982; Roth, Meisel, and Lidz, 1977). In practice, the most commonly applied test of competency is that which requires individuals to comprehend basic factual information disclosed to them (that is, factual understanding) (Appelbaum and Roth, 1982; Weithorn, 1982). Factual understanding requires basic comprehension of the nature of the condition requiring treatment, the nature of the proposed treatment interventions or research procedures, and the interventions' or procedures' possible risks and benefits. Individuals must have the basic vocabulary skills and experience within the health care context to make sense of the information. Some of the information may be concrete and familiar (as is an injection) and may not require sophisticated intellectual abilities to be understood. Other pieces of information may be more abstract and unfamiliar (a coma, the notion of randomization) and require higher cognitive abilities for comprehension.

The standard that dominates legal theory, however, is that of appreciation of inferential understanding (Appelbaum and Roth, 1982; Weithorn, 1982).[4] This standard requires individuals to go beyond the facts and to make inferences and abstractions about the relevance of those facts for their own situations. Thus, for example, if we inform a patient that a proposed medication's side effect is drowsiness, competency according to the factual understanding test requires basic comprehension of that fact. By contrast, competency according to the inferential understanding standard requires the individual to appreciate that this side effect could hamper her ability to perform certain functions such as driving a car, or if a child, that it might interfere with attention in school (Weithorn and Campbell, 1982). Such thought is characterized by the presence of hypothetico-deductive reasoning and inferences characterized by "if . . . then," which allow one to imagine the possibilities that might follow from the occurrence of specific events or circumstances (Inhelder and Piaget, 1958).

The definition of the third requirement of informed consent, voluntariness, is even more elusive than specification of what constitutes adequate disclosure or competency. The notion of volition is a common concept in American culture and people have strong intuitive feelings about what acting voluntarily means. Yet legal scholars, health care professionals, researchers, and ethicists still struggle to arrive at a definition that can be put into operation and broadly applied. The language and intent of the Nuremberg Code and the Declaration of Helsinki, which assert that voluntary consent to research is ethically mandatory, have influenced various statutory and regulatory proposals, as well as the ethical guidelines of various professional groups (Faden and Beauchamp, 1986; Levine, 1980).

A voluntary consent requires a substantial absence of control by others. Controlling influences that could adversely affect volition come in three guises (Faden and Beauchamp, 1986). *Coercion* is the intrusion of a credible and irresistible threat from another. *Manipulations* of individuals' options, information, or psychological states are resistible but potentially controlling. *Persuasion or appeals to reason* are resistible and by definition rarely controlling. The threshold at which an influence becomes irresistible and controlling may vary from one individual or class of persons to another. For example, as we will discuss below, children may be more susceptible than are adults to the influences of others.

Because of the psychological components of the legal and ethical notions of voluntariness, behavioral scientists have attempted to shed light on what constitutes volition and to find a comprehensive definition. Social scientists argue among themselves as to whether volition in human behavior exists (Deci and Ryan, 1987; Ford, 1987; Hayes, 1987; Hershberger, 1987; Howard and Conway, 1986, 1987; Lazarick et al., 1988; Skinner, 1971; Staats, 1987). Renowned psychologists, such as William James (1890/1950), Kurt Lewin (1951), and Jean Piaget (1967) developed theories of will and voluntary action. Behaviorists, however, proposed a more deterministic view of human behavior, asserting that notions of free will are but illusions (Skinner, 1971). Contemporary psychologists are renewing investigations of voluntary behavior with the view that volition can be experimentally validated without resorting to deterministic empiricism (Deci and Ryan, 1987; Howard and Conway, 1986; Lazarick et al., 1988).

We believe that voluntariness is both an intrinsic capacity of an individual and a social act, defined and constrained by the social ecology or context in which an individual is embedded (Deci and Ryan, 1987; Grisso and Vierling, 1978; Meisel, Roth, and Lidz, 1977; Scherer and Reppucci, 1988; Scherer, 1991). Consequently, voluntariness is a condition that varies depending on the capacities and attitudes of an individual and the constraints and demands of a person's environment. We must blend intrinsic and extrinsic concepts of voluntariness to derive an integrated and comprehensive view of volition in human behavior. Behavior is most likely to be voluntary when the demands of the environment are minimized and the capacities of the individual to respond to choice are optimal. By contrast, behavior is least likely to be voluntary when the press of the environment is great and the capacities of the individual to choose are limited.

Voluntariness, in essence, is a "psychological climate" arrived at through the interaction of individuals and their environments. To act voluntarily, one must be emotionally, cognitively, and physically capable of purposefully and intentionally deliberating about a decision and articulating a choice. Furthermore, one must believe or perceive that one has a choice and this belief must be supported by the dictates of one's social context. Finally, one's environment must be void of coercive or exploitive influences.

Legally Effective Assent to Research

The 1983 regulations define assent as "a child's affirmative agreement to participate in research. Mere failure to object should not, absent affirmative agreement, be construed as assent" (45 *CFR* §46.402[b]). In the late 1970s, the National Commission introduced the term *assent* in its reports on involving children and mentally disabled persons in research. In its report on research with children, the National Commission proposed a collateral consent formula requiring parental permission plus participant assent for children aged seven and older (National Commission, 1977, Recommendation 7). This proposal was ultimately adopted by the Department of Health and Human Services (HHS) in the 1983 regulations. The commission had distinguished "consent" from "permission," asserting that whereas consent requires an autonomous decision from the prospective subject, permission refers to what one may grant on behalf of another. Likewise, assent was distinguished from consent on the basis that the former referred to a child's agreement, which was not necessarily synonymous with a legally valid consent. In determining what constitutes legally valid assent, as contrasted with consent, we examine the three components reviewed above: information disclosure, competence, and voluntariness.

The National Commission proposed that the disclosure requirements for assent be the same as those for consent (1977). Yet we stress that an important distinction between assent and consent is that researchers disclosing information to children must ensure that their disclosures are geared to the children's levels of comprehension. The way in which information is presented can contribute to or hinder understanding. Repetition, concrete examples, and response to quizzical expressions and explicit questions during disclosure can facilitate children's understanding.

HHS did not adopt the National Commission's recommendation that the assent of children age seven and older be required. Rather, it left the determination of capacity more flexible and to the discretion of the IRB. Yet, the commission's recommendation sheds light on what level of competency it intended be required when it introduced the term "assent."

The National Commission clearly meant to signal that competent assent requires significantly lower levels of decision-making skill than is typically required for legally valid consent. For example, it explained its choice of the age seven as follows: "[C]hildren who are seven years of age or older are generally capable of understanding the procedures and general purpose of research and of indicating their wishes regarding participation" (National Commission, 1977, p. 16). Thus, a competent assent is one that reveals (1) a rudimentary understanding of the procedures, that is, what subjects will be required to do, or what will be done to them, if they participate; (2) basic comprehension of the general purpose of the research; and (3) an expression of a preference to participate in the research (Weithorn, 1983a, 1984; Weithorn and McCabe, 1988). Or, to reformulate, the standard appears to require a "low level" of factual understanding and the ability to express a preference (Appelbaum and Roth, 1982; Weithorn, 1983a, 1984).

But what of competency to dissent[5]? Are the standards of competency the same? According to the National Commission, "No." The commission recommended "the objection of a child of *any age* to participation in research should be binding *except*" where the research offers the prospect of significant direct benefit necessary to the children's health or welfare that is available only in the research context (National Commission, 1977, p. 16, emphasis added). In all other cases, the comprehension elements of the assent requirement are not required for dissent; a child needs only to express the desire not to participate. Thus, the commission apparently concluded, upon balancing ethical imperatives, that competency was irrelevant to dissent; that is, even children need not justify a decision not to participate.

HHS, in its formulation of the regulations, does not distinguish between assent and dissent. If a child is capable of providing assent, then a child's choice not to participate is respected. By contrast, if the child is not capable of providing assent, whether or not that child registers a preference for or against participation, the IRB can allow the investigator to bypass the child in the consent process. Thus, a protesting child who does not meet the standard of competence to assent set forth above may be required to participate in research on the basis of parental permission. Individual IRBs may, in their discretion, choose to adopt different requirements for assent versus dissent, as did the National Commission. And certainly, individual researchers can decide to do the same.

Clearly, the nature and intensity of and reasons for a child's protest are germane to the determination of how much weight to give a veto. We may view quite differently the protests of a toddler who resists leaving a toy in the waiting room to go into the research room from the protests of a toddler who is frightened of the research apparatus and reacts violently despite attempts to reassure her. In the former case, the protest is unrelated to the study and may be viewed more as part of the child's normal reactions to everyday life. In the latter case, the child finds the participation experience aversive. In our view, irrespective of that child's capacity for comprehension, any child's implicit or explicit objection should be respected. In deciding whether to override an objection, however, it may be necessary to balance it against other factors, such as the degree to which the study provides a potential benefit necessary to the child's well-being.

This leads to the third requirement of assent and consent—voluntariness. The National Commission recommended that the same standards apply, whether assent or consent be considered. Federal regulations are silent as to this issue. The National Commission's recommendation makes sense, however, and should be applied to the parental permission requirement as well (as should the disclosure and competency to consent requirements) in order fully to protect children. We suggest a "floating" or flexible standard of voluntariness, which may vary with the type of protocol involved. Thus, the greater the potential risks associated with participation, the greater the burden on the investigator to demonstrate that participation decisions were voluntarily made. Similarly, the greater the needed benefits to subjects associated with participation, the greater the burden on those refusing participation to show that nonparticipation decisions were voluntarily made. It follows that minimal demonstrations of voluntariness are necessary where the potential consequences of participation or nonparticipation are insignificant to the well-being of the prospective participants.

Should an assent and a dissent be viewed the same way from the standpoint of voluntariness? No. Children are more likely to acquiesce than protest (Grisso and Vierling, 1978; Pence, 1980; Scherer, 1991). An assent may reflect a true desire to participate, a desire to please an adult, the absence of a perception of choice, or many other things. By contrast, children are less likely to dissent, and a dissent is more likely to reflect a true desire not to participate (Pence, 1980; Scherer, 1991). Therefore, dissents should be weighted more heavily than assents because our society's rejection of forced altruism mandates a respect for participation dissents.

The Capacities of Children to Provide Effective Consent and Assent

Federal regulations set forth quite clearly that children's roles as decision makers in research participation choices hinge, to a large extent, on their capacities for such decision making. Ironically, despite the critical importance of the notion of capacity, the regulations do not guide investigators or IRBs in how to determine who is capable and who is not. Guidance from some source appears to be necessary, however, because there exists no consensus among IRBs as to which children are and are not capable. For example, one study found that when IRBs set a minimum age at which assent would be required, that age ranged from five to fifteen years of age (Janofsky and Starfield, 1981). Compare this range with the recommendations of the National Commission, which introduced the concept of assent and set a minimum age of seven.

There are two approaches to determining the capacity of members of a group whose capacity is uncertain. One approach, which we pursue in this section, recognizes there are general trends, such as those related to cognitive and emotional development, that allow us to use age as a yardstick. Thus, given what we know about developmental trends, we can hypothesize how children of various ages would function when presented with various tasks or situations. Using an age-based model has substantial practical value. Investigators who are studying adolescents, for example, can predict generally the informed consent requirements that they must consider when planning the study. The second approach, which we pursue in the next section, recognizes that there are individual differences, even among children or adults of the same age. Thus, this approach allows for the individual assessment of competency and/or voluntariness for each prospective participant. In general, we advocate a two-pronged approach that considers population trends and individual differences when determining the competency of children to take part.

In this section, we review the current state of knowledge about children's capacities to make decisions about research participation. Our review focuses on two dimensions of psychological functioning—the capacity to make competent participation decisions and the capacity to make voluntary participation decisions.

Capacities to Provide Competent Assent and Consent

Although the regulations speak only of children's assent, we consider also children's competence to consent. We do so because there are contexts in which the IRB may need to know whether a child is capable of consenting independently to research participation.[6]

Most of the research and scholarly analysis to which we refer concerns competency to make treatment participation decisions, not research participation decisions. The similarities between consent in the treatment and research contexts are sufficiently strong to render the results of the treatment-related research highly relevant. In both cases, we are interested in the capacities of individuals to decide whether to take part in a biomedical or behavioral procedure that will be described to them, that may have certain benefits, risks, discomforts or side effects, and possibly alternatives. The cognitive and emotional processes necessary to understand and appreciate the information presented are the same, whether the procedures are part of a treatment or research endeavor.

Research and treatment do differ, however, in some ways that are applicable to a discussion of competency (Weithorn, 1983a). Research necessarily entails the prospect of aiding society through contributions to generalizable knowledge, whereas treatment or practice necessarily entails the prospect of direct benefit to the participant. Of course, research involving nonvalidated practices includes both elements. Thus, research participation decisions involve understanding of some additional concepts and also may tap children's developing concepts of altruism and empathy. Investigations involving nonvalidated practices invoke complex concepts such as those related to randomized trials, not invoked by run-of-the-mill treatment. Investigations involving nonvalidated practices also require patient-subjects to comprehend the dual roles that clinician-investigators must play.

Thus, the research we review below concerning competency to consent to treatment is apropos, but may leave some gaps in our understanding of children's capacities to make research participation decisions. Although some studies have focused directly on research consent decisions, and we will review them below, these studies are few and do not address all of these issues.

In the 1970s and 1980s, several authors conducted reviews of basic behavioral science research germane to children's decision-making capacities in research or treatment contexts (Ferguson, 1978; Gardner, Scherer, and Tester, 1989; Grisso and Vierling, 1978; Weithorn, 1982, 1983a, 1984). In general these authors concluded that the cognitive capacities required for consent to biomedical and behavioral treatment or research mature during adolescence. Some authors concluded that the cognitive capacities required for consent to biomedical and behavioral treatment or research typically mature to adult levels or near-adult levels by midadolescence (that is, ages fourteen or fifteen) (Ferguson, 1978; Grisso and Vierling, 1978; Weithorn, 1982, 1984). Others urged greater caution in reaching conclusions as to adolescents' competency, arguing that additional research is necessary before behavioral scientists offer such conclusions to policymakers (Gardner, Scherer, and Tester, 1989). However, all of these authors would agree that there is no empirical support for an across-the-board legal presumption that adolescents are incapable of competent decision-making. And those who addressed specifically children's capacities in the research context (Ferguson, 1978; Weithorn, 1983a, 1984; Weithorn and McCabe, 1988) concluded that most children in elementary school are capable of providing what is now labeled *assent* by the federal regulations.

In the past decade or so, some investigations have focused directly on children's decision making and understanding concerning treatment or research decisions (see, e.g., Weithorn and Campbell, 1982; C. C. Lewis, 1980, 1981; C. E. Lewis, M. Lewis and Ifekwunigue, 1978; Adelman et al., 1985; Kaser-Boyd, Adelman, and Taylor, 1985). In addition, other investigators, while not examining treatment or research decision making per se, have examined the development of particular decision making skills (see, e.g., Davidson and Hudson, 1988; Gardner and Herman, 1991; Klayman, 1985; Knight et al., 1987; Nakajima & Hotta, 1989; Tester, Gardner, and Wilfong, 1987). Taken as a whole, this body of developmental research leads us to several conclusions.

First, adolescents, particularly those in mid- to late-adolescence (aged fourteen and older) generally do not differ from adults in their capacities to provide consent. We qualify this conclusion with the following more specific findings. Adolescents fourteen and older do not differ significantly from adults in their understanding of health care and related decision making. And, in general, these adolescents also do not differ from adults in the decision-making processes they use in such situations. Some studies, however, have found that from mid- to late adolescence, continued maturation in decision-making skills occurs (Lewis, 1981; Nakajima and Hotta, 1989). How pertinent the subtle differences found by these latter studies are to research or treatment consent contexts is not completely clear. In general, the nature and magnitude of those differences are not sufficient to alter our conclusions. From a policy standpoint, mid- to late adolescents' competency to consent compares favorably with that of adults on the critical dimensions.

Second, most school-aged children are capable of providing assent as defined above. Empirical findings support the conclusions that these children are capable of rudimentary understanding of the basic information about research participation that regulations require researchers to disclose. These children are also capable of expressing a preference regarding participation.

Third, some studies have found that the decision-making processes employed by younger adolescents (such as those ages twelve and thirteen) are not as mature as those evidenced by older adolescents and adults. Again, the relevance of these differences is not clear. Perhaps the most important conclusion we can draw from within-adolescence differences is that, contrary to earlier views in the field, the development of adult-like thinking is not necessarily complete by age twelve (Klayman, 1985; Tester, Gardner and Wilfong, 1987). Depending upon the nature, implications, and demands of a decision, there may be instances where older and younger adolescents should be treated differently with respect to decision-making responsibility.

Children's Capacities to Consent
We use a study conducted by one of us as the springboard for elaborating on the qualitative differences found among age groups. Weithorn and Campbell (1982) examined the relative performance of subjects ages nine, fourteen, eighteen, and twenty-one according to several standards of competency to consent. The subjects, all healthy nonpatient volunteers, responded to standardized questions concerning a series of hypothetical treatment dilemmas presented to them. The inquiry procedure was developed to allow assessment of the subjects' factual understanding, inferential understanding, reasoning, actual choices, and ability to evidence a choice.

Adolescent subjects in Weithorn and Campbell's study did not differ significantly from adults in their demonstrated levels of factual and inferential understanding. In fact, adolescents seemed to understand about the same quantity and types of information as did adults, and appeared equally skilled at drawing inferences about the treatment situation. By contrast, statistically significant differences between the nine-year-old subjects and the adults were observed. That is, the nine-year-olds systematically revealed that they understood fewer of the facts explained to them or understood facts only partially, and were less able to make inferences about those facts than were the adults. The Weithorn and Campbell findings suggest that adolescents aged fourteen and older may be competent to provide legally effective consent to a range of biomedical procedures, whereas the legal competency to consent of children aged nine and younger does not meet adult standards.

Weithorn and Campbell also looked at subjects' reasoning ability. The ability to reason about the information provided in a health care or research participation situation requires one to consider the disclosed facts, together with any other variables of idiosyncratic import. One must weigh and balance this information and imagine the consequences of each possible option. The adolescents did not differ significantly from the adults according to this standard, while significant differences between the children and adults were observed.

In the reasoning assessment, Weithorn and Campbell's nine-year-olds were less able than were adults to consider multiple bits of information when making their decision. The tendencies of younger children to focus on a single dimension of a stimulus complex, or on fewer aspects of a stimulus situation than do adolescents or adults, has been observed by many researchers (Greuneich, 1982; Leon, 1980; Piaget, 1976; Tester, Gardner and Wilfong, 1987). By contrast, the adolescents, like the adults, apparently considered multiple bits of information when reaching their decisions.

In a nonlaboratory study examining adolescents' reasoning about health care dilemmas, Catherine Lewis (1980) found no significant differences between pregnant minors (aged thirteen to seventeen) and pregnant adults (aged eighteen to twenty-five) who were interviewed at pregnancy clinics. She concluded that the minors did not differ from the adults in their " 'competence' . . . to imagine the various ramifications of their pregnancy decision" (p. 449). Given the broad age span within the sample groups, as well as other limitations of the study set forth by the investigator, Lewis' study can be viewed as providing only incremental additional support to the general conclusion of the parity between adolescents and adults in their reasoning about health care dilemmas.

In a laboratory study by the same investigator, Lewis (1981) found differences among three groups of subjects ranging in age from twelve to eighteen years of age in their responses to certain personal or social dilemmas. In particular, she found differences in the degree to which they considered risks inherent in decisions, future consequences of decisions, and recognition of the possible vested interests of adults. One of the dilemmas concerned a decision about whether to have cosmetic surgery. Comparing these findings of differences with the lack of such findings in her earlier field study, Lewis (1987) suggests that field studies may reflect more accurately the competence of minors to decide, while laboratory studies may be more a reflection of social expectations than of competence. She cites Dragastin (1975) for the assertion that key differences in cognitive maturity observed between adolescents and adults in studies of adolescent cognitive development may relate more to adolescent perceptions of what they are allowed to do than to true cognitive differences.

We note that Lewis' findings concerning increased awareness from grades seven to twelve of the possible vested interests of adults, however, is extremely pertinent to our conclusions. Her dilemma concerned a scientist seeking subjects for research. The participant learned, however, that this hypothetical researcher might have deceived subjects. Lewis (1981) found that 35 percent of seventh and eighth graders, 48 percent of tenth graders, and 74 percent of twelfth graders mentioned the potential vested interests of the scientist when discussing the dilemma. This study suggests that younger and even middle adolescents may be more trusting of investigators than are older adolescents. It is also possible that the younger groups are less likely to be perceptive of the reality that clinician-researchers have dual roles and are struggling to balance the needs of their patients and the potential benefits of their research for society against their own desires for professional success and career advancement.

As noted above, some laboratory studies have found differences among adolescents, or between adolescents of particular ages and adults, with respect to particular aspects of decision making. For example, Tester, Gardner, and Wilfong (1987) found that even eleven- to thirteen-year-olds were more likely to focus on multiple dimensions of a stimulus complex when decision making than were seven- to nine-year-olds. Yet, the pre- and early adolescents also differed from adults. Tester and colleagues found that as age increased, more efficient decision-making strategies were employed. The authors state that it is not clear that their findings have implications for policy-relevant conclusions about younger adolescents, but note that their findings contradict global assertions that younger adolescents are indistinguishable from adults.

We agree that there is much we do not know about the thinking of adolescents, and that it is likely that adolescents' cognitive processes continue to mature as they age. In addition, adolescents are experiencing unique developmental phenomena that may differentiate their perceptions or choices from those of adults. For example, Weithorn and Campbell (1982) found that adolescents typically did not differ from adults with respect to the treatment options they chose. For three of four dilemmas, no significant differences between the fourteen-year-olds and adults were observed. On the fourth dilemma, which involved a medication that could affect physical appearance somewhat, some adolescents deviated from the tendency observed across-the-board in all other sample groups to choose that medication. The investigators concluded that the unique socioemotional concerns of adolescents about physical attractiveness and body image affected their decisions on this dilemma. This finding is noteworthy because it reveals how individuals who demonstrate the cognitive capacity for competent decision making may deviate from expected results when certain personal concerns cause them to weigh some considerations more heavily than others.

Despite these observations, the cognitive functioning of fourteen-year-olds clearly appears sophisticated enough and sufficiently grounded in reason to meet legal criteria of competency to consent to most types of treatment and research.

Children's Capacities to Assent
Weithorn and Campbell found that their nine-year-old subjects understood significantly less information, or understood information less fully, than did adult subjects. This observation held true for assessment with both the factual and inferential understanding tests. Yet were the levels of understanding sufficiently high to suggest that the nine-year-olds were capable of providing effective assent? Yes. Weithorn and Campbell's nine-year-old subjects, as a group, attained 69 percent of the maximum possible score on the combined understanding scales, whereas adults responded correctly to 89 percent of the items (Weithorn 1983a). An almost 70 perecent level of comprehension of disclosed information appears to satisfy the criteria of competent assent we set forth earlier in this chapter. Furthermore, Weithorn and Campbell found that the nine-year-olds' reasoning, while less mature than that of adults, was effective. Despite an inability to focus on multiple elements of each stimulus complex, the nine-year-olds still tended to select what were arguably the most important variables for consideration. In addition, the reasoning skills they employed, while not fully matured, displayed logical and practical problem-solving strategies.

Other studies have examined the reasoning skills of school-aged children. For example, Davidson and Hudson (1988) presented preschoolers, first graders, and third graders with decision-making dilemmas. They found that the older the children, the more time the children took to make their decisions. They also found that the children took more time with a decision they were told was irreversible than with one they were told was reversible. The children also tended to make more consistent decisions in the irreversibility condition, and first and third graders were found to be more consistent than were preschoolers. The study also revealed that older children used more information about the decision than did younger ones, and that both groups used more information in the irreversibility condition. Finally, the investigators concluded that the first and third graders seemed to understand that more time should be spent and more options considered as the importance of a decision increased.

Although Davidson and Hudson's study did not compare children with adolescents or adults, its findings are relevant. School children display a growing awareness of how certain aspects of decisions, such as reversibility or importance, should affect the time and attention given to that decision. The results support the anecdotal observations of many clinicians and researchers that children who might appear to make hasty, foolish, or oppositional decisions about some things (such as how to wear their hair) are capable of making thoughtful and careful decisions about those things they view as important to their health and well-being (such as treatment or research participation).

Other studies also support the conclusion that most elementary school-aged children are mature enough to assent to research. For example, Lewis, Lewis, and Ifekwunigue (1978) examined the expressed preferences of children aged six to nine who were asked to participate in a swine flu vaccine trial. All the children registered a preference (some chose participation, some rejected participation, and some chose to talk with their parents before deciding further). This, along with the nature of the children's inquiries during a question and answer session, supported the notion that these children were capable of meaningful participation in such decisions. Furthermore, the nine-year-olds in Weithorn and Campbell's study did not differ from the adults in the ultimate choices they selected on three of four dilemmas. On the fourth dilemma— which concerned a choice of in-patient treatment, out-patient treatment, or no treatment for depression—the younger children were more likely than the adults to select in-patient treatment. Their interview responses revealed that they tended to perceive in-patient treatment as "more" treatment, and therefore necessarily "better" treatment, not considering some of the nuances germane to the choice picked up by the other age groups. Again, the lack of difference on three of the four dilemmas and the nature of the one observed difference supports the conclusion that children in this age group make reasonable choices when posed with treatment or research participation decisions. Even when they don't understand all of the information provided or reason about it in as sophisticated manner as do adults, they typically reach the same decision as do adults, perhaps because they focus on important, highly critical information.

Conclusions
The literature reviews and empirical studies reviewed, as well as other studies examining children's and pre-adolescents' research participation decision making (Haber and Stephen-Brens, 1981; Korsch, 1974), support the conclusion that school-aged children are competent to provide assent. The preferences of these children should probably be given less weight than the preferences of adolescents where the research holds out the prospect of necessary benefits not available elsewhere. We emphasize, however, that younger children should not be bypassed completely or routinely in the decision-making process. We discuss below how parents and investigators might involve these children in the decision-making process short of providing them with absolute veto power.

The critical question that remains is at what point minors reach more adult-like levels of thinking, qualifying them to be viewed as competent to consent. Most mid- to late adolescents (ages fourteen and older) are probably competent to provide informed consent for research at a level commensurate with that observed in adults. Where the nature of a particular study or other factors suggest that independent consent of an adolescent would best serve that adolescent and the investigation, IRBs and investigators can assume that most older adolescents are competent to provide it. This is clearly the case for research presenting no greater than minimal risk. Although adolescents may be capable cognitively of providing independent consent for studies presenting greater than minimal risk, additional safeguards should be provided in the absence of parental involvement, particularly considering the conclusions we reach in the section below on voluntariness.

The regulations permit researchers and IRBs to waive the assent requirement where studies offer the prospect of benefits necessary to an adolescent's well-being and not available outside of research context. We suggest the IRB and investigator not routinely dismiss the assent requirement. Given adolescents' capacities to decide and the likely meaning of the decision to them (as well as to their parents), their involvement may be important to their physical and emotional welfare. Although parents can override a clearly unreasonable decision by an adolescent, outright bypass of the adolescent in the decision-making process does not appear justified.

We conclude further that younger adolescents may be somewhat less sophisticated than older adolescents and adults in certain aspects of decision making. Most of the observed differences are subtle, and it is not clear whether most are observed in or are even pertinent to the real-world decision-making dilemmas posed by research participation choices. Further research clearly is necessary. Yet, at the moment, it is probably most useful that investigators and IRBs regard early adolescence as a period of transition. Some younger adolescents may be capable of providing independent consent or of influencing a decision concerning a needed intervention available only in the research context and some may not. The difficulty, complexity, and ramifications of each decision, including the potential risk entailed, should influence decisions of IRBs and investigators in how much to rely on the choices of younger adolescents. Furthermore, in this age group possibly more than any other, individualized assessment as to minors' capacities may be needed when questions of independent consent or interventions necessary to health and well-being arise.

The demands of each research participation context necessarily render each consent situation different. Some studies place higher demands on prospective participants' decision-making skills than do others. It is easier for a child to understand that a blood specimen taken may help scientists find a cure for a certain disease than to understand that one's own doctor is conducting a randomized clinical trial and that even she does not know which of the treatments studied is more effective or safe. We note also that when prospective subjects are ill, anxious, confused, tired, or experiencing other symptoms related to the condition that brings them to the research context, their competency may be impaired. Similarly, prospective subjects who are patients may have greater motivation and concern about their research participation decision than may prospective subjects of research not involving the prospect of direct benefit. In general, we must keep in mind that adults serve as our standard of competency to consent. If many adults don't understand randomization, for example, we should not expect adolescents to exhibit a greater understanding.

Capacities to Provide Voluntary Assent and Consent

In this section, we consider the constitutional attributes that individuals contribute to their potential to act voluntarily (*person* factors) and the constraints that stem from the environment (*situation* factors). *Person* factors reflect tendencies or modes of functioning that individuals bring with them to situations. Of course, particular situations inhibit, strengthen, or modify these tendencies, and in our discussion of situation factors, we examine some of the ways in which contexts may affect behavior. Environmental factors may have played an important, or even dominant, role in the initial development or the maintenance of the tendencies. But at the moment when consent or assent is sought, it is the *person* who brings these tendencies into the situation.

In our analysis of *person* variables, we focus primarily on the role that developmental factors play in determining children's capacities to make voluntary research participation decisions. We do so because what distinguishes the decision-making capacities of normal children from those of normal adults is children's not-yet-fully-matured cognitive and socioemotional functioning. We recognize that many other *person* factors, (e.g., intellectual level, emotional disorders) affect capacity. However, those factors typically do not distinguish children from adults and are the type that may be assessed individually by methods discussed in the following section of this chapter.

In our discussion of *situation* variables, we focus on variables external to the prospective research participant. Theorists from a variety of perspectives have contended that to understand and anticipate human behavior, we must consider the ecological context in which the individual is embedded (Bandura, 1978; Bateson, 1972, 1979; Bronfenbrenner, 1977, 1979; Garbarino, 1982; Jackson, 1967; Jaeger and Rosnow, 1988; Keeney, 1979; Magnusson, 1981; Veroff, 1983). These social ecologists, interactionists, and systems theorists assert that individuals' functioning is influenced by cultural heritages, institutional interfaces, and personal relationships. In an informed consent situation, there are a myriad of environmental factors that affect the degree of volition that an individual may exercise. Some of the more prominent factors include the nature of the request for participation, the authority of the consent seeker and her relationship to the prospective participant, social and familial support (or lack thereof), rewards or incentives to participate, and constraints imposed by institutional affiliation (as for prisoners, students, members of the military, or hospital patients).

There is little empirical research directly examining the capacities of children and adolescents to provide voluntary consent or assent. Thus, many of our analyses below examine related psychological constructs from which we draw inferences about the developmental progression of the capacity to consent or assent voluntarily.

Person Factors

While explanations emphasizing the intrapsychic development of volition and the expression of autonomy vary from one theoretical perspective to the next, in general, these formulations suggest that older children and young adolescents begin to demonstrate rudimentary capacities for self-determination. Children begin to individuate from their parents and families and develop increasingly stronger self-awareness and social insight. Furthermore, older children and young adolescents are more apt than younger children to infer that they can exercise control over their immediate environments. On the other hand, some theorists note that some adolescents remain keenly susceptible to social influence, particularly that of peers. Young adolescents typically exhibit the highest levels of conformity. Moreover, even older adolescents and adults continue to defer to the controlling influences of other people they feel to be more powerful or authoritative than themselves.

Older adolescents, however, rely less on external cues and more on self-reflection and social comparison when choosing a course of action. Consequently, they tend to be more realistic about their capacities to manipulate their social environment and the limitations of volition than their younger counterparts. Still, situational factors such as illness or social-economic status may modify what one might ordinarily expect from an individual. In sum, older adolescents are more likely than are younger minors to have the personal characteristics necessary to exercise self-determination given the proper conditions. Children and younger adolescents, prior to age fourteen, are more susceptible to compromising social influence and may require continued supervision in their research participation decisions. Below, we review in more detail the specific theoretical analyses and empirical investigations that bear on children's and adolescents' capacities to make voluntary decisions.

Psychodynamic formulations. Psychoanalytic theorists posit that children acquire distance from their parents as the children enter adolescence, and true autonomy begins to emerge during this period. The more traditional analytic view is that adolescents detach from their parents (Freud, 1958), which results in conflict between adolescents and their caregivers. Analysts assert that adolescents are vulnerable to "seduction by autonomy needs" (Douvan, 1974) and that their actions are predictably oppositional. Despite the common lay acceptance of this view, there is no empirical support for it.

More contemporary psychoanalytic perspectives suggest that genuine autonomy evolves through a process of individuation and may not develop until late adolescence together with an integral sense of self (Blos, 1979; Steinberg and Silverberg, 1986). Empirical research has revealed that as adolescents age, they espouse a greater sense of emotional autonomy from parents, experiencing less dependence, more separation and differentiation, and less idealization of parents (Steinberg and Silverberg, 1986). Moreover, adolescents report that they feel an increased subjective sense of self-reliance. However, young adolescents appear to trade their dependence on parents for a reliance on peers (Steinberg and Silverberg, 1986). Thus, young adolescents may merely shift from parental to peer influences and may fail to develop genuine autonomy in the sense of attaining freedom from salient social influence.

Self-understanding. The capacity for performing intentional, goal-directed, volitional behavior may parallel the development of self-understanding (comprehension of subjective interpretations of one's self) and may emerge gradually as children age (Bullock and Lutkenhaus, 1988; Damon and Hart, 1982; Deci and Ryan, 1987). As children enter later childhood and early adolescence they evolve a more psychological and social awareness of who they are. They also acquire abilities to manipulate their behavior and emotions, and engage in social comparison. By later adolescence, youth develop a deeper psychological comprehension of their thoughts, feelings, and actions that enables them to be more effective at monitoring and manipulating their inner states and behavior. Older adolescents also become increasingly reliant on self-reflection and self-evaluation and develop a belief in and respect for the powers and limitations of volition.

A corollary to the issue of self-understanding that pertains directly to the research participation context involves the development of altruism (Batson et al., 1987; Froming, Allen, and Jensen, 1985). Altruism is a self-directed incentive and requires sufficient self-awareness to allow social feelings to predominate over egocentrism (Kamps et al., 1987). Altruistic behavior evolves in stages as children age (Bar-Tal, Sharabany, and Raviv, 1982; Cialdini, Baumann, and Kenrick, 1981; Froming, Allen, and Jensen, 1985). The altruistic acts of young children are performed most often without an awareness of the social value of their conduct. By age six or seven children begin to appreciate that altruistic behavior is valued by others and they will respond altruistically to gain social rewards (Cialdini, Baumann, and Kenrick, 1981; Froming, Allen and Jensen, 1985; Kamps et al., 1987; Perry, Perry, and Weiss, 1986). Not until adolescence do children behave altruistically because they have learned of its self-rewarding value (Batson et al., 1987; Cialdini, Baumann, and Kenrick, 1981; Kamps et al., 1987; Perry, Perry and Weiss, 1986). Altruism can be inhibited or moderated by a variety of situational factors. Parental attitudes toward altruism (Peterson, Reaven, and Homer, 1984) or the presence of extrinsic rewards or pressure (Batson et al., 1987; Kim and Stevens, 1987) can undermine altruistic motivation.

Perceived control. Locus of control theory, like several other theories of perceived control, considers how and when people develop their beliefs about sources of causation and control for important personal life events (Connell, 1985; Skinner, Chapman, and Baltes, 1988a). According to locus of control theory, an individual attributes the reinforcements that derive from situations either to external influences (such as fate, chance, or luck) or to internal influences (such as those deriving from cognitive abilities and personal talents) (Rotter, 1966). Individuals prone to an external locus of control are likely to be passively accepting, deferential, and acquiescent; they tend to rely more on external cues to guide their behavior. They may be less capable of performing self-determined or voluntary behavior. Individuals with an internal locus of control are apt to perceive themselves as the agents for change in their lives and are more likely to act voluntarily.

Recent research suggests that developmental differences in locus of control are nonlinear. Internal and external attributions develop at different rates, and developmental characteristics of internal and external attributions vary across the cognitive, social, and physical domains (Connell, 1985; Skinner and Chapman, 1987; Skinner, Chapman, and Baltes, 1988b; Weisz and Stipek, 1982). In other words, a child might feel confident about her personal control over her athletic ability, but not her scholastic ability. Another child the same age might feel in control in social situations but not in sports.

Moreover, as children age, they explain events in their lives by attributing causation to different kinds of internal and external factors such as personal effort, individual qualities, the role of powerful others, luck, and unknown factors (Connell, 1985; Skinner and Chapman, 1987; Skinner, Chapman, and Baltes, 1988a). The inclination to attribute events to luck and unknown factors declines in later childhood and the early adolescent years (enhancing the potential for volition), while a belief in the role of powerful others' control does not appear to change over these ages (Krampen, 1989; Skinner and Chapman, 1987).

We do not know what types of changes in beliefs about personal control occur during the adolescent and young adult years. Nor do we have empirical evidence concerning how various changes in these beliefs alter their capacity for exercising volition in a consent situation. Research findings on obedience (Milgram, 1974) suggest that authority figures wield considerable influence over adults. Milgram's research implies that older adolescents and young adults may continue to use powerful others attributions. Furthermore, the authority figure in Milgram's famous study was a researcher. His findings suggest that adults may be quite deferential when confronted with the requests, instructions, or demands of a researcher. It is reasonable to assume that the clinician-researcher, whom people expect to have the patient-subject's best interests at heart, would have even greater power over individuals than do other researchers.

Social psychological constructs.   The constructs of conformity, compliance, and reactance may be particularly important to our understanding of the capacities of minors to consent voluntarily (Grisso and Vierling, 1978; Melton, 1983a; Scherer and Reppucci, 1988; Scherer, 1991). If minors respond systematically to social influence with conformity, compliance, or reactance more so than adults, it may indicate that minors have a lesser capacity for volition.

Conformity.   This factor connotes an actor's intention to seek uniformity with a social norm or influence. Conforming behavior peaks in early adolescence (between the ages of twelve and fifteen) and then declines as adolescents mature (Berndt, 1979; Steinberg and Silverberg, 1986). An act of *compliance* is a way of obeying a social norm or expectation. Research on compliance has found a strong tendency for both children and adults to acquiesce to authority even if they do not accept the social norm emotionally or attitudinally (Brehm, 1977; Milgram, 1974). According to *reactance* theory, individuals may respond to the actual or threatened loss of a perceived freedom by opposing the perceived source of the loss. Children as young as two have been observed to respond to parental or other adult control with such oppositional behavior. In general, however, children are most apt to respond to adult influence with compliance (Brehm and Brehm, 1981). In most consent situations, minors may not have the legal right or the requisite perception of psychological freedom to induce reactance. There is speculation (although no empirical support) that increases in autonomy during adolescence may heighten a sensitivity to potential threats to freedom. If so, adolescents might respond by revealing nonconformity of behavior and attitude.

Person factors that interact with situational factors.   Individuals' attributional styles (such as whether they view themselves as active agents controlling their environment or passive recipients of environmental influences) are apt to change depending on the situations in which they find themselves. For example, Connell (1985) suggests that attributions of control to unknown factors may be more prevalent among children with various types of somatic illness. Somatic illness may alter the quality of perceived control and, hence, ability to act voluntarily. Grodin and Alpert (1983) also note that children and adolescents may be particularly vulnerable to external influences in medical consent situations because of their very real physical, emotional, and financial dependency upon adults. Magnifying their vulnerability is children's lack of familiarity, experience, and practice with making health care and research participation decisions. Given these factors, minors may be apt to revert to dependency on significant others rather than to act with self-determination.

An individual's background may lead to the development of certain characteristics that affect volition. An ethnic or cultural heritage, or a family ethic, may support the expression of volition and autonomy among children, whereas other cultures and families may place a higher value on community standards than individual freedoms and may regard a child's assertion of independence as inappropriate. Socioeconomic status may also be relevant: Melton (1980) found that children from less privileged socioeconomic groups develop an awareness of their civil liberties later in life than do other children.

Conclusions. Most relevant theory and research suggests that children develop the capacity for autonomous decision making during adolescence. True individuation accompanies the development of an integrated sense of self in mid- to late-adolescence. Not until this point are minors more self-reliant than are younger adolescents and less responsive to the pressures of social factors. There is little research to support the notion that adolescents are systematically oppositional. Children and adolescents may resist efforts to control their everyday behavior (such as cleaning their rooms), but on life's larger issues, they typically espouse values similar to those of their parents and families and respect the influence of and defer to valid authority figures (Hill and Holmbeck, 1986; Larson, 1972; Lewis, 1981). Researchers seeking to involve children and younger adolescents in their studies need to be attentive to the effects of social persuasion. Incentives such as stipends, appeals involving peer pressure, or citing social desirability are apt to constrain the voluntariness for these individuals.

Theories of social cognition and social behavior identify a variety of conditions that mitigate the expression and development of voluntary decision making. As children become adolescents they develop stronger internal loci of control and a reduced propensity to conform to social norms. These changes enable them to act with greater autonomy. However, a belief in powerful others persists throughout adolescence, and deference to authority seems to be strong, even in adults. Moreover, other factors also may influence adolescents' capacity to act voluntarily, such as: lack of familiarity with the research context, the nature and gravity of the participation decision, and adolescents' ethnic or socioeconomic backgrounds. Correspondingly, researchers must use caution in their expressions of authority and attend to the social ecology of the consent decision.

Situation Factors

Situation factors constitute strong influences capable of compromising the voluntariness of participation decisions. Specific social roles or particular institutional identities ascribed to individuals may prescribe or proscribe those individuals' behavior. Children are typically relegated to subservient roles in our society, in families, and in most institutional settings (such as hospitals, schools, juvenile correction facilities) and may have much less potential for exercising volition in decision making. Because it is in these contexts that most research is conducted, social scientists have become increasingly concerned about the effects of social institutions on the decision-making capacities of individuals (Faden and Beauchamp, 1986; Grisso, in press; Koocher and Keith-Speigel, 1990). There is a danger that children of all ages will fail to perceive a freedom to decide about research participation because they have been socialized to comply with the requests and demands of adults.

Families are the chief socializing agent in a child's life. Parental influence over their offspring's decisions extends well into adulthood. Individuals of all ages tend to mirror their parents' values (Hill and Holmbeck, 1986; Rutter et al., 1976). Studies testing the quantity and quality of family influence over the decision making of children indicate that multiple variables must be considered to fully understand the impact of parental influence on children and adolescents (deTurck and Miller, 1983; Larson, 1972; Rollins and Thomas, 1975; Smith, 1983; White, Pearson, and Flint, 1989). However, few studies compare the differential effects of parental influence on children, adolescents, and adults. A recent study of medical consent (Scherer and Reppucci, 1988; Scherer, 1991) found differences between the capacities of children and adolescents to make and maintain an autonomous medical decision in the face of potentially coercive parental influence. The research also indicated that adolescents may exercise less voluntariness than do young adults.

The actions and attitudes of researchers may exert irresistible influences on child participants. Many factors, such as the phrasing of requests for participation or the use of rewards or inducements, may constrain a child's expression of self-determination. In this section, we elaborate upon various situational factors and how they support or mitigate children's and adolescents' abilities to act voluntarily in the research consent context.

Role constraints. The potential for controlling manipulation and coercion is present in specific social or institutional contexts. When one is part of an institution (such as hospital, school, correctional facility, group home, the military), one assumes an identity that corresponds to her role in the institution (such as patient, student, prisoner). These identities and the constraints imposed by these contexts may hinder the possibilities for obtaining voluntary consent (Faden and Beauchamp, 1986). Individuals locked into a subservient role are apt to experience a relative powerlessness vis-a-vis authority and may respond with characteristic passivity. Grisso (in press) refers to this subordination of individuals by an institution as a *normative power residual.* This is a mind-set or expectation formed by members of an institution for what will occur in their interactions with the officials of the institution.

Research on this issue is scant and there is even less information about the reactions of minors to institutional power. Grisso (in press) notes that with adults, normative power residual is pervasive and difficult to undermine. Presumably, children and adolescents also will be significantly influenced by the institutional milieus in which they are socialized. The institutions may exert even greater control over children's and adolescents' decisions because of the greater dependency minors experience. Role constraints also may pose an additional dilemma for research involving children because most research involving minors is conducted under the auspices, or with the approval, of an institution (often schools or hospitals).

Family factors. Family influence, specifically parental influence, has the potential to interfere seriously with children's ability to act voluntarily in research participation decisions. Family systems theorists assert that the degree of autonomy experienced by an individual develops in response to family relationships and the social context (Grotevant and Cooper, 1986). Family systems theorists believe that parent–child relationships are transformed over the course of adolescence, moving from unilateral parental authority to a sense of greater mutuality of parent-child influence (Bell and Bell, 1983; Grotevant and Cooper, 1986; Hill and Holmbeck, 1986; White, Speisman, and Costos, 1983; Youniss, 1983). Research suggests that adolescents who perceive themselves as being able to act with the greatest autonomy feel a positive closeness to their parents and view them as role models and consultants (Kandel and Lesser, 1969). In addition, parents continue to exert influence even over their adult children.

The quality of parental nurturance and adolescents' perceptions of parental power determine adolescents' responses to parental authority (deTurck and Miller, 1983; Rollins and Thomas, 1975). Parental persuasion attempts are more likely to attain an adolescent's emotional acceptance of a parent's petition. Parental commands that are imperative and unqualified and commands qualified by reason or concern are the most likely to achieve compliance with parental demands (Smith, 1983). On the other hand, inducing fear or employing coercion reduces an adolescent's perception of parental power and potential for influence, and ultimately may reduce compliance (deTurck and Miller, 1983).

These findings enable us to make inferences about the role of parental influence on children's ability to act voluntarily in situations involving decisions about participation in research. The nature of children's responses to parental attempts at influence may depend on the nature of the parent–child relationship and how the parents interact with the children around the decision. For many research and treatment decisions, children and parents will concur. They may concur because children have internalized their parents' values and preferences. Or, children and parents may concur on health care decisions because the children respect their parents. Parents who are actively involved in nurturing and structuring their children's lives are more likely to find their children positively influenced by the parents' own points of view. We view concurrence based on these factors as predominantly voluntary. By contrast, children of distant and peripheral parents may comply with parental choices, but often because of a sense of pressure to comply. Children of these parents may dissent if they view the parent as capricious, self-centered, or demanding. Finally, parents who are forceful, controlling, or coercive in their demands may gain their children's compliance, but at the expense of the child's volition.

Scherer (Scherer and Reppucci, 1988; Scherer, 1991) studied the effects of parental influence on treatment decision making regarding hypothetical medical dilemmas. Children (ages nine and ten), adolescents (ages fourteen and fifteen), and young adults (ages twenty-one to twenty-five) responded in similar manners to increasingly coercive parental influence for two types of fairly routine medical treatment. In each case, even young adults were deferential to parental persuasion and dictates. However, the investigators found differences among age groups responses to a hypothetical medical dilemma involving an organ donation that was designed to require an emotionally and morally complex deliberation. The investigators concluded that responses to parental influence in treatment decision making will vary depending upon the nature and gravity of the decision, the type of influence attempt by the parents, and the age of the minor. Developmental differences appear as the decisions become more serious and complex. Young adults exercised more self-determination than did adolescents who, in turn, were more likely than were children to perceive choice in the face of parental influence.

Consent-seeker factors. Researchers must guard against attempting, consciously or unknowingly, to influence the decisions of prospective participants because several types of consent-seeker power may interfere with a person's ability to decide voluntarily about research participation (Rodin and Janis,

1979; Smith, 1970). This power may turn consent or assent into an act of submission, rather than a self-determined choice. Consent may be obtained using coercive power (having the potential to punish), legitimate power (where control is granted to the influence agent out of obligation or a social norm), expert power, or the power to control the dispensing of rewards, any of which may alter volition in a consent situation. Perhaps the least intrusive social power is referent power, which is authority derived from the influencer's benevolence and admirability. Yet even this type of power may negatively affect the ability to decide voluntarily, since the decision may result from a desire to please a respected authority rather than from a desire to participate in the investigation. Children may be more easily controlled by each of these forms of power than are adults, but clearly adults, too, are quite vulnerable.

The ways in which consent seekers phrase participation requests may compromise volition. People appear to perceive interrogative, declarative, specific, and nonspecific requests as permitting different degrees of voluntariness. Specific requests stated in an interrogative form are most likely to leave people perceiving that they are free to choose (Kagehiro, 1988). Yet, we do not know how these different forms of request in treatment and research contexts affect children versus adults.

The use of rewards for participating in research may constitute a coercive or manipulative influence compromising the voluntariness of an individual's choice. Research indicates that the more equal the alternatives in a decision, the more freedom an individual perceives (Steiner, 1970). Offering rewards to children may tip the balance unfairly in favor of participation. Minors may find even modest rewards so compelling that they feel incapable of refusing the request for research participation. Compliance may also be induced through the "foot-in-the-door" technique (Saks, 1983). By gaining consent for small and simple procedures and gradually increasing complexity and frequency of consent, the desired consent can often be attained.

Conclusions

Obtaining voluntary research participation decisions from minors requires researchers and IRBs to consider both situational and person factors. Children and young adolescents typically exercise less autonomy and less resistance to social influence than do adults (Grisso and Vierling, 1978). They are apt to be more vulnerable to the manipulative and controlling potential of rewards and inducements and are less likely to view themselves as being in control of their destiny. Therefore, they are unlikely to be capable of giving voluntary consent.

Older adolescents, by contrast, are more able to regard a request for research participation in a manner similar to that of adults. The degree of volition they exercise will vary depending on the nature of the decision and the context in which it takes place. Researchers must exercise caution, however. Adolescents may defer to researcher's authority and to institutional conventions. In addition, these prospective subjects remain vulnerable to induced consent as a consequence of family expectations or researcher manipulation.

The collateral consent procedure required by the federal regulations provides some safeguards against many situational factors that could impinge upon adolescents' exercise of voluntary behavior. On the other hand, the use of collateral consent does not rule out the potential for coercive or excessive parental or family pressure to volunteer. Researchers and IRBs must be sensitive to this possibility and, where feasible, provide opportunities for child research participants to express their dissent while not incurring parental disapproval. We make suggestions concerning this issue in the next section of this chapter.

We recommend that the same standards of voluntariness discussed above relative to older adolescents apply when seeking assent from children and younger adolescents. The reduced capacities of children and younger adolescents for self-determination does not preclude them from assenting to research. However, the researcher seeking assent from a child must be aware of potentially controlling social influences. In most cases, the collateral consent requirement will protect children from participating in research when such a decision is unwise. If there is any question about parents' or guardians' abilities to serve in this role, researchers should provide additional protections for children. Yet even when parents acquiesce to their children's participation, children's dissents should be respected. The weight of a dissent is magnified by findings that children, even adolescents, do not routinely or lightly dissent to the requests of adults, including their parents, on important questions.

Discussion: Assessment and Promotion of Competency and Voluntariness

The preceding section provided an overview of patterns of developmental differences in the capabilities of children, adolescents, and adults to provide competent and voluntary consent and assent for research participation. We must remember, however, that individuals differ from one another. Although the recommendations above are guidelines, researchers must be flexible enough to identify and address those situations when individuals' capacities deviate from the norm. The need to be sure that child participants and their parents are making competent and voluntary decisions becomes greater with the increase in potential benefits or risks of participation. Investigators should, of course, attempt to enhance the decision-makers' abilities and opportunities to make competent and voluntary decisions. We provide some suggestions for how this may be done below.

It is equally important that researchers and IRBs assess the consent-seeking situation. Ideally, the situation should enhance a person's capacities to provide competent and voluntary consent. Yet as we noted above, situations may hinder or preclude demonstrations of competence or voluntariness. Where pertinent situational variables are under the control of the investigator, they should be modified to maximize competence and voluntariness. Where these variables are not under the control of the investigator, special protections should be instituted to ensure that prospective participants are not inappropriately included or excluded from studies.

Assessment and Promotion of Competent Decision Making

Assessment and promotion of competency are closely linked. For prospective participants of all ages—not just children—researchers can enhance individuals' capacities for understanding and reasoning by taking the time to provide thoughtful, careful, and comprehensible explanations of the information relevant to decision making. The way in which information is disclosed should be consistent with prospective subjects' ages, experience with similar procedures or interventions, and intellectual levels. When dealing with children or those with less-developed intellectual skills, researchers should define unfamiliar terms, make the abstract more concrete, and use repetition as much as possible.

The provision of information should be regarded as a process. This is increasingly important as research participation entails greater risks and prospective benefits to the participants. For example, if a study is a randomized clinical trial investigating the safety and efficacy of drugs for childhood leukemia, information provision should be individualized and part of a discussion process between a member of the research team and prospective decision makers. Written consent forms, although necessary, should be viewed as supplemental in this process, not as the primary mode of transmitting information.

In these discussion sessions, assessment and promotion of competency go hand in hand. Thus, as information about one concept is provided, such as the chances an experimental drug will have a possible side effect, the information provider should inquire as to the prospective subjects' comprehension. In complex situations such as this one, the research team member should not proceed to the discussion of new information until she has satisfactorily assessed comprehension of information just provided. Researchers and IRBs should remember that competency can and should be enhanced. It is irrelevant to the ultimate determination of competency how a prospective subject understood the relevant concepts before information provision. What is relevant is how the individual understands the information at the time she makes the participation decision. For this reason also, recall of information at a later date is also not a good measure of competency.

Depending on the standard of competency applied in the particular context, one may be satisfied with higher or lower demonstrations of competency. For example, if we expect a child to be capable of providing assent only, a researcher may consider that child competent if the child reveals a rudimentary understanding of the factual information provided and expresses clear preference for or against participation. By contrast, if one is assessing the parents' capacity to decide, or an older adolescents' capacity to provide independent consent, higher standards, such as demonstration of fuller comprehension of factual information and appreciation, are necessary. As noted, assessment of factual understanding involves asking questions whose answers reveal comprehension of the basic information provided. Assessment of appreciation involves asking questions that require individuals to make inferences about the factual information and to apply that information to their personal situations.

Assessment and promotion of competency also involve sensitivity to those factors that may hinder demonstrations of competency. If a child (or adult) is tired, in pain, anxious, depressed, hungry, distracted, or on medications that affect cognitive functioning, competency may be impaired. Obviously when a child is ill, and that illness is the reason for seeking consent for that child's participation in research, there are limits to what a researcher can do to maximize competency. However, where possible, the child should be educated about prospective participation. This should occur at that child's best time of the day (from a physical comfort standpoint), at a time that neither follows nor precedes some stressful procedure or intervention, and when the child agrees to discuss participation. The discussion should occur in a quiet location, away from distractions and interruptions, and where the child can be as physically comfortable as possible. Most younger children and some adolescents will prefer their parents to be present, and the presence of the parents will assist comprehension. Yet in some cases, parental presence will hinder the process. Researchers must be sensitive to these factors as well.

Assessment and Promotion of Voluntary Decision Making

Researchers are ethically bound to support the autonomy of their research participants. Researchers should be conservative in their estimates of a subject's volition for a range of reasons. There is a substantial difference in power between researchers and their subjects; researchers are capable of engineering consent decisions, and researchers may misunderstand their subjects' needs and preferences. When the subject is a minor, even more caution must be exercised.

Assessing a child's capacity for volition should begin with an evaluation of the child's maturity. Estimating a child's experience with the exercise of volition will assist a responsible researcher in determining a minor's current capacity for autonomous consent. Children who have had practice with research consent protocols might be more likely than naive subjects to understand their rights to dissent or volunteer. We qualify the preceding statement, however, in that children whose prior research experiences failed to respect their opportunities for choice will only reinforce their beliefs that they do not have a choice. Ideally, as part of the discussion and inquiry described in the preceding section on assessment and promotion of competency, investigators should query children about their expectations. Indirect questions might be most productive here. Although one may inquire "Whose choice is it to decide whether you take part?", one should also inquire about the child's perceptions of "What do you think your mother will do if you decide not to participate?", "What do you think your doctor will do?", or "What do you think will happen to your treatment here at the hospital?" Regardless of what they are told, children may fear that adults will be displeased with them, or that if they refuse research participation in an institutional setting, there will be other negative consequences. A child with cancer may fear the hospital staff will no longer treat her. A child in school may fear the teachers will be angry. A child in a correctional setting may fear reprisals from staff or loss of privileges. Often, indirect questions may be the only way of obtaining information about such beliefs and will allow researchers the opportunity to try to correct misapprehensions. As noted, assessment and promotion of voluntariness (and competency) are related. As researchers evaluate voluntariness, they should use the interchange with the subjects to help promote voluntariness.

In addition, researchers should be sensitive to the effect prospective subjects' cultural, ethnic, and economic backgrounds might have on capacities to decide voluntarily. Children from minority cultures or from lower socioeconomic backgrounds may be even more fearful than children from majority or middle class backgrounds to dissent, for fear of losing needed treatment, privileges, or of becoming victims of reprisal. Where necessary, researchers should reassure children about such concerns.

One must also attend to situational factors that may compromise voluntariness. Researchers must be alert to the influence of families and parents on decisions made by minors. Depending upon researchers' hunches about and observations of parent-child interactions, one may choose to conduct the interview session in the presence of absence of the parent. The parent who encourages a child's choice will assist that child in overcoming pressures inherent in institutional settings and relationships with caregiver-researchers. The parent who discourages a child's choice and tries to promote or demand compliance is likely to reduce the child's ability to decide voluntarily. In the latter case, participation of the parent in the interview may interfere in the examiners' effort to obtain a clearer picture of the child's preference. By contrast, it will provide a very clear picture of the pressures the child may be coping with from the parent-child relationship when trying to decide.

When dealing with minors for whom parental permission for participation is required, it is prudent to seek parental consent before seeking a child's assent. Since parental veto power is absolute, this procedure respects parental authority and protects the children from going through a process that may lead to disappointment or a sense of powerlessness (if, for example, they choose participation and their parents veto participation). Researchers, however, must be sensitive to children's perceptions that parental approval has made participation mandatory. Wherever possible, requests for participation to children should be introduced by the sentence "Your parents have indicated that it is okay with them if you take part if it is also okay with you." Researchers should of course obtain parental approval for such statements.

Research with children requires the researcher to be especially sensitive to the effects of role constraints and the institutional milieu. Children in many institutions (such as schools, hospitals, group homes, corrections facilities) may not assert their rights to dissent because of the powerful norms that exist in these settings. Grisso (in press) suggests that researchers in these settings make a formal assessment of the institutional milieu. In this way they can more accurately evaluate how power is wielded in the setting and how members characteristically respond. With this information a researcher will be better able to estimate the impact of her request for research participation and make necessary adjustments.

Researchers should pay careful attention to how they word requests for participation, and to how the child responds to these requests (Koocher and Keith-Spiegel, 1990). Subjects are more likely to make a voluntary decision when investigators articulate subjects' alternatives, including the subjects' rights to dissent. Researchers should avoid mixed messages, such as where they verbally state that a minor is free to choose but contradict that assertion in voice tones or nonverbal communications. Asking a minor to consent ("Would you like to take part?") is more respectful than asserting or declaring that a minor wants to consent ("I think you will want to take part"). Using social persuasion ("Many of your friends and classmates have done it") may hinder a minor's capacity to respond voluntarily.

Even more importantly, conducting research with children requires the researcher to be particularly sensitive and responsive to both a child's active dissent and potential passive resistance. Children may want to stop their involvement in a research project although they are not directly stating a wish to discontinue. When a child is distracted, fidgeting, or complaining about the length of the procedure, she may be indicating that she is no longer a willing participant in the research (Koocher and Keith-Spiegel, 1990).

Researchers must also consider how they wield authority. The use of coercion, expertise, or institutionally sanctioned power will inhibit the capacities of children to consent voluntarily. Investigators must minimize role confusion that arises when they serve as both clinicians and researchers. Dual roles may not only confuse patient-subjects but may create conflicts of interest; professionals need to be sensitive to that. Subject-patients may have difficulty understanding that their physicians' requests for participation are not necessarily recommendations made solely because participation is in the patients' best interests. Individuals may base their research consent on their expectations and faith that their clinician would only recommend the single best treatment for them, while not understanding the particulars of the research protocol.

The problem of disentangling the provider-clinician's dual roles poses particularly great difficulties for children. In some situations, it may be helpful if consent for research from children is obtained by someone other than the direct care provider. On the other hand, the primary provider may be the person with whom the child has the best and most open communication. In these situations, it may also be advisable to provide minors with a consultant or advocate aside from people involved with the study. This can enhance the likelihood that children's agreement is not based on a misunderstanding that the request for participation is purely in their best interests. Children should also be reassured that dissents will not lead to the provider's refusal to continue to treat them, or to their disapproval.

Rewards or payments for participation should be used sparingly. Where the potential benefits or risks of participation are great, researchers should resist the temptation to use rewards and incentives. These motivators tend to thwart the possibilities of a truly voluntary decision. Rewards and incentives are probably most appropriate in research with the prospect of less than minimal risk, which also does not hold out the possibility of needed benefits to the subjects. Thus, in nonrisky "pure" research, when one is asking subjects primarily for their time and where there are no institutional constraints that impinge directly on voluntariness, some minimal and age-appropriate compensation is acceptable (such as a small box of crayons for children and/or financial compensation to adults that might be viewed as hourly payment for time spent in the laboratory instead of the workplace). Of course, when providing such compensation to children, parental approval should be sought in advance.

Lastly, researchers can promote volition by empowering children and adolescents from the very beginning of their contact. For example, the investigator can give a child the choice of chairs to sit in or pencils to use. If researchers provide minors with even small choices throughout the consent and research protocol, the children will more readily infer or perceive their freedom to act with volition. By carefully adopting behaviors that establish an atmosphere of choice, investigators can do their best to maximize the possibility that children will respond to requests for participation in as competent and voluntary a manner as possible.

Notes

1. The formal ethical standards of those professional organizations that address children's participation in research are consistent with the commands of the federal regulations. For example, the American Academy of Pediatrics' *Guidelines for the Ethical Conduct of Studies to Evaluate Drugs in Pediatric Populations* (1977; see *Pediatrics 60*:91–101, 1977) reinforces the concept that children capable of providing assent have the right to refuse research participation. This right is limited only by the principle that children may not refuse therapy deemed necessary for their well-being. If that therapy is available only in a research context, children may be required to take part, but only to the extent necessary for effective therapy. The Society for Research in Child Development, in its *Ethical Standards for Research with Children* (*SRCD Newsletter Winter*, 5–7, 1990), likewise states that "[T]he investigator should respect the child's freedom to choose to participate in the research or not by giving the child the opportunity to give or not to give assent to participation as well as to choose to discontinue participation at any time." These standards underscore again how critical judgments of minors' capacities are in determining minors' decision-making role. The American Psychological Association's 1992 ethical code also provides for a collateral "assent-permission" formula.

2. Legally, in our society, citizens typically have no responsibility to help anyone else. There are exceptions, of course, where we bear special relationships to others (such as parents to children or doctors to patients) or where we take on special obligations to help others (such as police officers who attempt to rescue someone). Yet, as heinous as failure to help another may seem, individuals are not penalized by law for failing to help an injured person, even when one could have helped at no risk or cost to oneself.

3. The regulations also describe additional elements of information required in particular circumstances or types of studies.

4. The Restatement (Second) of Torts, chapter 45, §892 A(2), 1979, a summary and analysis of American tort law, proposes that a child can be considered competent if the child is "capable of appreciating the nature, extent and probable consequences of the conduct consented to."

5. Pence defines dissent as "more then (sic) lack of assent or consent: it is active disagreement, signified either verbally or nonverbally" (G. E. Pence, Children's dissent to research—A minor matter? *IRB: A Review of Human Subjects Research*

2(10):2,1980). Even refusal to move or other refusals to cooperate are evidence of dissent.

6. There are two contexts that follow directly from the regulations. First, the regulations' provision for waiver of the parental permission requirement where the requirement is not reasonable to protect the subjects indicates that in some situations a minor may be the sole decision maker. As such, her consent must meet the same standards as an adult's autonomous consent.

Second, if the research offers the prospect of a direct benefit necessary to the well-being of the subject not available outside of the research context, an IRB may choose to waive the participant-assent requirement. We recommend, however, that the IRB instead choose to require the child's agreement only where the subject demonstrates a higher level of competency than that required for assent. How stringent a standard to apply may depend upon how critical the benefits of participation are to the child's health and well-being. Thus, if they are potentially life-saving and no suitable alternatives are available outside of the research context, the investigator and IRB may allow children to decline participation only if they demonstrate the same levels of competency we would require of adults in a similar situation.

References

Abramson, L., Seligman, M., and Teasdale, J. (1978). Learned helplessness in humans: Critique and reformulation. *Journal of Abnormal Psychology 87:*49–74.

Adelman, H. S., Kaser-Boyd, N., and Taylor, L. (1984). Noncompulsory versus legally mandated placement, perceived choice and response to treatment among adolescents. *Journal of Clinical Child Psychology 131:*170–178.

Adelman, H. S., Lusk, R., Alvarez, V., and Acosta, N. K. (1985). Competence of minors to understand, evaluate, and communicate about their psychoeducational problems. *Professional Psychology Research and Practice 16:*426–434.

Appelbaum, P. S., Lidz, C. W., and Meisel, A. (1987). *Informed Consent: Legal Theory and Clinical Practice.* New York: Oxford University Press.

Appelbaum, P. S., and Roth, L. H. (1982). Competency to consent to research. *Archives of General Psychiatry 39:*951–958.

Arnkoff, D. B., and Mahoney, M. J. (1979). The role of perceived control in psychopathology. In *Choice and Perceived Control,* ed. L. C. Perlmuter and R. A. Monty. Hillsdale, N.J.: Lawrence Erlbaum, pp. 155–174.

Averill, J. R. (1973). Personal control over aversive stimuli and its relationship to stress. *Psychological Bulletin 80:*286–303.

Bandura, A. (1978). The self system in reciprocal determinism. *American Psychologist 33:*344–358.

Bar-Tal, D., Sharabany, R., and Raviv, A. (1982). Cognitive basis for the development of altruistic behavior. In *Cooperation and Helping Behavior: Theories and Research,* ed. V. J. Derlega and J. Grzelak. New York: Academic Press, pp. 377–396.

Bastien, R., and Adelman, H. (1984). Children's participation in consent for psychotherapy and their subsequent response to treatment. *Journal of Consulting and Clinical Psychology 52:*171–179.

Bateson, G. (1972). *Steps to an Ecology of Mind.* New York: Chandler.

Bateson, G. (1979). *Mind and Nature.* New York: Dutton.

Batson, C. D., Fultz, J., Schoenrade, P. A., and Paduano, A. (1987). Critical self-reflection and self-perceived altruism: When self-reward fails. *Journal of Personality and Social Psychology 53:*594–602.

Beauchamp, T. L., and Childress, J. (1983). *Principles of Biomedical Ethics,* 2d ed. New York: Oxford University Press.

Bell, D. C., and Bell, L. G. (1983). Parental validation and support in the development of adolescent daughters. In *Adolescent Development in the Family,* ed. H. D. Grotevant and C. P. Cooper. San Francisco: Jossey-Bass, pp. 27–42.

Berndt, T. J. (1979). Developmental changes in conformity to peers and parents. *Developmental Psychology 15:*608–616.

Blos, P. (1979). *The Adolescent Passage.* New York: International University Press.

Bluebond-Langer, M. (1978). *The Private Worlds of Dying Children.* Princeton: Princeton University Press.

Brehm, S. S. (1977). The effect of adult influence on children's preferences: Compliance versus opposition. *Journal of Abnormal Child Psychology 5:*31–41.

Brehm, S. S., and Brehm, J. W. (1981). *Psychological Reactance.* New York: Academic Press.

Bronfenbrenner, U. (1977). Toward an experimental ecology of human development. *American Psychologist 32:*513–531.

Bronfenbrenner, U. (1979). Contexts of child-rearing: Problems and prospects. *American Psychologist 34:*844–850.

Bullock, M., and Lutkenhaus, P. (1988). The development of volitional behavior in the toddler years. *Child Development 59:*664–674.

Cassileth, B. R., Zupkis, R. V., Sutton-Smith, K., and March, V. (1980). Informed consent—Why are its goals imperfectly realized? *New England Journal of Medicine 302:*832–836.

Cialdini, R. B., Baumann, D. J., and Kenrick, D. T. (1981). Insights from sadness: A three step model of the development of altruism as hedonism. *Developmental Review 1:*207–223.

Connell, J. P. (1985). A new multidimensional measure of children's perceptions of control. *Child Development 56:*1018–1041.

Damon, W., and Hart, D. (1982). The development of self-understanding from infancy through adolescence. *Child Development 53:*841–864.

Davidson, D., and Hudson, J. (1988). The effects of decision reversibility and decision importance on children's decision making. *Journal of Experimental Child Psychology 46:*35–40.

Day, L., and Reznikoff, M. (1980). Social class, the treatment process, and parents' and children's expectations about child psychotherapy. *Journal of Clinical Child Psychology 9:*195–198.

Deci, E. L. (1980). *The Psychology of Self-determination.* Lexington, Mass.: Lexington Books.

Deci, E. L., and Ryan, R. M. (1987). The support of autonomy and the control of behavior. *Journal of Personality and Social Psychology 53:*1024–1037.

deTurck, M. A., and Miller, G. R. (1983). Adolescent perceptions of parental persuasive message strategies. *Journal of Marriage and the Family 45:*543–551.

Devine, D. A., and Fernald, P. S. (1973). Outcome effects of receiving a preferred, randomly assigned, or nonpreferred therapy. *Journal of Consulting and Clinical Psychology 41:*104–107.

Douvan, E. (1974). Commitment and social contract in adolescents. *Psychiatry 37:*22–36.

Dragastin, S. E. (1975). Research themes and priorities, in *Adolescence in the Life Cycle,* ed. S. E. Dragastin and G. M. Elder, Jr. Hillsdale, N.J.: Erlbaum, pp. 291–301.

Faden, R. R., and Beauchamp, T. L. (1986). *A History and Theory of Informed Consent.* New York: Oxford University Press.

Ferguson, L. R. (1978). The competence and freedom of children to make choices regarding participation in research: A statement. *Journal of Social Issues 14:*114–121.

Ford, J. D. (1987). Whither volition? *American Psychologist 42:*1033–1034.

Frank, J. D. (1976). Psychotherapy and the sense of mastery. In *Evaluation of Psychological Therapies,* ed. R. L. Spitzer and D. F. Klein. Baltimore: Johns Hopkins University Press, pp. 47–56.

Freud, A. (1958). Adolescence. *The Psychoanalytic Study of the Child 13:*255–278.

Froming, W. L., Allen, L., and Jensen, R. (1985). Altruism, role-taking, and self-awareness: The acquisition of norms governing altruistic behavior. *Child Development 56:*1223–1228.

Garbarino, J. (1982). *Children and Families in the Social Environment.* Hawthorne, N.Y.: Aldine de Gruyter.

Gardner, W. P., and Herman, J. (1991). The developmental change in decision-making: Use of multiplicative strategies and sensitivity to losses. Paper presented at the biannual Meeting of the Society for Research and Child Development, April 19, 1991, Seattle, Wa.; printed version April 24, 1991.

Gardner, W. P., Scherer, D. G., and Tester, M. (1989). Asserting scientific authority: Cognitive development and adolescent legal rights. *American Psychologist 44:*895–902.

Glantz, L. H., Annas, G. J., and Katz, B. F. (1977). Scientific research with children: Legal incapacity and proxy consent. *Family Law Quarterly 11:*253–295.

Gordon, R. M. (1976). Effects of volunteering and responsibility on the perceived value and effectiveness of a clinical treatment. *Journal of Consulting and Clinical Psychology 44:*799–801.

Greuneich, R. (1982). The development of children's integration rules for making moral judgments. *Child Development 53:*887–894.

Grisso, T. (in press). Voluntary consent to research participation in the institutional context. In *Research Ethics: A Psychological Approach,* ed. B. Stanley and J. Sieber. Lincoln: University of Nebraska Press.

Grisso, T. (1986). *Evaluating Competencies.* New York: Plenum.

Grisso, T., and Vierling, L. (1978). Minors' consent to treatment: A developmental perspective. *Professional Psychology: Research and Practice 9:*412–427.

Grodin, M. A., and Alpert, J. J. (1983). Informed consent and pediatric care. In *Children's Competence to Consent,* ed. G. B. Melton, G. P. Koocher, and M. J. Saks. New York: Plenum Press, pp. 93–110.

Grotevant, H. D., and Cooper, C. R. (1986). Individuation in family relationships: A perspective on individual differences in the development of identity and role-taking skill in adolescence. *Human Development 29:*82–100.

Haber, S., and Stephen-Brens, S. (1981). Do children understand enough to consent to participate in research? Paper presented at the Wester Psychological Association Convention, Los Angeles.

Hart, S. N. (1991). From property to person status: Historical perspective on children's rights. *American Psychologist 46:*53–59.

Hayes, S. C. (1987). Contextual determinants of "volitional action": A reply to Howard and Conway. *American Psychologist 42:*1029–1030.

Hershberger, W. (1987). Of course there can be an empirical science of volitional action. *American Psychologist 42:*1032.

Hill, J. P., and Holmbeck, G. N. (1986). Attachment and autonomy during adolescence. *Annals of Child Development 3:*145–189.

Howard, G. S., and Conway, C. G. (1986). Can there be an empirical science of volitional action? *American Psychologist 41:*1241–1251.

Howard, G. S., and Conway, C. G. (1987). The next steps toward a science of agency. *American Psychologist 42:*1034–1036.

Inhelder, B., and Piaget, J. (1965). *The Growth of Logical Thinking.* New York: Basic Books.

Jackson, D. (1967). The individual and the larger contexts. *Family Process 6:*139–147.

Jaeger, M., and Rosnow, R. (1988). Contextualism and its implications for psychological inquiry. *British Journal of Psychology 79:*63–75.

James, W. (1890/1950). *The Principles of Psychology,* Vol. II. New York: Dover.

Janofsky, J., and Starfield, B. (1981). Assessment of risk in research on children. *Pediatrics 98:*842–846.

Jantzen, W. B., and Love, W. (1977). Involving adolescents as active participants in their own treatment plans. *Psychological Reports 41:*931–934.

Kagehiro, D. K. (1988). Perceived voluntariness of consent to warrantless police searches. *Journal of Applied Social Psychology 18:*38–49.

Kamps, W. A., Akkerboom, J. C., Nitschke, R., Kingma, A., Holmes, H. B., Caldwell, S., and Humphrey, G. B. (1987). Altruism and informed consent in chemotherapy trials of childhood cancer. *Loss, Grief and Care 1:*93–110.

Kandel, D., and Lesser, G. S. (1969). Parent-adolescent relationships and adolescent independence in the United States and Denmark. *Journal of Marriage and the Family 31:*348–358.

Kaser-Boyd, N., Adelman, H. S., and Taylor, L. (1985). Minors' ability to identify risks and benefits of therapy. *Professional Psychology 16:*411–417.

Keeney, B. P. (1979). Ecosystemic epistomology: An alternative paradigm for diagnosis. *Family Process 18:*117–129.

Kellerman, J., and Katz, E. (1977). The adolescent with cancer: Theoretical, clinical and research issues. *Journal of Pediatric Psychology 2:*127–131.

Kendall, P. C., Williams, L., Pechacek, T. F., Graham, L. E., Shisslak, C., and Herzoff, N. (1979). Cognitive-behavioral and patient education interventions in cardiac catheterization procedures: The Palo Alto Medical Psychology Project. *Journal of Consulting and Clinical Psychology 47:*49–58.

Kim, Y., and Stevens, J. H. (1987). The socialization of prosocial behavior in children. *Childhood Education 65:*200–206.

Klayman, J. (1985). Children's decision strategies and their adaptation to task characteristics. *Organizational Behavior and Human Decision Processes 35:*179–201.

Knight, G. P., Berning, A. L., Wilson, S. L., and Chao, Chia-Chen (1987). The effects of information processing demands and social-situational factors on the social decision making of children. *Journal of Experimental Psychology 43:*244–259.

Koocher, G. P., and Keith-Spiegel, P. C. (1990). *Children, Ethics, and the Law.* Lincoln: University of Nebraska Press.

Korsch, B. M. (1974). The Armstrong lecture: Physicians, patients and decisions. *American Journal of Diseases of Children 127:*328–332.

Krampen, G. (1989). Perceived childrearing practices and the development of locus of control in early adolescence. *International Journal of Behavioral Development 12:*177–193.

Larson, L. E. (1972). The influence of parents and peers during adolescence: The situation-hypothesis revisited. *Journal of Marriage and the Family 34:*67–74.

Lazarick, D. L., Fishbein, S. S., Loiello, M. A., and Howard, G. S. (1988). Practical investigations of volition. *Journal of Counseling Psychology 35:*15–26.

Leon, M. (1980). Coordination of intent and consequence information in children's moral judgment. In *The Integration of Information by Children,* ed. F. Wilkenberg, J. Becker and T. Trabasso. Hillsdale, N.J.: Erlbaum.

Levine, R. J. (1980). The senate's proposed statutory definition of "voluntary and informed consent." *IRB: A Review of Human Subjects Research 2(4):*8–10.

Levine, R. J. (1981). *Ethics and Regulation of Clinical Research.* Baltimore: Urban and Schwarzenberg.

Lewin, K. (1951). Intention, will, and need. In *Organization and Pathology of Thought,* ed. D. Rappaport. New York: Columbia University, pp. 95–150.

Lewis, C. C. (1980). A comparison of minors' and adults' pregnancy decisions. *American Journal of Orthopsychiatry 50:*446–453.

Lewis, C. C. (1981). How adolescents approach decisions: Changes over grades seven to twelve and policy implications. *Child Development 52:*538–544.

Lewis, C. C. (1987). Minors' competence to consent to abortion. *American Psychologist 42:*84–88.

Lewis, C. E., Lewis, M. A., and Ifekwunigue, M. (1978). Informed consent by children and participation in an influenza vaccine trial. *American Journal of Public Health 68:*1079–1082.

Lewis, C. E., Lewis, M. W., Lorimer, A., and Palmer, B. B. (1977). Child-initiated care: The use of school nursing services by children in an "adult free" system. *Pediatrics 60:*499–507.

Magnusson, D., ed. (1981). *Toward a Psychology of Situations.* Hillsdale, N.J.: Erlbaum.

Meisel, A. (1979). The "exceptions" to the informed consent doctrine: Striking a balance between competing values in medical decisionmaking. *Wisconsin Law Review,* pp. 413–488.

Meisel, A., Roth, L. H., and Lidz, C. W. (1977). Toward a model of the legal doctrine of informed consent. *American Journal of Psychiatry 134:*285–289.

Melton, G. B. (1980). Children's concepts of their rights. *Journal of Clinical Child Psychology 9:*186–190.

Melton, G. B. (1983a). Decision making by children: Psychological risks and benefits. In *Children's Competence to Consent,* ed. G. B. Melton, G. P. Koocher, and M. J. Saks. New York: Plenum, pp. 93–110.

Melton, G. B. (1983b). Toward "personhood" for adolescents. *American Psychologist 38:*99–103.

Melton, G. B. (1991). Socialization in the global community: Respect for the dignity of children. *American Psychologist 46*:66–71.

Milgram, S. (1974). *Obedience to Authority.* New York: Harper and Row.

Nakajima, Y., and Hotta, M. (1989). A developmental study of cognitive processes in decision making: Information searching as a function of task complexity. *Psychological Reports 64*:67–79.

Nannis, E. D., Susman, E. J., Strope, B. E., Wodruff, P. J., Hersh, S. P., Levine, A., and Pizzo, P. A. (1982). Correlates of control in pediatric cancer patients and their families. *Journal of Pediatric Psychology 7*:75–84.

National Commission for the Protection of Human Subjects of Biomedical and Behavioral Research (1977). *Report and Recommendations: Research Involving Children* (Publ. No. [OS] 77–0004). Rockville, Md.: Dept. of Health, Education and Welfare.

National Commission for the Protection of Human Subjects of Biomedical and Behavioral Research (1978). *Belmont Report* (Publ. No. [OS] 78–0012). Rockville, Md.: Dept. of Health, Education and Welfare.

Pence, G. E. (1980). Children's dissent to research—A minor matter? *IRB: A Review of Human Subjects Research 2(10)*:1–4.

Perry, L. C., Perry, D. G., and Weiss, R. J. (1986). Age differences in children's beliefs about whether altruism makes the actor feel good. *Social Cognition 4*:261–269.

Peterson, L., Reaven, N., and Homer, A. L. (1984). Limitations imposed by parents on children's altruism. *Merrill-Palmer Quarterly 30*:269–286.

Piaget, J. (1976). *The Psychology of Intelligence.* Totowa, N.J.: Littlefield, Adams & Co.

Piaget, J. (1967). *Six Psychological Studies.* New York: Random House.

President's Commission for the Study of Ethical Problems in Medicine and Biomedical and Behavioral Research (1982). *Making Health Care Decisions,* Vol. 1. Washington, D.C.: U.S. Government Printing Office.

Rickett, M., and Sheppard, M. A. (1988). Decision-making and young people. *Journal of Drug Education 18*:109–114.

Rodin, J., and Janis, I. L. (1979). The social power of health care practitioners as agents of change. *Journal of Social Issues 35*:60–81.

Rodin, J., and Langer, E. J. (1977). Long-term effects of a control-relevant intervention with the institutionalized aged. *Journal of Personality and Social Psychology 35*:897–902.

Rollins, B. C., and Thomas, D. L. (1975). A theory of parental power and child compliance. In *Power in Families,* ed. R. E. Cromwell and D. H. Olsen. Beverly Hills: Sage, pp. 38–60.

Roth, L. H., Meisel, A., and Lidz, C. W. (1977). Tests of competency to consent to treatment. *American Journal of Psychiatry 134*:279–284.

Rotter, J. (1966). Generalized expectancies for internal versus external control of reinforcement. *Psychological Monographs No. 609, 80*(1).

Rutter, M., Graham, P., Chadwick, O., and Yule, W. (1976). Adolescent turmoil: Fact or fiction. *Journal of Child Psychology and Psychiatry 17*:35–56.

Saks, M. J. (1983). Social psychological perspectives on the problem of consent. In *Children's Competence to Consent,* ed. G. B. Melton, G. P. Koocher, and M. J. Saks. New York: Plenum Press, pp. 93–110.

Scherer, D. G. (1991). The capacities of minors to exercise voluntariness in medical treatment decisions. *Law and Human Behavior 15*:431–449.

Scherer, D. G. and Reppucci, N. D. (1988). Adolescents' capacities to provide voluntary informed consent: The effect of parental influence and medical dilemmas. *Law and Human Behavior 12*:123–141.

Schulz, R. (1976). Effects of control and predictability on the physical and psychological well-being of the institutionalized aged. *Journal of Personality and Social Psychology 33*:563–573.

Seligman, M. E. P. (1975). *Helplessness: On Depression, Development and Death*. San Francisco: W. H. Freeman.

Skinner, B. F. (1971). *Beyond Freedom and Dignity*. New York: Knopf.

Skinner, E. A., and Chapman, M. (1987). Resolution of a developmental paradox: How can perceived internality increase, decrease, and remain the same across middle childhood? *Developmental Psychology 23*:44–48.

Skinner, E. A., Chapman, M., and Baltes, P. B. (1988a). Control, means-ends, and agency beliefs: A new conceptualization and its measurement during childhood. *Journal of Personality and Social Psychology 54*:117–133.

Skinner, E. A., Chapman, M., and Baltes, P. B. (1988b). Children's beliefs about control, means-ends, and agency: Developmental differences during middle childhood. *International Journal of Behavioral Development 11*:369–388.

Smith, T. E. (1970). Foundations of parental influence upon adolescents: An application of social power theory. *American Sociological Review 35*:860–872.

Smith, T. E. (1983). Adolescent reactions to attempted parental control and influence techniques. *Journal of Marriage and the Family 45*:533–542.

Spinetta, J. J. (1974). The dying child's awareness of death: A review. *Psychological Bulletin 81*:256–260.

Spinetta, J. J., Rigler, D., and Karon, M. (1974). Personal space as a measure of a dying child's sense of isolation. *Journal of Consulting and Clinical Psychology 42*:751–756.

Staats, A. W. (1987). Humanistic versus behavioristic determinism: Disunified psychology's schism problem and its solution. *American Psychologist 42*:1030–1032.

Steinberg, L., and Silverberg, S. B. (1986). The vicissitudes of autonomy in early adolescence. *Child Development 57*:841–851.

Steiner, I. (1970). Perceived freedom. In *Advances in Experimental Social Psychology,* ed. L. Berkowitz. New York: Academic Press, pp. 187–248.

Taylor, L., and Adelman, H. S. (1986). Facilitating children's participation in decisions that affect them: From concept to practice. *Journal of Clinical Child Psychology 15*:346–351.

Taylor, L., Adelman, H. S., and Kaser-Boyd, N. (1983). Perspectives of children regarding their participation in psychoeducational treatment decision making. *Professional Psychology 14*:882–894.

Taylor, L., Adelman, H. S., and Kaser-Boyd, N. (1985). Minors' attitudes and competence toward participation in psychoeducational decisions. *Professional Psychology: Research and Practice 16*:226–235.

Tester, M., Gardner, W., and Wilfong, E. (1987). Experimental studies of the development of decision making competence. Paper presented at American Psychological Association Convention, New York.

Thoresen, C. E., and Mahoney, M. J. (1974). *Behavioral Self-control.* New York: Holt, Rinehart and Winston.

Vernick, J., and Karon, M. (1965). Who's afraid of death on a leukemia ward? *American Journal of Diseases of Children 109:*393–397.

Veroff, J. (1983). Contextual determinants of personality. *Personality and Social Psychology Bulletin 9:*331–343.

Weisz, J. R., and Stipek, D. J. (1982). Competence, contingency, and the development of perceived control. *Human Development 26:*250–281.

Weithorn, L. A. (1982). Developmental factors and competence to make informed treatment decisions. *Child and Youth Services 5:*85–100.

Weithorn, L. A. (1983a). Children's capacities to decide about participation in research. *IRB: A Review of Human Subject's Research 5*(4).

Weithorn, L. A. (1983b). Involving children in decisions affecting their own welfare. In *Children's Competence to Consent,* ed. G. B. Melton, G. P. Koocher, and M. J. Saks. New York: Plenum Press, pp. 235–260.

Weithorn, L. A. (1984). Children's capacities in legal contexts. In *Children, Mental Health and the Law,* ed. N. D. Reppucci, L. A. Weithorn, E. P. Mulvey, and J. Monahan. Beverly Hills: Sage, pp. 25–55.

Weithorn, L. A. (1985). Children's capacities for participation in treatment decisionmaking. In *Emerging Issues in Child Psychiatry and the Law,* ed. D. H. Schetky and E. P. Benedek. New York: Bruner/Mazel, pp. 22–36.

Weithorn, L. A., and Campbell, S. (1982). The competency of children and adolescents to make informed treatment decisions. *Child Development 53:*1589–1599.

Weithorn, L. A., and McCabe, M. A. (1988). Emerging ethical and legal issues in pediatric psychology. In *Handbook of Pediatric Psychology,* ed. D. Routh. New York: The Guilford Press, pp. 567–606.

White, K. D., Pearson, J. C., and Flint, L. (1989). Adolescents' compliance-resistance: Effects of parents' compliance strategy and gender. *Adolescence 24:*595–621.

White, K. M., Speisman, J. C., and Costos, D. (1983). Young adults and their parents: Individuation to mutuality. In *Adolescent Development in the Family,* eds. H. D. Grotevant and C. P. Cooper. San Francisco: Jossey-Bass, pp. 61–76.

Wilson, G. T. (1979). Perceived control and the theory and practice of behavior therapy. In *Choice and Perceived Control,* ed. L. C. Perlmuter and R. A. Monty. Hillsdale, N.J.: Erlbaum, pp. 392–407.

Youniss, J. (1983). Social construction of adolescence by adolescents and parents. In *Adolescent Development in the Family,* ed. H. D. Grotevant and C. P. Cooper. San Francisco: Jossey-Bass, pp. 93–109.

6

Assessment of Risk
to Children

ESTHER H. WENDER

The assessment of risk to children is different from judgments regarding risk in adults. In this context, risk refers to the possibility of harmful outcome from procedures involved in research studies. One of the assumptions of this analysis is that the assessment of medical risk in children is relatively straightforward and differs from such assessment in adults only because of differences in physiology and disease susceptibility in children, issues that are the substance of pediatric medicine and have been previously well researched. When assessing risk as it uniquely affects children, however, the primary issues are psychological, and the psychological issues vary both with the progress of development and with environmental circumstance.

A review of those experiences likely to produce pain, anxiety and fear in children is given below. The impact of these experiences on children is greatly affected by developmental issues (Thompson, 1990). In addition, evidence suggests that children who have already experienced illness may react differently from children who have remained healthy. The ensuing discussion initially addresses the major developmental stages in children and how children of different ages can be expected to react to the experiences associated with research procedures. This is followed by a brief review of the impact that prior illness may have on the child's reactions.

Relationship Between Present Stress and Future Outcome

One of the critical issues in the psychological assessment of risk is whether, or to what extent, present discomfort, anxiety, or fear have a harmful effect on future outcome. Much is known about the circumstances that produce fear, anxiety, and discomfort in children, but very little is known about the direct connections between present stress and later outcome. Where such evidence does exist, this is mentioned in the ensuing discussion. However, in the absence of clear evidence of future harm the controversy remains whether, or to what extent, present fear, anxiety, or pain engendered by research procedures should be tolerated or considered unacceptable.

There is some direct evidence that current stress may not necessarily produce future harm. For example, a large literature in pediatrics demonstrates that children with a variety of chronic illnesses, presumably resulting in stressful experiences, have outcomes that are generally no different from those of healthy children (Pless, 1979). When chronic illness does result in adverse outcome, two factors have been identified as likely to produce such outcomes: (1) illnesses that are known to affect the central nervous system are likely to result in future problems (Rutter, 1970; Seidel, 1975); and (2) illnesses that are not outwardly visible, but require treatment or restrictions that affect the patient's lifestyle are more likely to produce poor outcome (McAnarney, 1974; Bruhn, 1971). A few studies suggest that present stress may actually protect the child from future problems. The evidence on this issue is meager and some of it comes from animal research (Friedman, 1966). However, it has been shown that some children with handicapping conditions use positive coping strategies and achieve outcomes that are extraordinary in the face of what would appear to be stressful obstacles to such achievements (Maccoby, 1983).

There is a body of research on later outcomes in children who were hospitalized early in life (Douglas 1975; Jessner, 1959; Lattimer, 1974; Schaffer, 1959; and Shannon, 1984). These studies have yielded contradictory findings. Douglas identified adverse outcomes, such as an increase in developmental and behavioral problems, in children hospitalized during the fi1st three years as compared to children never hospitalized. However, this study did not control for the fact that children who require hospitalization may already come from a group at risk for developmental or behavioral problems. Shannon did not identify any greater adversity at outcome in the hospitalized group compared to controls. Lattimer combined outcome data with information regarding normal child development to recommend an optimal age for certain types of elective surgical procedures. The authors recommended that orchiopexy (surgery for undescended testicle) be scheduled when the patient was developmentally able to tolerate separation and was able to understand the reason for the procedure (i.e., early elementary school age).

Thus the relationship between current stress and later outcome is not clear and probably varies depending upon a number of complex, interacting factors. In the ensuing review of stressful experiences in children and the factors that produce them, the reader should keep in mind the complex nature of the relationships between these experiences and future outcomes, including the possibility that stressful experiences, under some circumstances, may actually be protective. When considering a specific research proposal, the reviewer should ask: What is the age of the children being studied? And, What are the special vulnerabilities at that age? The reviewer should also ask what has been done to protect children from the potentially harmful effects of the proposed research.

Infancy (birth to approximately age two)

Both theoretical and experimental evidence tells us that the very young mammal thrives, and even depends for survival, upon the ready availability and responsiveness of the caregiver (Hinde, 1977). Conversely, the greatest stress in this period of life is abandonment, either physically or psychologically. Studies looking at infants' response to painful procedures and to hospitalization reveal that the presence of the caregiver is essential and protective (Robertson, 1968; Schaffer, 1959). In the early months of this period any caregiver who is available and responsive will do. However, once the infant has become clearly aware of familiar versus strange (five to seven months in the normal child), the availability of the familiar caregiver is essential (Stern, 1987; Prugh, 1983). The profound effect of abandonment on the infant suggests that separation for other than brief periods is highly likely to produce an adverse outcome later. For example, prolonged periods of separation from the caregiver without the substitution of another will usually result in apathy, weight loss, and finally an increased susceptibility to disease and even death (Bowlby, 1980). The message relating to the assessment of risk in research settings is that the infant should always have a responsive caregiver available; after the age of approximately six months, that caregiver should be familiar to the child. In addition, a research procedure that involves a prolonged separation of the infant from its caregiver cannot be justified.

A second issue in this infancy period relates to the impact of painful procedures on the infant. Much controversy has surrounded the question of whether the young organism, particularly the very young infant, will be adversely affected by painful procedures that the child apparently does not remember later in development. Recent research clearly verifies the pain experience of the infant as physiologically identical to pain experience in later development (Amand, 1987; Owens, 1984). However, a question remains unanswered: Do painful experiences in infancy, if they are not remembered, adversely affect later outcome? The current consensus of opinion is that pain reduction procedures, that is, anesthesia, should be used to protect infants to the same degree that they are used to protect older children and adults (Williamson, 1983). In the context of research, if painful procedures are required and can be justified for the purpose of obtaining important information, they should be accompanied by anesthesia with the outcome of anesthesia monitored as it would be in older children and adults, that is by its ability to reduce visible and physiological signs of distress.

Certain experiences are known to produce fear in the infant that may not produce fear in older children and adults. Loud noises are clearly a source of stress in the younger child as compared to older children and adults. This is probably because of the combination of the impact of loud noises on sensory structures plus the lack of cognitive experience with, and understanding of, the source of the noise. Another source of stress to infants is the perceived loss of structural support that comes from the immature visual perceptual system. Thus infants will not venture out onto a transparent surface (i.e., glass) when it appears to them that they might fall (the "visual cliff"). Again, researchers and review boards should be aware of this source of potential distress in young children. Finally, studies have shown that everyday visual and auditory experiences are well tolerated by infants, but unfamiliar sensory stimuli are not. Thus robots, distorted images and nonenvironmental noises may produce intense fear at this age (Mussen, 1980). Researchers and review boards should consider these special vulnerabilities of infants when planning or reviewing research studies involving this age group.

Preschool (approximately two- to five-years old)

This period of development is characterized by a delightful capacity for imaginative thinking that results in certain types of psychological vulnerability. This vulnerability is due, in large part, to the egocentric thinking that characterizes this age group. The perceptions of preschool children are not modified by a cause-effect analysis because of their inability to think in terms of causal inference (Inhelder, 1958). Children of this age also have a distorted sense of time as compared to older children and adults. Thus, the concept of future gain is not understood by preschool children. These egocentric and immature thought processes distort preschool children's perception of verbal explanations and reassurances given by adults (Bibace, 1980; Perrin, 1981). Also, what may seem to the adult as actions designed to entertain and distract may produce fear and anxiety in the child of this age. For example, life-size dolls, especially of fanciful creatures, may produce fear in preschool children who often lack clear boundaries between what is reality and fantasy (Dixon, 1987). Preschool children may be particularly vulnerable to the following types of experience:

1. Preschool children are often disturbed by what they perceive to be mutilations of their usual experience of objects and people. Thus, the doll who is missing its head or the stuffed animal whose limb is torn off may be anxiety provoking. It is known that children of this age can perceive their own bowel movement as a loss of a body part, or interpret a plaster cast as an anxiety provoking distortion of the affected limb. Intravenous tubes and the sight of bleeding can also provoke intense anxiety and fear.
2. Unfamiliar sights and noises, often presented with the intention of entertaining or distracting, can instead be anxiety provoking. The noise of a medical machine or the sight of a person wearing a hospital uniform or mask may be intensely frightening. Even puppets and toys made to look like animals or characters from books or television may provoke anxiety.
3. Preschool children are particularly likely to perceive painful procedures as acts of aggression or punishment for bad behavior. This is due in part to their difficulty understanding the explanations given for procedures that inflict pain. Thus preschool children cannot usually understand the concept that an intravenous needle or the injection of medicine will "make them feel better."

The presence of the familiar caregiver is also a significant issue for the preschool child. Although the preschool child, in comparison to the infant, can more easily adjust to temporary separation from the caregiver whenever the surroundings are unfamiliar or the activity produces pain or anxiety, the alleviation of these emotions is heavily dependent upon the supportive presence of the familiar caregiver (Prugh, 1983; Visitainer, 1975). Recent studies have shown that physiologic responses to pain can be greatly reduced by the skillful efforts of the supportive caregiver. The fact that children of this age are also verbal and can bargain and verbally provoke guilt in adults has often led to decisions by medical personnel to exclude caregivers when necessarily painful procedures are performed. Recent research, however, suggests that exclusion of the caregiver often heightens the anxiety of the preschool child (Ross, 1984; Zeltzer, 1989). Therefore, when painful procedures are necessary in a research study involving preschool children, attention should be given to including caregivers in the procedure and training them to provide support to the child.

How should these issues affect the assessment of research risk in the pre-school child? First, an understanding of the developmental issues known to affect the reaction of preschool children to research procedures should inform the choice of procedures to be followed and should provide guidelines for re-ducing the risk of provoking fear and anxiety whenever possible. Secondly, those in the position of assessing risk and balancing the benefits versus risks of research protocols involving preschool children should include in their evalua-tion an assessment of how that research is likely to affect the preschool child and how well these children are protected from the potential harmful affects.

School-age (approximately ages six through eleven)

The school-age child loses some of the vulnerability of the infant and preschool child. Verbal skills are increasingly well developed and children of this age can more realistically appraise the explanations of procedures and better under-stand the difference between fantasy and reality. School-age children increas-ingly tolerate the absence of the familiar caregivers for longer periods of sepa-ration. Children of this age also are increasingly able to benefit from psychological support outside the immediate family, that is, the nurse or re-search assistant.

However, new issues of vulnerability appear at this age that need to be un-derstood by the researcher and those who review the risk of research proce-dures.

Children of this age are highly influenced by the evaluation of their own performance relative to that of their peers. They are also affected by the evalua-tion of the important adults in their own family as well as those in their relevant community, for example teachers and youth group leaders. Also, these children are at a sensitive stage in the development of their self-image (Damon, 1983). Their self-concept is largely influenced by a sense of accomplishment in the "work" of school-age children—namely academic performance, physical ac-tivity, and the development of specific talents such as musical, constructional, or artistic skills (Nicholls, 1978).

Therefore, any medical illnesses or procedures that affect their ability to perform these age-related tasks are particularly threatening to school-age chil-dren. For example, medical procedures that are visible to peers (e.g., the use of nebulizers to treat asthma) are particularly burdensome. Also, any medical conditions that restrict activity may be especially stressful. Any treatment or procedure that makes school-age children look different to their peers is likely to be problematic. Psychological research involving deception must be viewed critically at this age. For example, some studies require that children knowingly be pushed beyond their limits in order to test the effects of stress on performance. Such studies should be viewed cautiously and attempts should be made to explain the procedures so as to reduce the potential for loss of self-esteem.

Another important issue for children of this age is loss of self-control or independence. Since both self-control (of temper, mood, etc.), and independence (e.g., bowel and bladder control; ability to be away from family at summer camps or overnight stays) are newly emerging skills at this age, any threat to independence or self-control may result in loss of self-esteem and developmental regression. Again, these issues need to be understood by researchers and review committees in order to evaluate risk-benefits and to provide adequate safeguards when procedures that affect these issues seem necessary.

Finally, the issue of children's understanding of what is meant by research becomes an important issue at this and at older ages. Most professionals would agree that permission to perform research on infants and preschool children resides with the relevant adults—that is the researchers, review committees, and parents. Infants and preschool children do not possess the relevant thought processes required to make decisions about their own involvement in research studies. However, most research regulations now require "assent" to the research procedure on the part of the school-age child and the young adolescent. (Older adolescents are frequently required to give informed consent.) Yet theoretical issues, plus data from one study, would suggest that school-age children do not understand research in the same way as most adults. The concepts of "being experimented upon" or "helping mankind understand disease" are not understood by school-age children in the same way as adults understand these concepts. One study has revealed that the concept of being experimented upon is extraordinarily anxiety provoking to children of this age (Schwartz, 1972). The findings of this study would suggest that explanations of research procedures to school-age children and younger adolescents should avoid the notion of "experiment," which is probably interpreted by many children in the context of science fiction stories to which they are exposed. Instead, research procedures should be explained as necessary to help doctors understand what makes children sick or what makes them better.

Adolescence (approximately ages twelve to eighteen)

Adolescents are gradually acquiring a much more sophisticated understanding of the nature of illness and a future perspective that enables them to perceive a sense of responsibility toward mankind. It is this sense of responsibility that often motivates adolescents and adults to participate willingly in research studies. However, there are special vulnerabilities typical of this stage of development that may lead to anxiety and fear and should be taken into the account of research risk.

Adolescents are especially vulnerable to any procedure that affects their appearance or sense of future capability (Kinnoth, 1983). Thus procedures such as those required to correct an orthopedic deformity might be particularly stressful and require special kinds of reassurance and explanation. Medications that alter appearance, such as steroids, are especially problematic at this age. Procedures that may affect one's sexual attractiveness will be extremely threatening at this time of emerging sexuality. Thus chemotherapy resulting in hair loss or hormones that alter body habitus may be particularly stressful. Adolescents are even more influenced than are school-age children by the evaluation of their peers. Any procedure or experience that makes adolescents feel different has the potential of damaging their newly emerging self-identity (Marcia, 1980). Thus, for example, a research study that requires adolescents to come to the hospital to participate in therapy and undergo a brief procedure will necessitate explanations to peers about their absence from peer activities. Such seemingly simple issues may pose problems for adolescents. Adolescents are typically self-conscious and may be much more sensitive than adults to even slight "differences" in appearance or ability. The adolescent's emerging sense of competence is also vulnerable and any procedure that shakes that confidence, such as studies that may make the patient feel dumb or clumsy, must be viewed with caution. Psychological studies that involve deceiving the patient must be viewed skeptically at this age and procedures should be instituted that reduce the potential loss of self-esteem.

Although adolescents are developing a perspective that includes a future (job, marriage, etc.), that future view can easily be shaken by any illness or injury that impairs present function. As compared to the adult who has passed through this vulnerable period, the adolescent has greater difficulty accepting a present setback as temporary. Thus research procedures in adolescent patients that will temporarily make them sicker—for example experimental chemotherapy—may be difficult to justify.

If these areas of vulnerability are understood by the researcher, research design can be altered to protect the adolescent's sense of self. For example, research can be done in settings (e.g., at home) or at times (e.g., early morning) that are least problematic to the adolescent.

The Impact of Prior Illness

Children who enter into research studies with a prior exposure to illness and medical procedures may react differently than the healthy child with no such prior experience. The most obvious negative impact of prior exposure to illness is a heightened sensitivity to potentially painful and frightening experiences (Tavormina, 1976). The child now knows what to expect. Health care personnel are familiar with the child with a chronic illness who begins to react negatively to a painful procedure long before it actually takes place. This negative anticipation can make the care of such patients an extremely difficult process. Also, the toddler or preschool child who is familiar with the immunization injection can be expected to react negatively to the nonpainful medical examination that precedes it.

However, there are positive effects of prior exposure especially as the child gets older. Fear of the unknown is reduced in children who have experienced a procedure and found that it "wasn't so bad" or that they survived the experience and could claim a sense of bravery from that survival. Many children develop positive coping strategies and gradually acquire a sense of control and mastery that produces confidence and positive self-esteem (Shantz, 1983; Maccoby, 1983; Damon, 1983). These thought processes may lead to positive outcomes as a direct result of stressful experience. Some professionals advocate a strategy of helping children develop positive coping skills as a way of protecting them from the potentially harmful impact of chronic illness. The same argument might be applied as an approach to the research setting that would help reduce the potential harmful impact of procedures that provoke anxiety or pain. Thus the impact of prior exposure on the assessment of risk must be individualized. In general, prior experience can be expected to increase the negative impact on toddlers and preschool children (Kopp, 1989). In school-age children and adolescents there is a possible beneficial effect of prior experience based upon the patient's coping strategies and the resulting sense of mastery, if coping has been effective. Previous exposure can either increase or reduce anticipatory fear depending upon the impact of the prior experience.

Summary

The assessment of the risk of harmful outcome in research procedures in children is a complex process. It begins, as in all research, with the assessment of the need for the information, the quality of the research design and the potential benefit of that research on the well-being of the general population. These factors must then be weighed against the potential for producing harmful effects in the research subject. In children, the potential for producing harmful effects is complicated by the process of development, which may obscure the issue of whether immediate negative impact is harmful in the long term. In addition, the potential for immediate negative impact changes with development. However, our understanding of the general factors that possess the potential for negative impact on children of various ages and stages of development is fairly well understood. These developmental issues should be part of every review committee's assessment of risk in children. In addition, researchers should employ strategies designed to reduce these risks whenever possible.

Infants, toddlers, and preschool children are adversely affected by any procedure that removes them from the supportive and familiar caregiver. Verbal explanations and strategies designed to distract and entertain must be chosen carefully; researchers should be sensitive to the distortions that characterize these children's perceptions. School-age children and adolescents are increasingly less dependent upon familiar caregivers and are increasingly supported by verbal explanations and potent distractors. However, children of this age are increasingly sensitive to procedures that affect function and distort body image. In addition, although less dependent upon the support of familiar adults, they are increasingly affected by their perception of the reaction of peers.

If these general principles are understood and if they are appropriately applied to research procedures, the harmful risk of research on children can be reduced.

References

Abramovitch, R., Freedman, J. L., Thoden, K., and Nikolich, C. (1991). Children's capacity to consent to participation in psychological research: Empirical findings. *Child Development 62:*1100–1109.

Amand, K. J. S., Sippeli, W. G., and Aynsley-Green, A. (1987). Randomized trial of fentanyl anesthesia in preterm babies undergoing surgery: Effects on the stress response. *Lancet 1:*243–247.

Bibace, R., and Walsh, M. (1980). Development of children's concept of illness. *Pediatrics 66:*912–917.

Bowlby, J. (1980). *Attachment and Loss: III. Loss, Sadness and Depression.* New York: Basic Books.

Bruhn, J. G., Hampton, J. W., and Chandler, G. C. (1971). Clinical marginality and psychological adjustment in hemophilia. *Journal of Psychosomatic Research 15:*207–213.

Damon, W., and Hart, D. (1983). The development of self-understanding from infancy through adolescence. *Child Development 53:*841–864.

Dixon, S. D. (1987). 2–1/2 Years: The emergence of magic. In *Encounters with Children,* ed. S. D. Dixon and M. T. Stein. Chicago: Year Book Medical Publishers,

Douglas, J. W. B. (1975). Early hospital admissions and later disturbances of behavior and learning. *Developmental Medicine and Child Neurology 17:*456–80.

Dweck, C. S., and Elliot, E. S. (1983). Achievement motivation. In *Handbook of Child Psychology: Volume 4: Socialization, Personality, and Social Development,* ed. E. M. Hetherington and P. H. Mussen. New York: Wiley, pp. 643–691.

Friedman, S. B., and Glasgow, L. A. (1966). Psychological factors and resistance to infectious disease. *Pediatriac Clinics of North America 13:*315–335.

Graham, P. J. (1981). Ethics and child psychiatry. In *Psychiatric Ethics,* ed. S. Block and P. Chodoff. Oxford: Oxford University Press, pp. 235–254.

Hinde, R. A., and McGinnis, L. (1977). Some factors influencing the effect of temporary mother-infant separation: Some experiments with rhesus monkeys. *Psychological Medicine 7:*197–212.

Inhelder, B., and Piaget, J. (1958). *The Growth of Logical Thinking.* New York: Basic Books.

Janofsky, J. and Starfield, B. (1981). Assessment of risk in research on children. *Journal of Pediatrics 98:*842–846.

Jessner, L. (1959). Some observations on children hospitalized during latency. In *Dynamic Psychopathology in Childhood,* ed. L. Jessner and E. Pavenstedt. New York: Grune & Stratton.

Kinnoth, A. L., Lindsay, M. K. M., and Baum, J. D. (1983). Social and emotional complications in a clinical trial among adolescents with diabetes mellitus. *British Medical Journal 286:*952–954.

Kopp, C. B. (1989). Regulation of distress and negative emotions: A developmental view. *Developmental Psychology 25:*343–354.

Lattimer, J. D, et al. (1974). The optimum time to operate for cryptorchidism. *Pediatrics 53:*46.

Maccoby, E. E. (1983). Social-emotional development and response to stressors. In *Stress, Coping and Development in Children,* ed. N. Garmezy and M. Rutter. New York: McGraw-Hill, pp. 217–234.

Marcia, J. E. (1980). Identity in adolescence. In *Handbook of Adolescent Psychology,* ed. J. Adelson. New York: Wiley, pp. 159–187.

McAnarney, E. R., Pless, I. B., Satterwhite, B. B., et al. (1974). Psychological problems of children with chronic juvenile arthritis. *Pediatrics 53:*523–528.

Mussen, P. H., Conger, J. J., and Kagan, J. (1980). *Essentials of Child Development and Personality.* New York: Harper and Row.

Nicholls, J. G. (1978). The development of the concepts of effort and ability, perception of academic attainment, and the understanding that difficult tasks require more ability. *Child Development 49:*800–814.

Owens, M. E., and Todt, E. H. (1984). Pain in infancy: Neonatal response to heel lance. *Pain 20:*77–86.

Perrin, E. C., and Gerrity, P. S. (1981). There's a demon in your belly: Children's understanding of concepts regarding illness. *Pediatrics 67:*841.

Pless, I. B. (1979). Adjustment of the young chronically ill. In *Research in Community and Mental Health,* ed. R. Simmons. Greenwich, Conn.: JAI Press.

Prugh, D. G. (1983). Reactions of children and families to hospitalization and medical and surgical procedures. In *The Psychosocial Aspects of Pediatrics.* Philadelphia: Lea & Febiger, pp. 508–509.

Rheingold, H. L. Ethics as an integral part of research in child development. In *Strategies and Techniques of Child Study,* ed. R. Vasta. New York: Academic Press, pp. 305–324.

Robertson, J. (1968). *Young Children in Hospitals.* New York: Basic Books.

Ross, D. M., and Ross, S. A. (1984). The importance of type of questions, psychological climate and subject set in interviewing children about pain. *Pain 19:*71–79.

Rutter, M., Graham, P., Yule, W., et al. (1970). *A Neuropsychiatric Study in Childhood.* London: Spastics International Medical Publications, p. 203.

Schaffer, H. R., and Callender, W. M. (1959). Psychologic effects of hospitalization in infancy. *Pediatrics 24:*528.

Schwartz, A. H. (1972). Children's concepts of research hospitalization. *New England Journal of Medicine 287*:589–592.

Seidel, U. P., Chadwick, O. F. D., and Rutter, M. (1975). Psychological disorders in crippled children: A comparative study of children with and without brain damage. *Developmental Medicine and Child Neurology 17*:563–573.

Shannon, F. T., Fergusson, D. M., and Dimond, M. E. (1984). Early hospital admissions and subsequent behavior problems in 6 year olds. *Archives of the Diseases of Childhood 59*:815–819.

Shantz, C. U. (1983). Social cognition. In *Handbook of Child Psychology: Vol 3. Cognitive Development,* ed. J. H. Flavell and E. M. Markman. New York: Wiley, pp. 495–555.

Stern, M. T. (1987). Children's encounters with illness: Hospitalization and procedures. In *Encounters with Children: Pediatric Behavior and Development,* ed. S. D. Dixon and M. T. Stein. Chicago: Year Book Medical Publishers, pp. 367–376.

Tavormina, J. B., et al. (1976). Chronically ill children—a psychologically and emotionally deviant population? *Journal of Abnormal Child Psychology 4*:99–110.

Thompson, R. A. (1990). Vulnerability in research: A developmental perspective on research risk. *Child Development 61*:1–16.

Visitainer, M. A., and Wolfer, J. A. (1975). Psychological preparation for surgical pediatric patients: The effects on children's and parents' stress responses and adjustment. *Pediatrics 56*:187–202.

Williamson, P. S., and Williamson, M. L. (1983). Physiologic stress reduction by a local anesthetic during newborn circumcision. *Pediatrics 71*:36–40.

Zeltzer, L. K., Jay, S. M., and Fisher, D. M. (1989). The management of pain associated with pediatric procedures. *Pediatric Clinics of North America 36*:941–964.

7

Vulnerable Children

ROBERT E. COOKE

Previous chapters deal with the vulnerability of children in general. This chapter identifies specific groups of children who are especially likely to suffer greater harm or benefit less from research unless specific safeguards are in place.

Most of the in-depth analysis of this problem was carried out ten to fifteen years ago when Public Law 93–348 established the National Commission for the Protection of Human Subjects in Biomedical and Behavioral Research concerning research participation by the institutionalized mentally infirm (mentally retarded and mentally ill). Since that time, society has tended to normalize the condition of the mentally infirm, particularly through deinstitutionalization and integration into the larger community. Despite these social changes, many if not all of the original recommendations published in 1978 still pertain except for the exemption of research on education practices such as educational techniques, effectiveness, curriculum, and so on (Henning, 1988). This exemption of educational research on the grounds that it is innocuous may not be justified in the minds of some since it has the potential of producing more damage to a child psychologically than some biomedical research (Holder, 1986).

Unfortunately, few if any investigators in the field of ethics research related to children have had the resources to carry out in-depth investigations into the problem of vulnerable children as participants in research. Many important questions have been raised (Grodin and Alpert, 1988) but most authors continue to use the information unearthed by the original National Commission (McClowry, 1987; Coulter, Murray, and Cerreto, 1988).

The designation of a group of children or a particular child as "vulnerable" is arbitrary and varies according to individual circumstances. There is no such thing as a textbook child; children are even more varied than adults. They range from the 600 gm premature infant to the 120 kg obese adolescent. Growth and development lead to enormous diversity among well infants and children and disease processes greatly accentuate these differences.

As a consequence, children cannot be considered a homogeneous group of research subjects, and society may not have the knowledge necessary to assure that certain groups of them would be adequately protected. In some instances, so few of a particular group of children may exist any place in the world that the distribution of burdens and benefits of a proposed research project would be very limited. In other circumstances, it may not be possible for third parties to give adequate consent to a certain research procedure, as, for example, in the case of some institutionalized mentally handicapped children. Regardless of status, all children by law have limited competence, namely limited ability to understand and limited capacity to make decisions. Vulnerable children are even more limited functionally and are incapable of protecting their own interest (Levine, 1981).

Who are these children who are especially vulnerable? Many of those who might qualify for such a designation can be categorized by *extrinsic* (social, cultural, and environmental) and *intrinsic* (inherent in the child) factors that lead to greater vulnerability to any child in research. Extrinsic factors, such as the following, result from a wide variety of environmental circumstances, principally those involving significant persons in the life of the child—parents, guardians, or caretakers.

> One or no parents
>
> Divorced parents
>
> Abusing parents
>
> Mentally retarded or disturbed parents
>
> Impoverished environment
>
> Poverty
>
> Migrant status
>
> Homeless status
>
> Ethnic or religious barriers
>
> Institutional placement
>
> Foster placement

Intrinsic factors include physical, psychological, and emotional factors, such as the following, that set the child apart or appear to set the child apart from his or her peers so that he is perceived as substantially different from the norm.

Cognitive deficiencies

Emotional instability, especially Attention Deficit Disorder

Physical defects

Sensory deficiencies

AIDS

Genetic disorders or medical orphans

Dying

The presence of any of these factors may make adjustment to research especially difficult and may result in inadequate understanding of research activities or inadequate appreciation of risks and benefits incurred by the children. Thus determination of such children's suitability as research subjects becomes even more difficult. Some groups or classes of subjects—by virtue of their socioeconomic status, race, genetic background, or by the nature of their disease—may be more likely to be selected as subjects of research than most children, so that the distribution of risks and benefits may be inequitable. Examples of such selection bias include homeless and migrant children, children with genetic diseases, and children who receive Medicaid. Hospitalized children are also more likely to be chosen as research subjects than nonhospitalized children simply for administrative convenience. Research may be performed on any of these groups of children for the benefit of children who are less vulnerable, even though the risks to the subject children may exceed their own possible benefit. There are times when benefit might accrue to a group that is vulnerable by subjecting them to only minimal risk of harm. The problem is that many suffer from conditions that require research but those potential subjects are not likely to receive that benefit. However, if research is not carried out with certain classes or groups of subjects, or even with individuals who are especially vulnerable, the benefits of modern research might not accrue to them even though their special needs and problems may require much research in order to be alleviated.

Extrinsic Factors

One or No Parents

A high percentage of children live in one-parent families or in settings with no mother and father. Some of these children may be regarded as particularly vulnerable because of family disruption. While children in two-parent families may have the advantage of two adults acting jointly on their behalf, for many children a single parent obviously makes most or all of the decisions affecting his or her child in everyday life. This point is incorporated into the federal regulations on research with children. For higher-risk, lower-benefit research involving children, the regulation requires the consent of both parents if both are available. However, the consent of one parent is sufficient where only one is available.

In the case of a divorced or separated couple, the noncustodial parent, although estranged, may well retain an interest in the well-being of the child. He or she might have some legal standing as regards litigation if an untoward event occurs during the research. Clearly the presence of two parents in the family is no guarantee of appropriate decision making and differences between the two parents can be anticipated. Yet these should be respected, and where there are differences the child should not be a subject of research that carries risk of harm and little chance of benefit. If the research offers substantial benefit to the subject, then a single parent should be able to give adequate permission. Children with no parents who are intimately involved with the care of the child—for example, the institutionalized child, the foster child or orphan—should be selected as subjects only if the research can be especially beneficial to the particular child, when special precautions are taken to protect the child, or when the study itself is directed at the problem of foster children, orphans, and the like.

The importance of an intact family from the standpoint of participation in research rests with the ethical and social concept of family autonomy. As has been discussed repeatedly in this text and elsewhere, consent is necessary to recognize the autonomy and dignity of the individual. When little or no autonomy can be recognized, as in the case of an infant, a substitute concept can be considered. Infants and children are usually part of a unit, the family, which society recognizes as a fairly autonomous unit. The family can care for the child in a variety of ways without societal interference unless distinct harm to the child results. Parents choose the religion, the physical location, the education, the medical care, and the nutrition of their children. Some families do not raise their children as well as one wishes, but society does not step in unless there is serious harm to the child. Some parents may be limited in their understanding because of emotional and cognitive problems, a situation made worse because consent forms are commonly written for comprehension at the academic or scholarly level. Therefore, uninformed and possibly irresponsible consent or denial to participation might result.

The notion of family in the decision-making process leading to participation in research is critical when there are no parents or when one parent may be overburdened, isolated, and highly vulnerable. Trust, love, and care for the child are integral parts of a family. The obtaining of consent by the family for actions toward that child is out of respect for these *bonds,* not out of respect for the child as an autonomous being. Proxy consent can be seen equally as an attempt to protect the integrity of the family. Infants and children are part of families and of the human race. They are not to be excluded automatically from research because they cannot make decisions on their own behalf.

If the family is not intact, if the decision to participate by caring parents is not unanimous, caution should be taken in enlisting such a child. There may be considerable differences when a divorce or separation exists. Abusing parents certainly cannot be considered ideal decision makers for the child. Hauerwas (1977) points out that the child ought to be seen as a family member because of the child's special position within the family and is cared for on that basis. Third-person consent may be regarded as an attempt to protect the integrity of the family by ensuring that whatever is done to a child is consistent with the moral convictions and traditions of the child's family. Care should be taken in the blanket acceptance of the parents' wishes. Reasonable decisions might not be possible when parents are absent, disturbed, irrational, unintelligent, or in-experienced. A protection committee has been suggested as an adjunct to the Institutional Review Board in order to assess the adequacy and reasonableness of parental consent and the assent of the child over six years of age and in order to supervise recruitment of subjects (Lowe, Alexander, and Mishkin, 1974). The National Commission (1977) in its report involving children indi-cated in Recommendation 5 that a minor increase over minimal risk was ac-ceptable in nontherapeutic research with the assent of the child and permission and participation of their parents or guardians. In the discussion of Recommen-dation 7, the Commission said that "parental or guardian permission should reflect the 'collective judgment of the family' that an infant or child may partic-ipate in the research." For minimal risk research or therapeutic research, per-mission of one parent seems adequate to reflect the family consensus.

The institutional review board should determine for each project whether permis-sion of one or both parents should be required. This decision would be dependent on the nature of the project's activities; the age and status of the subject should also be considered. The institutional review board should also assure that children who will be asked to participate will have a good relationship with the parents and receive care in supportive surroundings. The institutional review board may appoint someone to assist in the selection of subjects and to review the quality and interaction between parents or guardians and the child. Because of the depen-dency of infants, the traditional role of parents as protectors and the general authority of parents to determine the care and upbringing of their children, the institutional review board may determine that small children should participate in research only if the parents or guardians participate themselves by being present during some or all of the conduct of the research. (National Commission, 1977, p.13).

If the infants or children are wards of the state, their participation in nontherapeutic research should be permitted only if there is an advocate appointed for each child to act like the parent. Unless a concerned adult is intimately involved with the child subject and is present whenever procedures are carried out, an advocate cannot function adequately and must depend on the judgment of the researcher thereby rendering the already vulnerable child even more vulnerable.

> As a general rule, when infants participate in research that may cause physical discomfort or emotional stress and involves a significant departure from normal routine, a parent or guardian should be present. Generally, parents or guardians should be sufficiently involved in the research to understand its effects on their child and be able to intervene if necessary. (National Commission, 1977, p.15).

The sociodemographic and motivational characteristics of parents who volunteer their children for clinical research have been studied in a controlled way by Harth and Thong (1990). They concluded that "parents who volunteer their children for medical research are significantly more socially disadvantaged and emotionally vulnerable" than a control group that did not volunteer their children. Only 15 percent of mothers and 16 percent of fathers who volunteered their children had a tertiary or university education compared with 26 percent of mothers and 45 percent of fathers who did not volunteer their children. Volunteering parents also exhibited greater substance abuse but they were motivated to find better ways to help their own children as well as others. Whether these results from Great Britain can be generalized to the United States is not clear, but caution should be exercised whenever parents seem overeager to have their children be research subjects.

Poverty and Minority Status

Although researchers do not intentionally discriminate against poor or minority children, such children are overrepresented in many research protocols, perhaps because university or university-affiliated hospitals where most biomedical research is conducted are located in inner cities close to centers of poverty. A study of research in children carried out by the University of Michigan found that hospital patients, in contrast to normal children living in the community, served as subjects in 84 percent of projects reviewed by institutional review boards in children's hospitals, while 72 percent of research projects in other biomedical settings used hospital patients (Tannenbaum and Cooke, 1977). Research carried out with subjects other than patients may show a similar over-representation of poor and minority children for exactly the same reasons, although some studies have been carried out in private practitioners' offices and there the distribution of white middle class children may be somewhat over-represented.

By contrast, behavioral research has a much broader selection of subjects and does not depend as much upon hospital patient populations. Because children of migrant families frequently lack familiarity with local medical facilities or personnel and lack support systems, they should be used as research subjects only when there is a particular medical or social problem that applies to them. Many migrants, and especially the homeless, lack consistent health care and may be at greater risk in biomedical research as a consequence. Migrant status also interferes with adequate follow-up and adds substantial administrative inconvenience to the conduct of the research. The homeless child provides even greater problems despite the fact that the study of the medical and psychological problems of homeless children may be critical to their well-being.

Religious and Ethnic Barriers

Children who are members of families who belong to religious groups that oppose some aspects of biomedical research or treatment are vulnerable in the sense that research directed at improving the treatment of the child, or therapeutic research, may not be permitted by the family. Out of respect for the autonomy of families, no participation is possible unless the family agrees after thorough study of all the arguments that have been presented. It is not reasonable to take legal action against the family when the therapeutic intervention is still highly experimental, although it may be reasonable to consider legal action in order to provide generally accepted lifesaving therapy.

Conducting research on children in other countries, particularly in underdeveloped countries, cannot be justified unless the same procedural rules are used as in the United States and there is a reasonable chance that the benefits of the research can equitably accrue to those children as well as to ours. The ethical principles of beneficence, justice, and respect for persons are universal and not constrained by national borders. Their application should not be restricted solely to the United States. These children should not be excluded from the benefits or the minimal risks of research arbitrarily but they should not be the targets for easy exploitation because their country has no guidelines for research comparable to those in the United States.

In all of these situations, research directed at the unique social aspects of the child—for example, the study of the effects of abusing parents, or the medical, psychological, and social needs of the homeless child—may be extremely difficult to carry out. Observation in public settings without intrusion is generally acceptable without family consent, but more intrusive studies should be carried out only if permission of the participants is obtained.

The American Academy of Pediatrics Committee on Drugs (1977) in its Guidelines for the Ethical Conduct of Studies to Evaluate Drugs in Pediatric Populations states:

> *General Considerations.* Subjects enrolled in clinical investigation should represent a cross section of society insofar as possible. The study should not rely exclusively or heavily on one socioeconomic, racial, or ethnic group when this type of selection is not a necessary part of the investigation. The institutional review committee must be uniquely sensitive to this principle and ask if there is an equitable distribution of risks and inconveniences of this investigation throughout all societal groups. This is especially important when the study group will be drawn from an institution or community frequented mainly by one socioeconomic, racial, and/or ethnic group. The institutional review committee must consider whether one group from the population at large will bear an undue portion of the burdens or will be able to avail itself of an undue portion of the benefits if the research is conducted at only one institution. If there is an imbalance, the institutional review committee must ask whether other population groups can be added to the study in the same community, as well as whether a multi-center program could distribute the risks and benefits more appropriately without adversely altering the study design. When studies are conducted at only one institution, ethical practice requires that a reasonable cross section of all groups in the community participate.
>
> *Special Consideration.* Institutionalized retarded children and other children who are confined in a residential facility may be selected as subjects of a study only if the study involves situations or conditions peculiar to these individuals and the information sought can only be obtained from their participation. Special safeguards may have to be provided to assure that appropriate consent is obtained for these children's participation.

Intrinsic Factors

Of all the intrinsic factors listed previously, the institutionalized mentally infirm child represents the most studied class of subjects since they were specifically identified by Congress for study and recommendation by the National Commission for the Protection of Human Subjects. The term *institutionalized mentally infirm* applied to both emotionally disturbed and mentally retarded persons who are not living in their own homes with parents. The Commission stated that:

> [I]n no other area of the Commission's mandate has the need for research been so clearly manifest, so little is known about the factors. From a review of the pertinent literature and site visits to institutions for the mentally ill and the retarded, the Commission is profoundly impressed by the paucity of knowledge relating to the care and treatment of persons institutionalized as mentally infirm and by the historical role of such persons as social outcasts. In no other area of the Commission's mandate is the need for research been so clearly manifest. So little is known about the factors that cause mental retardation and the conditions known as mental illness that efforts to prevent such disabilities are in the primitive stages. Clearly, improvements are in order and these improvements are strongly dependent upon research. (National Commission, 1978, p. 155)

In 1985, the federal government spent more than $7.7 billion for programs serving the retarded, yet only 0.85 percent ($64 million) was spent on research (Braddock, 1986). What part of these research funds applied to children with mental retardation is unknown, but it was substantially less than was needed. More than half the projects funded were behavioral, with less than 5 percent of the total with risks considered more than minimal.

Public interest in the propriety of research on the mentally retarded (infirm) first appeared in relation to the trial of hepatitis vaccine on residents of Willowbrook State School in Staten Island, New York, by Krugman and associates in 1955 (Krugman and Ward, 1958). These trials were called "scandalous" by some, good science by others, and humanitarian by others. Politicians expressed public outrage. Willowbrook was cited as one of the reasons for the legislation creating the National Commission for the Protection of Human Subjects in Biological and Behavioral Research. In 1986 Krugman stated that "I am as convinced today as I was at that time that our studies were ethical and justifiable. This judgment is based on knowledge of the extraordinary conditions that existed in the institution as well as on an assessment of the potential risks and benefits to the participants" (Krugman, 1986). In 1973, the *New England Journal of Medicine* agreed and stated its editorial policy this way: "Reports of investigations performed unethically are not accepted for publication. Thus, appearance of another Willowbrook report in this issue indicates that the study, on balance, is not rated as unethical" (Ingelfinger, 1973).

The facts are that Willowbrook was built for 3000 mentally retarded infants and children in 1942 but it was used by the U.S. Army as Halloran General Hospital for the first five years of its existence. By 1955 there were 4000 residents, and later, 6000. The conditions are described by a director at that time:

Of the 6,000, 77% were severely and profoundly retarded, 60% were not toilet trained, 39% were not ambulatory, 30% had seizures, 64% were incapable of feeding themselves. The hepatitis rate (clinical jaundice) was 25 per 1,000 among children and 40 per 1,000 among adults. By the use of improved tests of hepatic function, it was found that most newly admitted children were destined to contract hepatitis infection under the conditions that existed in the institution as shown by the fact that 79 percent of the residents had hepatitis A and B markers of past infection. (Krugman, 1986).

Krugman further states that extensive efforts were made to obtain informed consent from the parents and that protocols were carefully reviewed by the New York University and Willowbrook—equivalents of institutional review boards in 1957. The scientific results of the epidemiologic and laboratory studies and of the clinical trials were valuable in the prevention of hepatitis worldwide and those immunized at Willowbrook were prevented from acquiring more serious natural infection.

However, in hindsight, it is appropriate to criticize the use of such vulnerable infants and children in studies that entailed more than minimal risk as the first recipients of possibly hazardous vaccines. Adult volunteers capable of giving informed consent could have been recruited as subjects. Staff volunteers instead of residents would have been more appropriate, but the numbers would not have been adequate to draw valid conclusions from the data. It is clear, however, that the motivation of all the investigators, although misguided and insensitive according to present day standards, was to help the residents of Willowbrook. Consent from parents was obtained, but the quality of the consent could be questioned because there was substantial indication that ties between residents and parents were relatively weak. Certainly the moral outrage that was expressed by so many publicly should have been directed not only at Krugman and his investigators but also at the state government, the public, and the parents for tolerating such outrageous living conditions for so many vulnerable infants, children, and adults.

Legal and Ethical Issues

Despite a paucity of case law, it is generally agreed that children who are mentally retarded or temporarily incapacitated by mental illness cannot assent to participate in research on their own, as older children without these handicaps might be able to do. Whether third-party consent is appropriate for this group has been argued vigorously. However, to prohibit the use of these children and the mentally ill as experimental subjects when no feasible alternatives are available is to continue the present level of ignorance that surrounds these conditions. Various studies have attempted to determine appropriate limits on the use of this class of subjects. The Nuremberg Code seemed to block such research, but the author of a memorandum to the War Crimes Court proposed that "in the case of mentally ill patients for the purpose of experiments concerning the nature and treatment of nervous and mental illness or related subjects, such consent of the next of kin or legal guardian is required. Whenever the mental state of the patient permits, that is, in those mentally ill patients who are not delirious or confused, his own consent should be obtained in addition (this obviously applied only to adults). There is a notation that such a provision was not included in the final Nuremberg Code possibly because it did not apply to the specific cases under trial" (National Commission, 1978).

Ramsey (1970) categorically rejects research on these patients unless it is for their specific benefit because they cannot consent. He states that "Nontherapeutic, non-diagnostic experimentation involving human subjects must be based on true consent if it is to proceed as a human enterprise." In the case of "beneficial research," Ramsey considers third-party consent a proper fulfillment of the obligation to protect vulnerable subjects; in the case of nonbeneficial research, he considered third-party permission a breach of the duty to care and protect. In *Wyatt vs. Stickney* (1972/73), a case involving an institution for the mentally ill and retarded in Alabama, the court mandated that, with regard to research, "patients shall have a right not to be subjected to experimental research without the express and informed consent of the patient if the patient is able to give such consent, and of his guardian or next of kin after opportunities for consultation with independent specialists and legal counsel." The 1975 Willowbrook decree carried an absolute prohibition against medical experimentation.

Hauerwas (1970) takes the position that the child, particularly the child with limited abilities, is owed protection as a moral responsibility of the child's family. When the child is ill, as with the mentally infirm, he feels that there is an even greater moral obligation of society to provide protection because of the kind of people we wish to be. Protection of children (under these circumstances) is not paternalism but is part of the responsibility of the community "doing what is best for children." In addition, the sick child, and frequently the mentally retarded, may have a reduced capacity to dissent. It is common for the mentally retarded to act passively and compliantly in an effort to avoid criticism for being considered uncooperative or deviant. The expression of even limited autonomy is commonly not encouraged by caretakers.

Under these circumstances, even protection by the family may be flawed since family judgment may be impaired by the emotional impact of having an ill or handicapped child. The child may be a burden physically, emotionally or financially, or parents may become dependent on the therapist or clinician, thereby altering their judgment. Unreal expectations of returning to normality may cloud the family's perception of therapeutic research. For example, in the 1950s, a number of parents of children with Down syndrome gave permission for a major and dangerous surgical procedure—jugular carotid anastomosis—in the vain hope that increased brain vascularization would improve intelligence. Likewise, numerous other therapeutic experiments have been undertaken, particularly with the mentally retarded, with the permission of caring parents, despite substantial risk of harm or discomfort, all in the vain hope that cognitive function could be improved or appearance normalized.

Emotional disorders in children introduce an additional complication in the conduct of research, as an example in the experimental treatment of attention deficit hyperactive disorder. This common disorder of childhood, which has been identified in 8–10 percent of school-age children, is not debilitating in the usual sense but hyperactivity, limited attention span, uncooperative behavior, and social inappropriateness is difficult for parents and teachers to cope with. The question can be asked is, To whom is the treatment directed, child or caretaker? Better control may improve school performance and socialization for the child, but it also may make life easier for teachers and parents. If treatment improves the long-term academic and social adjustment of the child either through his or her improved performance or through improved regard by teachers or parents, research on drug therapy may be justified providing the risks of harm are minimal. The toxic side effects should have been studied in adult volunteers prior to their use with vulnerable children. How much risk the child should be subjected to in such a situation should be reviewed carefully on a case-by-case basis in drug trials for this condition, especially since tics may appear and Gilles de la Tourette syndrome may be uncovered as a complication of stimulant therapy (Wilens and Biederman, 1992).

One of the more difficult issues that the National Commission for the Protection of Human Subjects contended with was research on a particular diagnostic category—for example, Down's syndrome—with no prospect of benefit to the group of subjects or the individual subject. In such a situation, non–Down syndrome subjects could not be used meaningfully since the biological or behavioral processes to be studied existed only in those children with Down syndrome. The moral question is whether or not any person, child, or adult with a particular disorder or diagnosis has any greater obligation to future generations with the same disorder than the average person. If normal healthy adults cannot be drafted for research to help others without their consent, should it be possible to give third-party proxy for research on more vulnerable people—the ill, handicapped, or disordered? Nevertheless the majority of the members of the National Commission (1978) recommended that nontherapeutic research could be carried out providing the risk of harm was only a minor degree above minimal. This recommendation was supported by the majority of commission members on the grounds that the anticipated knowledge would be of vital importance for the understanding or amelioration of the type of disorder or condition of the subjects or might possibly benefit the subject in the future.

At the time I disagreed with the recommendation and I still disagree. Unless the anticipated knowledge might reasonably benefit the individual subject, any risk that is greater than minimal as defined for nonvulnerable children is unacceptable. There is no greater moral obligation for a mentally infirm subject toward others of his disease class, present or future, than for any other person in society, even though in biological terms (for example chromosome number) there may be some closer relationship. Since it is accepted that normal persons should not be enrolled in nontherapeutic research with more than minimal risk unless they can give informed and meaningful consent, it is doubly unreasonable that the mentally infirm should be so enrolled. The mentally infirm, especially the mentally retarded, have few opportunities for decision making even when normalization is the accepted principle of care. Furthermore, it is often the case that the nature of their condition weakens their capacity to make responsible choices on their own behalf.

Although some members of the National Commission felt that the opportunity to participate in research might enrich the somewhat impoverished lives of the mentally retarded, it is very unlikely that there is a great deal of psychic benefit for children whose participation in ordinary daily life is so limited. Such an approach projects onto disabled children a willingness to take risks for the benefit of others—a value not considered important by most people in our society. Vulnerable children should be given greater protection, not less.

The Law Reform Commission of Canada has banned experimentation on confined mentally disordered people when the choice of subjects is based solely on grounds of ease of observation and analysis of results. However, the commission did approve nontherapeutic biomedical experimentation on mentally deficient persons providing certain conditions were met, namely: that the research was important; that it could not be done on consenting adults; that it did not involve serious risks; that there is consent of the person's representatives; that a third party's (judge, lawyer, or ombudsman) approval was obtained; and that the person's refusal was respected (Law Reform Commission of Canada, 1989).

Sex research involving the mentally retarded is a special case that also requires additional protection since understanding of the procedures may be substantially more difficult (Jonsen and Mann, 1980).

All of the recommendations from the work of the National Commission, unfortunately, carry no official governmental force since no regulations regarding the mentally infirm have been promulgated. Neither the administration nor the Congress has moved to demand a set of regulations over the past thirteen years. Institutional review boards (IRBs) therefore operate without firm guidelines; substantial deviations from one research setting to another exist in research protocols using mentally infirm subjects, including children.

The Dying Child

Research conducted on children with terminal illness presents many of the problems discussed earlier. Parents are understandably distraught. Their judgment may be clouded by grief and, at times, guilt. Some parents may even feel that their child's death can be rationalized if the research helps others. The death of an ill child or the life of a profoundly handicapped child may be considered more "meaningful" if the child makes a contribution to other children. Although these are noble sentiments and may reduce the grief of the parents, the terminally ill child may not appreciate or benefit from their wishes. Hauerwas (1977) expresses the belief of many that the sick child, especially the dying child, needs greater, not less, protection. The late Robert Turtle, Esq., a valuable member of the commission, expresses the problem succinctly when he said that "sick children cannot be deemed to be a morally relevant separate class for purposes of relaxing protective measures. The concept of minimal risk, that is, like usual experience, is not applicable because sick children already are or have been exposed to a good deal of discomfort and risk" (Turtle, 1977). Investigators also see the dying child as someone who cannot be hurt further or who can have no lasting memory. Such an approach makes the dying child even more vulnerable and ignores the need for greater protection rather than less for such children.

On the other hand some may view the administration of a Phase I drug (a drug whose safety and efficacy in humans has not been determined) as a last hope worthy of pursuit (Cogliano-Shutta, 1986). Allowing the dying child to participate in making an informed choice between the use of research drugs and no further chemotherapy also recognizes the matured autonomy of that child and would seem to be a reasonable approach borne out by empiric studies (Nitschke et al., 1982).

Genetic Disorder

Reference has already been made to the use of children with Down syndrome as research subjects. Because of the great number of genetic possibilities and the enormous genetic heterogeneity that exist in humans, certain children may be one of a handful of potential subjects for research that could lead to future prevention or alleviation of the disorder. As noted earlier in this chapter, Do such children, or do their parents, have any special obligation to participation in nontherapeutic research? And yet how will such problems be solved if ignorance continues? Adult subjects who can give valid consent would be preferable but, if the disorder is lethal in childhood, that relief would not pertain. The collection of research information that is part of routine care with no additional risk or discomfort might provide valuable information. The development of tissue culture techniques as an in vitro representation of the human genome seems to be the ultimate solution of this moral dilemma. When a genetic abnormality is largely, if not exclusively, limited to a given ethnic or racial group (Tay Sach's disease or sickle cell disease, for example), a burden may be placed on that group in the selection of subjects without benefit to the particular individual, even though others might benefit subsequently from the knowledge gained. Again, the use of tissue culture as a representation of the individual or the discovery or even creation of animal models might obviate the problems. It seems reasonable to carry out research on subjects with particular problems, but they have no obligation to accept more risk than unaffected children (so-called normal children).

When environmental factors that increase vulnerability are complicated by intrinsic factors that do the same, much care must be given in the selection of human subjects. For example, a child with a genetic disorder living in a single-parent home or institution with multiple caretakers or abusing parents should rank very low in priority during the selection of research subjects unless that research has a good probability of helping that individual.

AIDS

Nowhere are these complications more evident than in the case of the study of infants and children with maternally acquired AIDS. The infants and children are commonly ill with recurrent infection and are chronically neurologically damaged. One or both parents may be dying; one or both parents may be drug abusers; and social deprivation may also be present. Quality foster care may be needed but difficult to obtain. In addition, privacy issues are important not only because of the stigma of AIDS in the public mind but because the child may be deprived of social, educational, or therapeutic opportunity as a consequence. On the other hand, the need for more knowledge concerning congenital AIDS is critical. Investigators must therefore exert extraordinary care in the selection of subjects and in the informing of parents, and in the conduct of the research.

Selection of Subjects

To avoid the inappropriate use of subjects who are vulnerable because of social limitations of the family, careful review of the selection process should be carried out by the investigator. Unfortunately, most research proposals are not scrutinized in great detail by institutional review boards as regards the selection of subjects. According to the last published report (Tannenbaum and Cooke, 1977), only 10 percent of research proposals were returned to investigators for clarification of subject selection. By contrast the consent portion of proposals was returned for correction 25 percent of the time. If a child is a patient in a hospital or clinic and there is a consenting parent or guardian, further investigation of the motives, capabilities, and socioeconomic standard, minority status, etc., is rarely carried out. The quality of the past parenting is almost never looked at unless there is physical evidence of abuse. Since alcohol or drug abuse is so common in the general population, an appraisal of the quality of parenting should be carried out to avoid overrepresentation of socially vulnerable children in nontherapeutic research. Charles Lowe and colleagues (1974) have suggested that a parent monitor is important, and children who have good relationships with parents and receive care in supportive surroundings are more appropriate subjects of nontherapeutic research.

Assent and Dissent of Vulnerable Children

Children with limited cognitive ability or emotional stability may not be able to provide the quality of assent or dissent appropriate for their chronological age. "The developmental level which will vary from child to child is a better determinant" (Group for the Advancement of Psychiatry, 1989). Language, cultural, or religious barriers may also interfere with the process of understanding the research or expressing the child's feelings.

The Medical Research Council of Canada distinguishes legal incapacity from incapacity to consent to a medical act. "Just because a person is under guardianship should not mean he should automatically be deprived of the right to express his opinion regarding a medical act, if at the time he possesses the necessary capacity and understanding" (Law Reform Commission of Canada, 1989).

Suggested Safeguards

The National Commission for the Protection of Human Subjects (1978) published formal recommendations regarding the participation of the mentally infirm in biomedical and behavioral research, as noted earlier in this chapter. Much of the reasoning and some of the recommendations that supplement those pertaining to research using children as subjects are applicable to other vulnerable children. However, a number of other measures need to be considered in the review of research protocols involving these children.

1. There should be improved scrutiny in the selection of subjects for research to ensure that the risk and benefits of research are distributed fairly throughout the child population. Hospital patients should be supplemented with office patients if possible; if not, a balance of private and insured patients should be attained along with Medicaid patients. Likewise, Medicaid should not be used as a funding vehicle for the support of the cost of hospitalization for research subjects since it may serve as an inducement to investigators to use socially vulnerable children. The possible overrepresentation of minorities in nontherapeutic research or occasional underrepresentation in therapeutic research must be addressed by each IRB. The American Academy of Pediatrics Committee on Drugs (1977) summarizes its position this way: "Subjects enrolled in clinical investigation should represent a cross-section of society insofar as possible. Investigators should not rely heavily on one social, racial or ethnic group when this type of selection is not a necessary part of the investigation."

2. It is important that each investigator proposing to recruit children who are vulnerable for any reason be required to justify the involvement of such subjects. These children should be permitted to participate only if the research is relevant to their condition; if the research is not potentially beneficial to the individual, participation should be allowed only if the risk is no more than minimal.

3. A consent auditor or parent monitor should be appointed to examine the quality of the proxy consent given when usual parental decision making is not possible or when the possibility of significant harm exists. Such a system would help to prevent the performance of untested therapeutic procedures that parents may wish to have carried out to help their disabled child such as carotid jugular anastomosis mentioned earlier in this chapter.

4. As a necessary precondition, enrollment of the highly vulnerable should not be undertaken unless they are the only relevant subjects. For example, recruitment of the homeless in research should be permitted only for the study of the problem of homeless children, not those of the average child, and there should be an order of preference in the selection of subjects that proceeds from less vulnerability to more. Unfortunately, no scale of vulnerability has been developed. The American Bar Association (1973) states the issue with clarity: "If there are two classes of subjects, one of which is already severely burdened and the other of which is much less burdened, then in order to equalize the distribution of burdens, the latter class ought to accept any additional risks.'' Members of the National Commission (1978) differed in their consideration of this issue as it pertained to the institutionalized mentally infirm. In the deliberations and conclusions of the National Commission:

> There was a difference of opinion among Commission members as to (1) whether institutionalized individuals should participate in research when suitable non-institutionalized subjects are available; and (2) whether institutionalized individuals should participate in research that is not relevant to their particular condition. Some members of the Commission felt strongly that an individual who is institutionalized as mentally infirm should not participate, or be asked to participate, in research for which non-institutionalized persons would be suitable subjects. The rationale for this position is two-fold: first, that institutionalized individuals are particularly vulnerable to exploitation and, second, that they already carry burdens from their disability and their institutionalization, and it is therefore unjust to ask them to assume any additional burdens. It is feared that persons in institutions will be involved disproportionately and unfairly in research because they are convenient and because their presence in an institutionalized setting might reduce the expense of conducting research. Further, it was suggested that those outside the institution, although perhaps also burdened by disabilities, are likely to have caring persons to assist and protect them, if necessary. Therefore, some members of the Commission proposed that even for research that is relevant to a mental disability, selection of subjects should be limited to individuals who are not institutionalized, where possible.
>
> On the other hand, some Commission members felt just as strongly that it is incorrect to assume that participation in research is always a burden or that being in an institution is always a damaging experience. They suggested that participation in research may have beneficial effects, such as interaction with people from outside the institution or, at least, additional attention. Research tasks may be interesting and a welcome change from the boredom of institutional life, although relief from boredom does not in itself justify participation in research.

Despite arguments that participation in research may offer new opportunities for choice for this class of people, this author remains convinced that there are other opportunities and experiences other than research that entails any risk or unfair distribution of benefits.

5. Inducements to participate in research, whether in foreign countries or the United States, should not be so great as to attract subjects from impoverished groups so that imbalance in the socioeconomic mix of subjects occurs. Compensation for expenses incurred seems fair, but payments or gifts to families or subjects that attract socially vulnerable people here or in other countries should not be allowed.

6. A substituted judgment—that is, third-party decisions as to what someone would wish—cannot be applied to children with a possible exception of older adolescents because children, unlike mentally ill or elderly adults, have never had the capacity to enumerate their own values or desires regarding participation in research. Paul Ramsey (1970) and others, have emphasized that proxy permission treats persons as means, not as ends in themselves, and is a violation of the ethical principle of respect for personhood. Beneficence requires that subjects be protected from harm and that there be positive benefits from the research. The possibility of good must justify the possibilities of harm. When there is to be no benefit, then any risk is excessive if the subject is vulnerable. From the practical standpoint, proxy permission with certain classes of children may be invalidated by differences in culture or language. Several of Levine's eleven elements of information needed to meet the requirements of "informed consent" may be invalidated when vulnerability is the consequence of environmental factors (Levine, 1977).

Parents who are themselves retarded may not understand the overall purpose of the research as well as the description of discomforts, risks, and benefits. They may not feel comfortable or be competent to ask appropriate questions.

7. The consent process in the case of research involving vulnerable children must be carried out with constant recognition that participation in research for the benefit of others cannot be imposed on anyone against their will without violating universal ethical principles. The argument that doing good for others is ennobling may be true, but only if the subject freely volunteers and is not conscripted. In addition, many vulnerable children will not understand the abstractions involved in *ennoblement*. Assent of the vulnerable subject is doubly important before research is undertaken and much time and effort should be devoted to assisting vulnerable children to understand what is involved in participation. Complete parental responsibility for the consent process assumes that parents always act with both good will and good sense. Since this may not always be true, the child's wishes should be respected.

8. In the conduct of the research, every effort should be made to use materials gained from procedures carried out in the usual treatment of the participants so that additional risk of harm or discomfort is minimized. Because genetic and biomedical research is critical for mentally vulnerable children, the value of tissue culture where feasible is immeasurable. The development of techniques for differentiating cells in culture should be strongly encouraged so that organ-specific biochemical studies can be carried out without the need for invasive procedures. Although such developments are not specific for vulnerable children they are more frequently applicable particularly to children with severe mental retardation where genetic defects are so common.

9. In the conduct of research, investigators should make certain that, in the case of institutionalized subjects or other children in unfavorable social situations, the research does not prolong residence in that inadequate setting in any way.

10. The privacy of subjects should be maintained with vulnerable children just as with the less vulnerable, only more so. Even though public wards or public programs (Medicaid) or public institutions are used, having fewer worldly goods should not diminish protection.

11. Whenever possible, parents should be present during all procedures so that they can make appropriate decisions regarding further participation or nonparticipation in research.

Marion Yarrow (1977) of the National Institute of Mental Health succinctly stated many of these issues: "To assure that scientific objectives do not overshadow an evaluation of the effects of a study on children, the investigator should be knowledgeable about their vulnerabilities and capacities, always attending to the social and psychological child as well as the biological child."

Conclusion

Although most IRBs have operated for fifteen years under guidelines promulgated by the National Commission but not formally approved by the Department of Health and Human Services, sensitivity to the need for special consideration for vulnerable children, whether on biological or social grounds, has not been characteristic of some review groups in the author's experience. Nowhere is the insensitivity more evident that in the selection of subjects who may be poor or a minority or with disrupted families. All of these classes are overrepresented in most university hospital inpatient units or outpatient clinics. Likewise the quality of the decision making process by families who agree to enroll their vulnerable children is rarely questioned even though many of these children come from families that have difficulty in coping with commonplace problems of everyday living.

IRBs need to take on an additional responsibility in the case of research that does not hold out the prospect of benefit to the subject—namely to investigate the motivation of the families who volunteer their children as well as the nature of the families both socially and economically so that vulnerable children do not assume an undue burden of risks in relation to benefits.

References

American Academy of Pediatrics Committee on Drugs (1977). Guidelines for the ethical conduct of studies to evaluate drugs in pediatric populations. *Pediatrics* 60:91–102.

American Bar Association (1973). Statement on the mentally disabled. *Mental Disability Law Reporter 1:*156.

Braddock, D. (1986). From Roosevelt to Reagan: Federal spending for mental retardation and developmental disabilities. *American Journal of Mental Deficiency* 90(5):479–489.

Cogliano-Shutta, W. A. (1986). Pediatric phase I clinical trials: Ethical issues and nursing considerations. *Oncology Nursing Forum 13*(2):29–32.

Conley, R. W. (1973). *The Economics of Mental Retardation.* Baltimore: Johns Hopkins Press.

Cooke, R. E. (1978). In *Asymmentrical Function of the Brain,* ed. M. Kinsbourne. New York: Cambridge University Press.

Cooke, R. E. (1978). *Dissenting Statement.* HEW Publication (OS) 78–0006, pp. 122–123. Washington, D.C.: Department of Health, Education, and Welfare.

Cooke, R. E. (1980). Clinical research on children. In *Issues in Research with Human Subjects.* NIH Publication 80–1858, pp. 109–117. Bethesda, Md.: National Institutes of Health.

Coulter, D. J., Murray, T. H., and Cerreto, M. L. (1988). Practical ethics in pediatrics. *Current Problems in Pediatrics 18*(3):143–195.

Grodin, M. A., and Alpert, J. J. (1988). Children as participants in medical research. *Pediatric Clinics of North America 35*(6):1389–1401.

Group for the Advancement of Psychiatry Committee on Child Psychiatry (1989). *The Ages of Rights and Responsibilities, Report No. 126.* New York: Brunner/Mazel, pp. 53–75.

Harth, S. C., and Thong, Y. H. (1990). Sociodemographic and motivational characteristics of parents who volunteer their children for clinical research: A controlled study. *British Medical Journal 300:*1372–1376.

Hauerwas, S. (1970). Must a patient be a person to be a patient. Or my Uncle Charlie may not be much of a person but he still is my Uncle Charlie. *Connecticut Medicine 39:*815–817.

Hauerwas, S. (1977). *Rights, Duties and Experimentation on Children: A Critical Response to Worsfold and Bartholome.* HEW Publication 77–0005, appendix, pp. 5–22.

Henning, J. S. (1988). *The Rights of Children.* Springfield, Ill.: Charles C Thomas, p. 190.

Holder, A. R. (1986). *Legal Issues in Pediatrics and Adolescent Medicine.* New Haven, Conn.: Yale University Press, p. 160.

Ingelfinger, F. J. (1973). Ethics of experiments on children. *New England Journal of Medicine 288:*791–792.

Jonsen, A. R., and Mann, R. (1980). Ethics of sex research involving children and the mentally retarded. In *Ethical Issues in Sex Therapy and Research,* vol. 2, ed. V. E. Johnson and W. H. Masters. Boston: Little Brown.

Krugman, S. (1986). The Willowbrook hepatitis studies revisited: Ethical aspects. *Review of Infectious Diseases 8:*157–162.

Krugman, S., and Ward, R. (1958). Clinical and experimental studies of infectious hepatitis. *Pediatrics 22:*1016–1022.

Law Reform Commission of Canada (1989). Working Paper 61, *Biomedical Experimentation Involving Human Subjects.* Ottawa, Canada.

Levine, R. J. (1977). *The Nature and Definition of Informed Consent in Various Re-*

search Settings. Cited by L. R. Ferguson, HEW Publication (OS) 77–005, p. 4–5. Washington, D.C.: Department of Health, Education, and Welfare.

Levine, R. J. (1981). *Ethics and Regulation of Clinical Research.* Baltimore: Urban and Schwarzenberg, pp. 54, 172.

Lowe, C., Alexander, D., and Mishkin, B. (1974). Non-therapeutic research in children: An ethical dilemma. *Journal of Pediatrics 84:*468.

McClowry, S. G. (1987). Research and treatment: ethical distinctions related to the care of children. *Journal of Pediatric Nursing 2*(1):23–9

National Commission for the Protection of Human Subjects of Biomedical and Behavioral Research (1977). *Research Involving Children.* HEW Publication (OS) 77–0004. Washington, D.C.: Department of Health, Education, and Welfare.

National Commission for the Protection of Human Subjects of Biomedical and Behavioral Research (1978). *Research Involving Those Institutionalized as Mentally Infirm.* HEW Publication (OS) 78–0006. Washington, D.C.: Department of Health, Education, and Welfare.

Nitschke, R., Bennett Humphrey, G., Saxaner, C. L., Catron, B., Wunder, S., and Jay, S. (1982). Therapeutic choices made by patients with end-stage cancer. *Journal of Pediatrics 101*(3):471–476.

Ramsey, P. (1970). *The Patient as a Person.* New Haven, Conn.: Yale University Press, p. 14.

Schwartz, A. H. (1972). Children's concepts of research hospitalization. *New England Journal of Medicine 287:*588–592.

Tannenbaum, A. S., and Cooke, R. A. (1977). *Research Involving Children.* HEW Publication No. (OS) 77–0005, Appendix, pp. 1–10. Washington, D.C.: Department of Health, Education, and Welfare.

Turtle, R. (1977). *Dissenting Statement.* HEW Publication No. (OS) 77–0004, pp. 146–153. Washington, D.C.: Department of Health, Education, and Welfare.

Wilens, T. E., and Biederman, J. (1992). The stimulants. *Psychiatric Clinics of North American 15*(1):191–222.

Wyatt vs. Stickney (MD. Ala. 1972), (M.D. Ala. 1973). 344 F. Supp. 373, 344 F. Supp. 387.

Yarrow, M. R. (1977). *Summary of Testimony before the National Commission for the Protection of Human Subjects of Biomedical and Behavioral Research.* HEW Publication No. (OS) 77–0004, p. 69. Washington, D.C.: Department of Health, Education, and Welfare.

Appendix A

Points to Consider in Proposing or Reviewing Research Involving Children

What follows is a set of issues that we think investigators and reviewers of research with children should consider before approving or conducting research. While several of these considerations should apply to all human subjects, they are particularly pertinent to the protection of children as subjects. It is assumed that all other aspects of review as required by the federal regulations have been complied with.

1. Is the use of children as research subjects justified in this instance?
   (a) Has research with animals been completed?
   (b) if the research question can be addressed first in adults, has research with adults been conducted?
   (c) has the adult research produced results that would indicate that the proposed research would benefit, or not be harmful to, the child-subjects?

2. Are the personnel involved in the research, and the facility in which it will be conducted knowledgeable about and sensitive to the physical and psychological needs of the children and their families?

3. Have the investigators taken into account the child-subject's previous experience with illness and medical interventions? Some children, particularly older ones, may cope better as a result of previous experiences with medical encounters. Other children may find that the research intervention adds too many additional burdens to what is required for their care.

4. Is the proposed number of child-subjects the fewest necessary to obtain statistically significant data from which valid conclusions can be drawn? Using too few subjects to obtain valid information, or more than the minimum necessary, puts subjects at risk without the counterbalancing benefits.

5. Are the proposed techniques the least invasive necessary, from both a physical and psychological perspective?

6. Have the potential risks been evaluated from a child-centered point of view, taking into account the developmental stages of the particular subjects? Children's reactions to pain, discomfort, anxiety, embarrassment, separation from parents and friends, body perception, fears and fantasies of mutilation and dying must be assessed in a developmentally sensitive manner.

7. Will the intervention directly benefit the individual child-subject? All potential benefits should be based on objective data from previous scientific work, and not merely be stated in terms of "possible" or "hoped for" benefits.

8. Where research will not benefit the particular child-subject, there is a presumption that it should not be conducted. This presumption can be only rebutted if the investigator can show either there is no risk to the individual child-subject, or the risk is minimal and the benefits to children as a group are great.

9. Have the investigators made clear how they will obtain the child's assent to research? Assent forms are not enough. What will the investigators say to the child? Where, when, and what actions by the child will the investigators take to mean the child has not assented or has withdrawn assent? This requires research personnel who are familiar with talking and listening to children.

10. Have the special concerns of preadolescents and adolescents about privacy been taken into account? It should be made clear to them what information, if any, will be shared with parents, health care providers, school personnel, or others.

11. Has every effort been made to ensure that a parent is present when the research intervention is conducted? This will not only comfort the child but will enable the parent to exercise the right to end the child's participation in the research project at any time. There are circumstances where parental presence may not be appropriate such as when preadolescents and adolescents are being interviewed about sensitive personal matters, or are undergoing physical examinations during which the parent would not ordinarily be present.

12. If the proposed subjects are members of a vulnerable class such as institutionalized children, dying children, children with cognitive or psychiatric disorders, homeless or impoverished children, what is the specific justification for using these additionally at-risk populations? Research on vulnerable populations should only be done when such research is directed at benefiting that population.

13. When children have a rare disease there is an understandable tendency for researchers to want to study them repeatedly. One must be vigilant in not turning these children into permanent research subjects.

14. While the use of deception in research, particularly psychological research, raises serious issues with all subjects, it raises particular concern for child-subjects. A child's sense of trust and security depends on how they are treated by adults. The use of deception can be particularly harmful at certain developmental stages. Deception should not be used unless absolutely necessary to obtain important information. The investigators must demonstrate the necessity for deception, why it will not be harmful to the subjects, and how subjects will be debriefed in an effective manner from the child's perspective.

15. Is money or are other rewards provided to the parents or the child-subjects? While parents may be compensated for out-of-pocket expenses such as travel or time away from work, it is inappropriate to pay parents for the use of their children as research subjects. It may be appropriate to provide the child with a small gift as a means of thanking the child for his or her participation as a research subject. However, this should be done after the child has completed the research study and should not be viewed as a condition or used as an enticement to participate as a subject.

16. Research with dying children raises especially difficult problems and therefore must be subject to especially close scrutiny. Dying children are particularly vulnerable for three reasons. First, they suffer from conditions that researchers feel a profound imperative to cure or ameliorate. Second, parents may be less capable of making protective decisions because they will often embrace any option that presents even the remote possibility of preserving or prolonging their child's life. Finally, dying children are subject to significant physical invasion and psychological stress as a result of their conditions. Additional invasions for research purposes constitute added burdens to an already burdened child. As a result of these factors, researchers and reviewers must be scrupulous in assuring that neither parents nor children are exploited.

If research with dying children involves pain, suffering, or the risk of physical or psychological harm, it should be conducted only if it has the intent and reasonable probability, based on scientific data, of directly improving the health or well-being of the child-subject, or of significantly increasing the child's length of life without significantly decreasing its quality. Where the research does not meet this standard, that is, the purpose or reasonable expectation is not to directly benefit the child, only the most benign interventions, such as those which may be reviewed through expedited procedures (see pages 242–243), may be conducted.

Researchers must be scrupulous in assuring that both the parents of dying children and the children or adolescents themselves truly understand the risks and discomforts of proposed research, and the likely impact of the procedures on both the quality and length of life. Researchers must be exceptionally careful not to overstate the likely benefits and not to understate the risks of participation.

Appendix B

The Nuremberg Code (1947)

1. The voluntary consent of the human subject is absolutely essential.

This means that the person involved should have legal capacity to give consent; should be so situated as to be able to exercise free power of choice, without the intervention of any element of force, fraud, deceit, duress, over-reaching, or other ulterior form of constraint or coercion; and should have sufficient knowledge and comprehension of the elements of the subject matter involved as to enable him to make an understanding and enlightened decision. This latter element requires that before the acceptance of an affirmative decision by the experimental subject there should be made known to him the nature, duration, and purpose of the experiment; the method and means by which it is to be conducted; all inconveniences and hazards reasonably to be expected; and the effects upon his health or person which may possibly come from his participation in the experiment.

The duty and responsibility for ascertaining the quality of the consent rests upon each individual who initiates, directs or engages in the experiment. It is a personal duty and responsibility which may not be delegated to another with impunity.

2. The experiment should be such as to yield fruitful results for the good of society, unprocurable by other methods or means of study, and not random and unnecessary in nature.

3. The experiment should be so designed and based on the results of animal experimentation and a knowledge of the natural history of the disease or other problem under study that the anticipated results will justify the performance of the experiment.

Reprinted from *Trials of War Criminals before the Nuremberg Military Tribunals under Control Council Law 10* (Washington, D.C.: Superintendant of Documents, U.S. Government Printing Office, 1950); Military Tribunal Case 1, *United States v. Karl Brandt et al.,* October 1946–April 1947. Vol. II, pp. 171–184.

4. The experiment should be so conducted as to avoid all unnecessary physical and mental suffering and injury.

5. No experiment should be conducted where there is an *a priori* reason to believe that death or disabling injury will occur; except, perhaps, in those experiments where the experimental physicians also serve as subjects.

6. The degree of risk to be taken should never exceed that determined by the humanitarian importance of the problem to be solved by the experiment.

7. Proper preparations should be made and adequate facilities provided to protect the experimental subject against even remote possibilities of injury, disability, or death.

8. The experiment should be conducted only by scientifically qualified persons. The highest degree of skill and care should be required through all stages of the experiment of those who conduct or engage in the experiment.

9. During the course of the experiment the human subject should be at liberty to bring the experiment to an end if he has reached the physical or mental state where continuation of the experiment seems to him to be impossible.

10. During the course of the experiment the scientist in charge must be prepared to terminate the experiment at any stage, if he has probable cause to believe, in the exercise of the good faith, superior skill, and careful judgment required of him, that a continuation of the experiment is likely to result in injury, disability, or death to the experimental subject.

Appendix C

World Medical Association Declaration of Helsinki IV 41st World Medical Assembly Hong Kong, September 1989

Introduction

It is the mission of the physician to safeguard the health of the people. His or her knowledge and conscience are dedicated to the fulfillment of this mission.

The Declaration of Geneva of the World Medical Association binds the physician with the words, 'The health of my patient will be my first consideration,' and the International Code of Medical Ethics declares that, 'A physician shall act only in the patient's interest when providing medical care which might have the effect of weakening the physical and mental condition of the patient.'

The purpose of biomedical research involving human subjects must be to improve diagnostic, therapeutic and prophylactic procedures and the understanding of the aetiology and pathogenesis of disease.

In current medical practice most diagnostic, therapeutic or prophylactic procedures involve hazards. This applies especially to biomedical research.

Medical progress is based on research which ultimately must rest in part on experimentation involving human subjects.

In the field of biomedical research a fundamental distinction must be recognized between medical research in which the aim is essentially diagnostic or therapeutic for a patient, and medical research, the essential object of which is purely scientific and without implying direct diagnostic or therapeutic value to the person subjected to the research.

Special caution must be exercised in the conduct of research which may affect the environment, and the welfare of animals used for research must be respected.

Because it is essential that the results of laboratory experiments be applied to human beings to further scientific knowledge and to help suffering humanity, the World Medical Association has prepared the following recommendations as a guide to every physician in biomedical research involving human subjects. They should be kept under review in the future. It must be stressed that the standards as drafted are only a guide to physicians all over the world. Physicians are not relieved from criminal, civil and ethical responsibilities under the laws of their own countries.

I. Basic Principles

1. Biomedical research involving human subjects must conform to generally accepted scientific principles and should be based on adequately performed laboratory and animal experimentation and on a thorough knowledge of the scientific literature.

2. The design and performance of each experimental procedure involving human subjects should be clearly formulated in an experimental protocol which should be transmitted for consideration, comment and guidance to a specially appointed committee independent of the investigator and the sponsor provided that this independent committee is in conformity with the laws and regulations of the country in which the research experiment is performed.

3. Biomedical research involving human subjects should be conducted only by scientifically qualified persons and under the supervision of a clinically competent medical person. The responsibility for the human subject must always rest with a medically qualified person and never rest on the subject of the research, even though the subject has given his or her consent.

4. Biomedical research involving human subjects cannot legitimately be carried out unless the importance of the objective is in proportion to the inherent risk to the subject.

5. Every biomedical research project involving human subjects should be preceded by careful assessment of predictable risks in comparison with foreseeable benefits to the subject or to others. Concern for the interests of the subject must always prevail over the interests of science and society.

6. The right of the research subject to safeguard his or her integrity must always be respected. Every precaution should be taken to respect the privacy of the subject and to minimize the impact of the study on the subject's physical and mental integrity and on the personality of the subject.

7. Physicians should abstain from engaging in research projects involving human subjects unless they are satisfied that the hazards involved are believed to be predictable. Physicians should cease any investigation if the hazards are found to outweigh the potential benefits.

8. In publication of the results of his or her research, the physician is obliged to preserve the accuracy of the results. Reports of experimentation not pin accordance with the principles laid down in this Declaration should not be accepted for publication.

9. In any research on human beings, each potential subject must be adequately informed of the aims, methods, anticipated benefits and potential hazards of the study and the discomfort it may entail. He or she should be informed that he or she is at liberty to abstain from participation in the study and that he or she is free to withdraw his or her consent to participation at any time. The physician should then obtain the subject's freely-given informed consent, preferably in writing.

10. When obtaining informed consent for the research project the physician should be particularly cautious if the subject is in a dependent relationship to him or her or may consent under duress. In that case the informed consent should be obtained by a physician who is not engaged in the investigation and who is completely independent of this official relationship.

11. In case of legal incompetence, informed consent should be obtained from the legal guardian in accordance with national legislation. Where physical or mental incapacity makes it impossible to obtain informed consent, or when the subject is a minor, permission from the responsible relative replaces that of the subject in accordance with national legislation.

Whenever the minor child is in fact able to give a consent, the minor's consent must be obtained in addition to the consent of the minor's legal guardian.

12. The research protocol should always contain a statement of the ethical considerations involved and should indicate that the principles enunciated in the present Declaration are complied with.

II. Medical Research Combined with Professional Care (clinical research)

1. In the treatment of the sick person, the physician must be free to use a new diagnostic and therapeutic measure, if in his or her judgment it offers hope of saving life, reestablishing health or alleviating suffering.

2. The potential benefits, hazards and discomfort of a new method should be weighed against the advantages of the best current diagnostic and therapeutic methods.

3. In any medical study, every patient—including those of a control group, if any—should be assured of the best proven diagnostic and therapeutic method.

4. The refusal of the patient to participate in a study must never interfere with the physician-patient relationship.

5. If the physician considers it essential not to obtain informed consent, the specific reasons for this proposal should be stated in the experimental protocol for transmission to the independent committee (I,2).

6. The physician can combine medical research with professional care, the objective being the acquisition of new medical knowledge, only to the extent that medical research is justified by its potential diagnostic or therapeutic value for the patient.

III. Non-therapeutic Biomedical Research Involving Human Subjects (non-clinical biomedical research)

1. In the purely scientific application of medical research carried out on a human being, it is the duty of the physician to remain the protector of the life and health of that person on whom biomedical research is being carried out.

2. The subjects should be volunteers—either healthy persons or patients for whom the experimental design is not related to the patient's illness.

3. The investigator or the investigating team should discontinue the research if in his/her or their judgment it may, if continued, be harmful to the individual.

4. In research on man, the interest of science and society should never take precedence over considerations related to the wellbeing of the subject.

Appendix D

Federal Regulations Pertaining to the Protection of Human Subjects

United States Federal Policy for the Protection of Human Subjects; Notices and Rules

56 **Federal Register** *28003 (June 18, 1991)*

§ 46.101 To what does this policy apply?

(a) Except as provided in paragraph (b) of this section, this policy applies to all research involving human subjects conducted, supported or otherwise subject to regulation by any Federal Department or Agency which takes appropriate administrative action to make the policy applicable to such research. This includes research conducted by Federal civilian employees or military personnel, except that each Department or Agency head may adopt such procedural modifications as may be appropriate from an administrative standpoint. It also includes research conducted, supported, or otherwise subject to regulation by the Federal Government outside the United States.

(1) Research that is conducted or supported by a Federal Department or Agency, whether or not it is regulated as defined in § 46.102(e), must comply with all sections of this policy.

(2) Research that is neither conducted nor supported by a Federal Department or Agency but is subject to regulation as defined in § 46.102(e) must be reviewed and approved, in compliance with § 46.101, § 46.102, and § 46.107

This is an excerpt from the Federal Regulations. We have retained the substantive provisions and have omitted some purely procedural matters. We have also deleted the regulations regarding research with pregnant women, fetuses or human in vitro fertilizaton, and research with prisoners. The regulations concerning research with children are printed in their entirety.

through § 46.117 of this policy, by an Institutional Review Board (IRB) that operates in accordance with the pertinent requirements of this policy.

(b) Unless otherwise required by Department or Agency heads, research activities in which the only involvement of human subjects will be in one or more of the following categories are exempt from this policy:

(1) Research conducted in established or commonly accepted educational settings, involving normal educational practices, such as:

(i) research on regular and special education instructional strategies; or (ii) research on the effectiveness of or the comparison among instructional techniques, curricula, or classroom management methods.

(2) Research involving the use of educational tests (cognitive, diagnostic, aptitude, achievement), survey procedures, interview procedures or observation of public behavior, unless:

(i) information obtained is recorded in such a manner that human subjects can be identified, directly or through identifiers linked to the subjects; and (ii) any disclosure of the human subjects' responses outside the research could reasonably place the subjects at risk of criminal or civil liability or be damaging to the subjects' financial standing, employability, or reputation.

(3) Research involving the use of educational tests (cognitive, diagnostic, aptitude, achievement), survey procedures, interview procedures, or observation of public behavior that is not exempt under paragraph (b)(2) of this section, if:

(i) the human subjects are elected or appointed public officials or candidates for public office; or (ii) Federal statute(s) require(s) without exception that the confidentiality of the personally identifiable information will be maintained throughout the research and thereafter.

(4) Research involving the collection or study of existing data, documents, records, pathological specimens, or diagnostic specimens, if these sources are publicly available or if the information is recorded by the investigator in such a manner that subjects cannot be identified, directly or through identifiers linked to the subjects.

(5) Research and demonstration projects which are conducted by or subject to the approval of Department or Agency heads, and which are designed to study, evaluate, or otherwise examine:

(i) Public benefit or service programs; (ii) procedures for obtaining benefits or services under those programs; (iii) possible changes in or alternatives to those programs or procedures; or (iv) possible changes in methods or levels of payment for benefits or services under those programs.

(6) Taste and food quality evaluation and consumer acceptance studies:

(i) if wholesome foods without additives are consumed; or (ii) if a food is consumed that contains a food ingredient at or below the level and for a use found to be safe, or agricultural chemical or environmental contaminant at or below the level found to be safe, by the Food and Drug Administration or approved by the Environmental Protection Agency or the Food Safety and Inspection Service of the U.S. Department of Agriculture.

(c) Department or Agency heads retain final judgment as to whether a particular activity is covered by this policy.

(d) Department or Agency heads may require that specific research activities or classes of research activities conducted, supported, or otherwise subject to regulation by the Department or Agency but not otherwise covered by this policy, comply with some or all of the requirements of this policy.

(e) Compliance with this policy requires compliance with pertinent Federal laws or regulations which provide additional protections for human subjects.

(f) This policy does not affect any state or local laws or regulations which may otherwise be applicable and which provide additional protections for human subjects.

(g) This policy does not affect any foreign laws or regulations which may otherwise be applicable and which provide additional protections to human subjects of research.

(h) When research covered by this policy takes place in foreign countries, procedures normally followed in the foreign countries to protect human subjects may differ from those set forth in this policy. [An example is a foreign institution which complies with guidelines consistent with the World Medical Assembly Declaration (Declaration of Helsinki amended 1989) issued either by sovereign states or by an organization whose function for the protection of human research subjects is internationally recognized.] In these circumstances, if a Department or Agency head determines that the procedures prescribed by the institution afford protections that are at least equivalent to those provided in this policy, the Department or Agency head may approve the substitution of the foreign procedures in lieu of the procedural requirements provided in this policy. Except when otherwise required by statute, Executive Order, or the Department or Agency head, notices of these actions as they occur will be published in the **Federal Register** or will be otherwise published as provided in Department or Agency procedures.

(i) Unless otherwise required by law, Department or Agency heads may waive the applicability of some or all of the provisions of this policy to specific research activities or classes of research activities otherwise covered by this policy. Except when otherwise required by statute or Executive Order, the Department or Agency head shall forward advance notices of these actions to the Office for Protection from Research Risks, National Institutes of Health, Department of Health and Human Services (DHHS), and shall also publish them in the **Federal Register** or in such other manner as provided in Department or Agency procedures.[1]

§ 46.102 Definitions.

(a) *Department or Agency head* means the head of any Federal Department or Agency and any other officer or employee of any Department or Agency to whom authority has been delegated.

(b) *Institution* means any public or private entity or Agency (including Federal, State, and other agencies).

(c) *Legally authorized representative* means an individual or judicial or other body authorized under applicable law to consent on behalf of a prospective subject to the subject's participation in the procedure(s) involved in the research.

(d) *Research* means a systematic investigation, including research development, testing and evaluation, designed to develop or contribute to generalizable knowledge. Activities which meet this definition constitute research for purposes of this policy, whether or not they are conducted or supported under a program which is considered research for other purposes. For example, some demonstration and service programs may include research activities.

(e) *Research subject to regulation,* and similar terms are intended to encompass those research activities for which a Federal Department or Agency has specific responsibility for regulating as a research activity, (for example, Investigational New Drug requirements administered by the Food and Drug Administration). It does not include research activities which are incidentally regulated by a Federal Department or Agency solely as part of the Department's or Agency's broader responsibility to regulate certain types of activities whether research or non-research in nature (for example, Wage and Hour requirements administered by the Department of Labor).

(f) *Human subject* means a living individual about whom an investigator (whether professional or student) conducting research obtains

(1) data through intervention or interaction with the individual; or

(2) identifiable private information. *Intervention* includes both physical procedures by which data are gathered (for example, venipuncture) and manipula-

---

1. Institutions with DHHS-approved assurances on file will abide by provisions of Title 45 *CFR* Part 46 subparts A-D. Some of the other departments and agencies have incorporated all provisions of Title 45 *CFR* Part 46 into their policies and procedures as well. However, the exemptions at 45 *CFR* 46.101(b) do not apply to research involving prisoners, fetuses, pregnant women, or human in vitro fertilization, Subparts B and C. The exemption at 45 *CFR* 46.101(b)(2), for research involving survey or interview procedures or observation of public behavior, does not apply to research with children, Subpart D, except for research involving observations of public behavior when the investigator(s) do not participate in the activities being observed.

tions of the subject or the subject's environment that are performed for research purposes. Interaction includes communication or interpersonal contact between investigator and subject. *Private information* includes information about behavior that occurs in a context in which an individual can reasonably expect that no observation or recording is taking place, and information which has been provided for specific purposes by an individual and which the individual can reasonably expect will not be made public (for example, a medical record). Private information must be individually identifiable (i.e., the identity of the subject is or may readily be ascertained by the investigator or associated with the information) in order for obtaining the information to constitute research involving human subjects.

(g) *IRB* means an Institutional Review Board established in accord with and for the purposes expressed in this policy.

(h) *IRB approval* means the determination of the IRB that the research has been reviewed and may be conducted at an institution within the constraints set forth by the IRB and by other institutional and Federal requirements.

(i) *Minimal risk* means that the probability and magnitude of harm or discomfort anticipated in the research are not greater in and of themselves than those ordinarily encountered in daily life or during the performance of routine physical or psychological examinations or tests.

(j) *Certification* means the official notification by the institution to the supporting Department or Agency, in accordance with the requirements of this policy, that a research project or activity involving human subjects has been reviewed and approved by an IRB in accordance with an approved assurance.

§ 46.103 Assuring compliance with this policy—research conducted or supported by any Federal Department or Agency.

(a) Each institution engaged in research which is covered by this policy and which is conducted or supported by a Federal Department or Agency shall provide written assurance satisfactory to the Department or Agency head that it will comply with the requirements set forth in this policy. In lieu of requiring submission of an assurance, individual Department or Agency heads shall accept the existence of a current assurance, appropriate for the research in question, on file with the Office for Protection from Research Risks, National Institutes of Health, DHHS, and approved for Federalwide use by that office. When the existence of an DHHS-approved assurance is accepted in lieu of requiring submission of an assurance, reports (except certification) required by this policy to be made to Department and Agency heads shall also be made to the Office for Protection from Research Risks, National Institutes of Health, DHHS.

(b) Departments and agencies will conduct or support research covered by this policy only if the institution has an assurance approved as provided in this section, and only if the institution has certified to the Department or Agency head that the research has been reviewed and approved by an IRB provided for in the assurance, and will be subject to continuing review by the IRB. Assurances applicable to federally supported or conducted research shall at a minimum include:

(1) A statement of principles governing the institution in the discharge of its responsibilities for protecting the rights and welfare of human subjects of research conducted at or sponsored by the institution, regardless of whether the research is subject to Federal regulation. This may include an appropriate existing code, declaration, or statement of ethical principles, or a statement formulated by the institution itself. This requirement does not preempt provisions of this policy applicable to Department- or Agency-supported or regulated research and need not be applicable to any research exempted or waived under § 46.101(b) or (i).

(2) Designation of one or more IRBs established in accordance with the requirements of this policy, and for which provisions are made for meeting space and sufficient staff to support the IRB's review and recordkeeping duties.

(3) A list of IRB members identified by name; earned degrees; representative capacity; indications of experience such as board certifications, licenses, etc., sufficient to describe each member's chief anticipated contributions to IRB deliberations; and any employment or other relationship between each member and the institution; for example: full-time employee, part-time employee, member of governing panel or board, stockholder, paid or unpaid consultant. Changes in IRB membership shall be reported to the Department or Agency head, unless in accord with § 46.103(a) of this policy, the existence of a DHHS-approved assurance is accepted. In this case, change in IRB membership shall be reported to the Office for Protection from Research Risks, National Institutes of Health, DHHS.

(4) Written procedures which the IRB will follow:

(i) for conducting its initial and continuing review of research and for reporting its findings and actions to the investigator and the institution; (ii) for determining which projects require review more often than annually and which projects need verification from sources other than the investigators that no material changes have occurred since previous IRB review; and (iii) for ensuring prompt reporting to the IRB of proposed changes in a research activity, and for ensuring that such changes in approved research, during the period for which IRB approval has already been given, may not be initiated without IRB review and approval except when necessary to eliminate apparent immediate hazards to the subject.

(5) Written procedures for ensuring prompt reporting to the IRB, appropriate institutional officials, and the Department or Agency head of: (i) any unantici-

pated problems involving risks to subjects or others or any serious or continuing noncompliance with this policy or the requirements or determinations of the IRB; and (ii) any suspension or termination of IRB approval.

(c) The assurance shall be executed by an individual authorized to act for the institution and to assume on behalf of the institution the obligations imposed by this policy and shall be filed in such form and manner as the Department or Agency head prescribes.

(d) The Department or Agency head will evaluate all assurances submitted in accordance with this policy through such officers and employees of the Department or Agency and such experts or consultants engaged for this purpose as the Department or Agency head determines to be appropriate. The Department or Agency head's evaluation will take into consideration the adequacy of the proposed IRB in light of the anticipated scope of the institution's research activities and the types of subject populations likely to be involved, the appropriateness of the proposed initial and continuing review procedures in light of the probable risks, and the size and complexity of the institution.

(e) On the basis of this evaluation, the Department or Agency head may approve or disapprove the assurance, or enter into negotiations to develop an approvable one. The Department or Agency head may limit the period during which any particular approved assurance or class of approved assurances shall remain effective or otherwise condition or restrict approval.

(f) Certification is required when the research is supported by a Federal Department or Agency and not otherwise exempted or waived under § 46.101(b) or (i). An institution with an approved assurance shall certify that each application or proposal for research covered by the assurance and by § 46.103 of this policy has been reviewed and approved by the IRB. Such certification must be submitted with the application or proposal or by such later date as may be prescribed by the Department or Agency to which the application or proposal is submitted. Under no condition shall research covered by § 46.103 of the policy be supported prior to receipt of the certification that the research has been reviewed and approved by the IRB. Institutions without an approved assurance covering the research shall certify within 30 days after receipt of a request for such a certification from the Department or Agency, that the application or proposal has been approved by the IRB. If the certification is not submitted within these time limits, the application or proposal may be returned to the institution.

§ 46.107 IRB membership.

(a) Each IRB shall have at least five members, with varying backgrounds to promote complete and adequate review of research activities commonly conducted by the institution. The IRB shall be sufficiently qualified through the experience and expertise of its members, and the diversity of the members, including consideration of race, gender, and cultural backgrounds and sensitivity to such issues as community attitudes, to promote respect for its advice and counsel in safeguarding the rights and welfare of human subjects. In addition to possessing the professional competence necessary to review specific research activities, the IRB shall be able to ascertain the acceptability of proposed research in terms of institutional commitments and regulations, applicable law, and standards of professional conduct and practice. The IRB shall therefore include persons knowledgeable in these areas. If an IRB regularly reviews research that involves a vulnerable category of subjects, such as children, prisoners, pregnant women, or handicapped or mentally disabled persons, consideration shall be given to the inclusion of one or more individuals who are knowledgeable about and experienced in working with these subjects.

(b) Every nondiscriminatory effort will be made to ensure that no IRB consists entirely of men or entirely of women, including the institution's consideration of qualified persons of both sexes, so long as no selection is made to the IRB on the basis of gender. No IRB may consist entirely of members of one profession.

(c) Each IRB shall include at least one member whose primary concerns are in scientific areas and at least one member whose primary concerns are in nonscientific areas.

(d) Each IRB shall include at least one member who is not otherwise affiliated with the institution and who is not part of the immediate family of a person who is affiliated with the institution.

(e) No IRB may have a member participate in the IRB's initial or continuing review of any project in which the member has a conflicting interest, except to provide information requested by the IRB.

(f) An IRB may, in its discretion, invite individuals with competence in special areas to assist in the review of issues which require expertise beyond or in addition to that available on the IRB. These individuals may not vote with the IRB.

§ 46.108 IRB functions and operations.

In order to fulfill the requirements of this policy each IRB shall:

(a) Follow written procedures in the same detail as described in § 46.103(b)(4) and to the extent required by § 46.103(b)(5).

(b) Except when an expedited review procedure is used (see § 46.110), review proposed research at convened meetings at which a majority of the members of the IRB are present, including at least one member whose primary concerns are in nonscientific areas. In order for the research to be approved, it shall receive the approval of a majority of those members present at the meeting.

§ 46.109 IRB review of research.

(a) An IRB shall review and have authority to approve, require modifications in (to secure approval), or disapprove all research activities covered by this policy.

(b) An IRB shall require that information given to subjects as part of informed consent is in accordance with § 46.116. The IRB may require that information, in addition to that specifically mentioned in § 46.116, be given to the subjects when in the IRB's judgment the information would meaningfully add to the protection of the rights and welfare of subjects.

(c) An IRB shall require documentation of informed consent or may waive documentation in accordance with § 46.117.

(d) An IRB shall notify investigators and the institution in writing of its decision to approve or disapprove the proposed research activity, or of modifications required to secure IRB approval of the research activity. If the IRB decides to disapprove a research activity, it shall include in its written notification a statement of the reasons for its decision and give the investigator an opportunity to respond in person or in writing.

(e) An IRB shall conduct continuing review of research covered by this policy at intervals appropriate to the degree of risk, but not less than once per year, and shall have authority to observe or have a third party observe the consent process and the research.

§ 46.110 Expedited review procedures for certain kinds of research involving no more than minimal risk, and for minor changes in approved research.

(a) The Secretary, HHS, has established, and published as a Notice in the **Federal Register,** a list of categories of research that may be reviewed by the IRB through an expedited review procedure. The list will be amended, as appropriate, after consultation with other departments and agencies, through periodic republication by the Secretary, HHS, in the **Federal Register.** A copy of the list is available from the Office for Protection from Research Risks, National Institutes of Health, DHHS, Bethesda, Maryland 20892.

(b) An IRB may use the expedited review procedure to review either or both of the following:

(1) some or all of the research appearing on the list and found by the reviewer(s) to involve no more than minimal risk;

(2) minor changes in previously approved research during the period (of one year or less) for which approval is authorized.

Under an expedited review procedure, the review may be carried out by the

IRB chairperson or by one or more experienced reviewers designated by the chairperson from among members of the IRB. In reviewing the research, the reviewers may exercise all of the authorities of the IRB except that the reviewers may not disapprove the research. A research activity may be disapproved only after review in accordance with the non-expedited procedure set forth in § 46.108(b).

(c) Each IRB which uses an expedited review procedure shall adopt a method for keeping all members advised of research proposals which have been approved under the procedure.

(d) The Department or Agency head may restrict, suspend, terminate, or choose not to authorize an institution's or IRB's use of the expedited review procedure.

§ 46.111 Criteria for IRB approval of research.

(a) In order to approve research covered by this policy the IRB shall determine that all the following requirements are satisfied:

(1) Risks to subjects are minimized:

(i) by using procedures which are consistent with sound research design and which do not unnecessarily expose subjects to risk; and (ii) whenever appropriate, by using procedures already being performed on the subjects for diagnostic or treatment purposes.

(2) Risks to subjects are reasonable in relation to anticipated benefits, if any, to subjects, and the importance of the knowledge that may reasonably be expected to result. In evaluating risks and benefits, the IRB should consider only those risks and benefits that may result from the research (as distinguished from risks and benefits of therapies subjects would receive even if not participating in the research). The IRB should not consider possible long-range effects of applying knowledge gained in the research (for example, the possible effects of the research on public policy) as among those research risks that fall within the purview of its responsibility.

(3) Selection of subjects is equitable. In making this assessment the IRB should take into account the purposes of the research and the setting in which the research will be conducted and should be particularly cognizant of the special problems of research involving vulnerable populations, such as children, prisoners, pregnant women, mentally disabled persons, or economically or educationally disadvantaged persons.

(4) Informed consent will be sought from each prospective subject or the subject's legally authorized representative, in accordance with, and to the extent required by § 46.116.

(5) Informed conse nt will be appropriately documented, in accordance with, and to the extent required by § 46.117.

(6) When appropriate, the research plan makes adequate provision for monitoring the data collected to ensure the safety of subjects.

(7) When appropriate, there are adequate provisions to protect the privacy of subjects and to maintain the confidentiality of data.

(b) When some or all of the subjects are likely to be vulnerable to coercion or undue influence, such as children, prisoners, pregnant women, mentally disabled persons, or economically or educationally disadvantaged persons, additional safeguards have been included in the study to protect the rights and welfare of these subjects.

§ 46.112 Review by institution.

Research covered by this policy that has been approved by an IRB may be subject to further appropriate review and approval or disapproval by officials of the institution. However, those officials may not approve the research if it has not been approved by an IRB.

§ 46.113 Suspension or termination of IRB approval of research.

An IRB shall have authority to suspend or terminate approval of research that is not being conducted in accordance with the IRB's requirements or that has been associated with unexpected serious harm to subjects. Any suspension or termination of approval shall include a statement of the reasons for the IRB's action and shall be reported promptly to the investigator, appropriate institutional officials, and the Department or Agency head.

§ 46.116 General requirements for informed consent.

Except as provided elsewhere in this policy, no investigator may involve a human being as a subject in research covered by this policy unless the investigator has obtained the legally effective informed consent of the subject or the subject's legally authorized representative. An investigator shall seek such consent only under circumstances that provide the prospective subject or the representative sufficient opportunity to consider whether or not to participate and that minimize the possibility of coercion or undue influence. The information that is given to the subject or the representative shall be in language understandable to the subject or the representative. No informed consent, whether oral or written, may include any exculpatory language through which the subject or the representative is made to waive or appear to waive any of the subject's legal rights, or releases or appears to release the investigator, the sponsor, the institution or its agents from liability for negligence.

(a) Basic elements of informed consent. Except as provided in paragraph (c) or (d) of this section, in seeking informed consent the following information shall be provided to each subject:

(1) a statement that the study involves research, an explanation of the purposes of the research and the expected duration of the subject's participation, a description of the procedures to be followed, and identification of any procedures which are experimental;

(2) a description of any reasonably foreseeable risks or discomforts to the subject;

(3) a description of any benefits to the subject or to others which may reasonably be expected from the research;

(4) a disclosure of appropriate alternative procedures or courses of treatment, if any, that might be advantageous to the subject;

(5) a statement describing the extent, if any, to which confidentiality of records identifying the subject will be maintained;

(6) for research involving more than minimal risk, an explanation as to whether any compensation and an explanation as to whether any medical treatments are available if injury occurs and, if so, what they consist of, or where further information may be obtained;

(7) an explanation of whom to contact for answers to pertinent questions about the research and research subjects' rights, and whom to contact in the event of a research-related injury to the subject; and

(8) a statement that participation is voluntary, refusal to participate will involve no penalty or loss of benefits to which the subject is otherwise entitled, and the subject may discontinue participation at any time without penalty or loss of benefits to which the subject is otherwise entitled.

(b) Additional elements of informed consent. When appropriate, one or more of the following elements of information shall also be provided to each subject:

(1) a statement that the particular treatment or procedure may involve risks to the subject (or to the embryo or fetus, if the subject is or may become pregnant) which are currently unforeseeable;

(2) anticipated circumstances under which the subject's participation may be terminated by the investigator without regard to the subject's consent;

(3) any additional costs to the subject that may result from participation in the research;

(4) the consequences of a subject's decision to withdraw from the research and procedures for orderly termination of participation by the subject;

(5) a statement that significant new findings developed during the course of the research which may relate to the subject's willingness to continue participation will be provided to the subject; and

(6) the approximate number of subjects involved in the study.

(c) An IRB may approve a consent procedure which does not include, or which alters, some or all of the elements of informed consent set forth above, or waive the requirement to obtain informed consent provided the IRB finds and documents that:

(1) the research or demonstration project is to be conducted by or subject to the approval of state or local government officials and is designed to study, evaluate, or otherwise examine:

(i) public benefit of service programs; (ii) procedures for obtaining benefits or services under those programs; (iii) possible changes in or alternatives to those programs or procedures; or (iv) possible changes in methods or levels of payment for benefits or services under those programs; and

(2) the research could not practicably be carried out without the waiver or alteration.

(d) An IRB may approve a consent procedure which does not include, or which alters, some or all of the elements of informed consent set forth in this section, or waive the requirements to obtain informed consent provided the IRB finds and documents that:

(1) the research involves no more than minimal risk to the subjects;

(2) the waiver or alteration will not adversely affect the rights and welfare of the subjects;

(3) the research could not practicably be carried out without the waiver or alteration; and

(4) whenever appropriate, the subjects will be provided with additional pertinent information after participation.

(e) The informed consent requirements in this policy are not intended to preempt any applicable Federal, State, or local laws which require additional information to be disclosed in order for informed consent to be legally effective.

(f) Nothing in this policy is intended to limit the authority of a physician to provide emergency medical care, to the extent the physician is permitted to do so under applicable Federal, State, or local law.

§ 46.117 Documentation of informed consent.

(a) Except as provided in paragraph (c) of this section, informed consent shall be documented by the use of a written consent form approved by the IRB and signed by the subject or the subject's legally authorized representative. A copy shall be given to the person signing the form.

(b) Except as provided in paragraph (c) of this section, the consent form may be either of the following:

(1) A written consent document that embodies the elements of informed consent required by § 46.116. This form may be read to the subject or the subject's

legally authorized representative, but in any event, the investigator shall give either the subject or the representative adequate opportunity to read it before it is signed; or

(2) A short form written consent document stating that the elements of informed consent required by § 46.116 have been presented orally to the subject or the subject's legally authorized representative. When this method is used, there shall be a witness to the oral presentation. Also, the IRB shall approve a written summary of what is to be said to the subject or the representative. Only the short form itself is to be signed by the subject or the representative. However, the witness shall sign both the short form and a copy of the summary, and the person actually obtaining consent shall sign a copy of the summary. A copy of the summary shall be given to the subject or the representative, in addition to a copy of the short form.

(c) An IRB may waive the requirement for the investigator to obtain a signed consent form for some or all subjects if it finds either:

(1) that the only record linking the subject and the research would be the consent document and the principal risk would be potential harm resulting from a breach of confidentiality. Each subject will be asked whether the subject wants documentation linking the subject with the research, and the subject's wishes will govern; or

(2) that the research presents no more than minimal risk of harm to subjects and involves no procedures for which written consent is normally required outside of the research context.

In cases in which the documentation requirement is waived, the IRB may require the investigator to provide subjects with a written statement regarding the research.

§ 46.122 Use of federal funds.

Federal funds administered by a Department or Agency may not be expended for research involving human subjects unless the requirements of this policy have been satisfied.

Subpart D—Additional DHHS Protections for Children Involved as Subjects in Research

48 Federal Register *9818* (March 8, 1983); 56 Federal Register 28032 (June 18, 1991)

§ 46.401 To what do these regulations apply?

(a) This subpart applies to all research involving children as subjects, conducted or supported by the Department of Health and Human Services.

(1) This includes research conducted by Department employees, except that each head of an Operating Division of the Department may adopt such nonsubstantive, procedural modifications as may be appropriate from an administrative standpoint.

(2) It also includes research conducted or supported by the Department of Health and Human Services outside the United States, but in appropriate circumstances, the Secretary may, under paragraph (e) of § 46.101 of Subpart A, waive the applicability of some or all of the requirements of these regulations for research of this type.

(b) Exemptions at § 46.101(b)(1) and (b)(3) through (b)(6) are applicable to this subpart. The exemption at § 46.101(b)(2) regarding educational tests is also applicable to this subpart. However, the exemption at § 46.101(b)(2) for research involving survey or interview procedures or observations of public behavior does not apply to research covered by this subpart, except for research involving observation of public behavior when the investigator(s) do not participate in the activities being observed.

(c) The exceptions, additions, and provisions for waiver as they appear in paragraphs (c) through (i) of § 46.101 of Subpart A are applicable to this subpart.

§ 46.402 Definitions.

The definitions in § 46.102 of Subpart A shall be applicable to this subpart as well. In addition, as used in this subpart:

(a) "Children" are persons who have not attained the legal age for consent to treatments or procedures involved in the research, under the applicable law of the jurisdiction in which the research will be conducted.

(b) "Assent" means a child's affirmative agreement to participate in research. Mere failure to object should not, absent affirmative agreement, be construed as assent.

(c) "Permission" means the agreement of parent(s) or guardian to the participation of their child or ward in research.

(d) "Parent" means a child's biological or adoptive parent.

(e) "Guardian" means an individual who is authorized under applicable State or local law to consent on behalf of a child to general medical care.

§ 46.403 IRB duties.

In addition to other responsibilities assigned to IRBs under this part, each IRB shall review research covered by this subpart and approve only research which satisfies the conditions of all applicable sections of this subpart.

§ 46.404 Research not involving greater than minimal risk.

DHHS will conduct or fund research in which the IRB finds that no greater than minimal risk to children is presented, only if the IRB finds that adequate provisions are made for soliciting the assent of the children and the permission of their parents or guardians, as set forth in § 46.408.

§ 46.405 Research involving greater than minimal risk but presenting
the prospect of direct benefit to the individual subjects.

DHHS will conduct or fund research in which the IRB finds that more than minimal risk to children is presented by an intervention or procedure that holds out the prospect of direct benefit for the individual subject, or by a monitoring procedure that is likely to contribute to the subject's well-being, only if the IRB finds that:

(a) the risk is justified by the anticipated benefit to the subjects;

(b) the relation of the anticipated benefit to the risk is at least as favorable to the subjects as that presented by available alternative approaches; and

(c) adequate provisions are made for soliciting the assent of the children and permission of their parents or guardians, as set forth in § 46.408.

§ 46.406 Research involving greater than minimal risk and no prospect of
direct benefit to individual subjects, but likely to yield generalizable
knowledge about the subject's disorder or condition.

DHHS will conduct or fund research in which the IRB finds that more than minimal risk to children is presented by an intervention or procedure that does not hold out the prospect of direct benefit for the individual subject, or by a monitoring procedure which is not likely to contribute to the well-being of the subject, only if the IRB finds that:

(a) the risk represents a minor increase over minimal risk;

(b) the intervention or procedure presents experiences to subjects that are reasonably commensurate with those inherent in their actual or expected medical, dental, psychological, social, or educational situations;

(c) the intervention or procedure is likely to yield generalizable knowledge about the subjects' disorder or condition which is of vital importance for the understanding or amelioration of the subjects' disorder or condition; and

(d) adequate provisions are made for soliciting assent of the children and permission of their parents or guardians, as set forth in § 46.408.

§ 46.407 Research not otherwise approvable which presents an opportunity to
understand, prevent, or alleviate a serious problem affecting the health or
welfare of children.

DHHS will conduct or fund research that the IRB does not believe meets the requirements of § 46.404, § 46.405, or § 46.406 only if:

(a) the IRB finds that the research presents a reasonable opportunity to further the understanding, prevention, or alleviation of a serious problem affecting the health or welfare of children; and

(b) the Secretary, after consultation with a panel of experts in pertinent disciplines (for example: science, medicine, education, ethics, law) and following opportunity for public review and comment, has determined either:

(1) that the research in fact satisfies the conditions of § 46.404, § 46.405, or § 46.406, as applicable; or

(2) the following:

(i) the research presents a reasonable opportunity to further the understanding, prevention, or alleviation of a serious problem affecting the health or welfare of children;

(ii) the research will be conducted in accordance with sound ethical principles;

(iii) adequate provisions are made for soliciting the assent of children and the permission of their parents or guardians, as set forth in § 46.408.

§ 46.408 Requirements for permission by parents or guardians and for assent by children.

(a) In addition to the determinations required under other applicable sections of this subpart, the IRB shall determine that adequate provisions are made for soliciting the assent of the children, when in the judgment of the IRB the children are capable of providing assent. In determining whether children are capable of assenting, the IRB shall take into account the ages, maturity, and psychological state of the children involved. This judgment may be made for all children to be involved in research under a particular protocol, or for each child, as the IRB deems appropriate. If the IRB determines that the capability of some or all of the children is so limited that they cannot reasonably be consulted or that the intervention or procedure involved in the research holds out a prospect of direct benefit that is important to the health or well-being of the children and is available only in the context of the research, the assent of the children is not a necessary condition for proceeding with the research. Even where the IRB determines that the subjects are capable of assenting, the IRB may still waive the assent requirement under circumstances in which consent may be waived in accord with § 46.116 of Subpart A.

(b) In addition to the determinations required under other applicable sections of this subpart, the IRB shall determine, in accordance with and to the extent that consent is required by § 46.116 of Subpart A, that adequate provisions are made for soliciting the permission of each child's parents or guardian. Where parental permission is to be obtained, the IRB may find that the permission of one parent is sufficient for research to be conducted under § 46.404 or § 46.405. Where research is covered by § 46.406 and § 46.407 and permission is to be obtained from parents, both parents must give their permission unless one parent is deceased, unknown, incompetent, or not reasonably available, or when only one parent has legal responsibility for the care and custody of the child.

(c) In addition to the provisions for waiver contained in § 46.116 of Subpart A, if the IRB determines that a research protocol is designed for conditions or for a subject population for which parental or guardian permission is not a reasonable requirement to protect the subjects (for example, neglected or abused children), it may waive the consent requirements in Subpart A of this part and paragraph (b) of this section, provided an appropriate mechanism for protecting the children who will participate as subjects in the research is substituted, and provided further that the waiver is not inconsistent with Federal, State, or local law. The choice of an appropriate mechanism would depend upon the nature and purpose of the activities described in the protocol, the risk and anticipated benefit to the research subjects, and their age, maturity, status, and condition.

(d) Permission by parents or guardians shall be documented in accordance with and to the extent required by § 46.117 of Subpart A.

(e) When the IRB determines that assent is required, it shall also determine whether and how assent must be documented.

§ 46.409 Wards.

(a) Children who are wards of the State or any other agency, institution, or entity can be included in research approved under § 46.406 or § 46.407 only if such research is:

(1) related to their status as wards; or

(2) conducted in schools, camps, hospitals, institutions, or similar settings in which the majority of children involved as subjects are not wards.

(b) If the research is approved under paragraph (a) of this section, the IRB shall require appointment of an advocate for each child who is a ward, in addition to any other individual acting on behalf of the child as guardian or in loco parentis. One individual may serve as advocate for more than one child. The advocate shall be an individual who has the background and experience to act in, and agrees to act in, the best interests of the child for the duration of the child's participation in the research and who is not associated in any way (except in the role as advocate or member of the IRB) with the research, the investigator(s), or the guardian organization.

**Research Activities Which May Be Reviewed Through
Expedited Review Procedures**

46 **Federal Register** *8392 (January 26, 1981)*

Research activities involving no more than minimal risk *and* in which the only involvement of human subjects will be in one or more of the following categories (carried out through standard methods) may be reviewed by the Institutional Review Board through the expedited review procedure authorized in § 46.110 of 45 CFR Part 46.

(1) Collection of: hair and nail clippings, in a nondisfiguring manner; deciduous teeth; and permanent teeth if patient care indicates a need for extraction.

(2) Collection of excreta and external secretions including sweat, uncannulated saliva, placenta removed at delivery, and amniotic fluid at the time of rupture of the membrane prior to or during labor.

(3) Recording of data from subjects 18 years of age or older using noninvasive procedures routinely employed in clinical practice. This includes the use of physical sensors that are applied either to the surface of the body or at a distance and do not involve input of matter or significant amounts of energy into the subject or an invasion of the subject's privacy. It also includes such procedures as weighing, testing sensory acuity, electrocardiography, electroencephalography, thermography, detection of naturally occurring radioactivity, diagnostic echography, and electroretinography. It does not include exposure to electromagnetic radiation outside the visible range (for example: X rays, microwaves).

(4) Collection of blood samples by venipuncture, in amounts not exceeding 450 milliliters in an eight-week period and no more often than two times per week, from subjects 18 years of age or older and who are in good health and not pregnant.

(5) Collection of both supra- and subgingival dental plaque and calculus, provided the procedure is not more invasive than routine prophylactic scaling of the teeth and the process is accomplished in accordance with accepted prophylactic techniques.

(6) Voice recordings made for research purposes such as investigations of speech defects.

(7) Moderate exercise by healthy volunteers.

(8) The study of existing data, documents, records, pathological specimens, or diagnostic specimens.

(9) Research on individual or group behavior or characteristics of individu-

als, such as studies of perception, cognition, game theory, or test development, where the investigator does not manipulate subjects' behavior and the research will not involve stress to subjects.

(10) Research on drugs or devices for which an investigational new drug exemption or an investigational device exemption is not required.

Index